A

Born in
(formerly Waugh) grew up in Ratho, a
small village on the western outskirts
of Edinburgh where she continued to
stay after her marriage to John in
1969. Her career in banking, which
began in 1957 with the Commercial
Bank of Scotland Ltd, was spent in
branch banking apart from four years in development and
marketing and a short secondment to the Commonwealth Games
Office in Edinburgh in 1986. She is a member of the Chartered
Institute of Bankers in Scotland. In 1993 when John's health
deteriorated she took early retirement from her position of
Advances Manager at the Royal Bank of Scotland's North Bridge
Branch, Edinburgh. After his death in 1997, she applied to
Voluntary Service Overseas and worked as a volunteer in Zambia
from October 2000 to February 2003. Since returning to the UK
she has taken part in a BBC Radio 4 programme, 'The Golden Age
of Aid,' and has spoken on the value of mature volunteers on radio,
television and to the press.

Wash My Bikini

Mwashibukeeni
'Good Morning' in Bemba

Working with Voluntary Service Overseas in Zambia

by

Anne Thomson

Librario

Published by

Librario Publishing Ltd.

ISBN: 978-1-906775-06-3

Copies can be ordered via the Internet
www.librario.com

or from:

Brough House, Milton Brodie, Kinloss
Moray IV36 2UA
Tel/Fax No 00 44 (0)1343 850 617

Printed and bound in the UK

Typeset by 3btype.com

All royalties due to the author from the sale of this book
will be donated to VSO.

For all VSO volunteers,
past, present and future.

Acknowledgements

My Zambian venture could never have taken place without the help and support of my family and friends; VSO's staff, both in the UK and in Zambia; colleagues at Prison Fellowship Zambia and my neighbours at Zawi. Then there were the volunteers themselves, my 'substitute family,' and those residents of Ndola who, appreciating what we were trying to do, took us to their hearts. A few of the photographs in this book were taken by fellow volunteers or VSO staff.

I thank Librario Publishing for its technical help and guidance, Jonathan Dimbleby, President, Voluntary Service Overseas, for providing the foreword to the book and Alex Good for the assistance and encouragement he gave as he read through my material.

Contents

Those who feature regularly in Wash My Bikini   ix
Foreword by Jonathan Dimbleby   xi
Map of Zambia   xii
Map of Ndola City Centre   xiii
Introduction   xv

1   Good Morning Zambia   1
2   Wash My Bikini   9
3   'Journey into a Far Country'   16
4   Ndola   23
5   'Getting to Know You'   32
6   Zawi   41
7   Settling In   49
8   The Funeral of Bishop Chikwamba   55
9   'Friendship begins with liking...'   59
10   Go to Prison   67
11   'Water, Water, Everywhere' – but not a trickle
      from the tap   72
12   A Woman's Place   79
13   Zambian Advent   85
14   Christmas by the Zambezi   96
15   Travelling Zambian Style   105
16   Pies and Birthday Pickles   119
17   Zambia 1 Nigeria 1   125
18   Christmas Comes Late   132
19   'Aids may kill me tomorrow...'   142
20   Visitors from Home   151
21   Lunch, Supper, Dinner   166
22   Total Eclipse plus A Sports Day   174
23   Medical Assistance   183
24   'When the Sun Rises in Africa'   196

25	'... And Sorrow and Sighing"	210
26	Wedding Bells	216
27	Slaves and Spices	226
28	Wheeling and Dealing	233
29	Shiwa Ng'andu	242
30	Highs and Lows	250
31	RAISA	262
32	The Ending of a Strategic Plan	279
33	Sharing Skills, Changing Lives	293
	Bibliography	297

Those who feature regularly in Wash My Bikini

Voluntary Service Overseas (VSO)

Volunteers

Ruth Brewer   Sue Clay   Dave Clinton
Carl Edmonds   Justin Highstead   Emily Kippax
Vicky Murgatroyd   Mirriam Vroonhof   Mike Bird
Dan Cashdan   Helen Gosnell (youth project)

Placement Officer in Lusaka
Dolores Long

Volunteers from Other Agencies

Mark Schroeder   Mennonite Church of Canada
Brian Higgins   Society of African Missions
Kevin McDonagh   Society of African Missions
Torunn Wilk   Voluntary Missionary Movement
Vicky Rowan   Ireland Aid
Susanne Bradley   Society of African Missions

Prison Fellowship Zambia (PFZ)

Dr Mathani   Chairman of Board
Rev George Chanda   Acting Executive Director (2000–June 2001)
Rev Lawrence Tenfwe Executive Director (Sept 2001–Sept 2002)
Rev Betlem Chonde   Executive Director (from Oct 2002)
Regina Kangwa   PA to Executive Director
Maurice Shakwamba   Health Co-ordinator/Programme Manager
Mutinta Mudenda   Secretary to the Projects/Park Projecct
Rev Francis Mpzeni   Chaplain
Rev Jim Mwewa   Chaplain
Robam Mukubwa   Accountant
Mellbin Simingola   Tailoring Project

Idah Nkari	Restaurant
Kanyanta Sambie	Micro Credit Project
Gift Njombe	Park Project
Knox	Gardener at Office
Chama	Messenger
Marjorie Fwolishi	
Newton Zulu	} PFZ Health Dept Volunteers
Charles Kachali	

People in Ndola

Anna Hovells	Teacher (previously VSO)
Tony Tompkins	Teacher (previously VSO)
Harriet Chiyanika	Maid
Brian	Harriet's baby son

Foreword by Jonathan Dimbleby

Anne Thomson is a remarkable woman and she tells a great story. Like thousands of VSO volunteers across Africa and Asia, she has not just talked about tackling poverty or promoting human rights, she has got on and done something about it. There are no magic bullets, but there is a shared struggle, and she is part of it.

Her story brings out the ups and downs of everyday life for Zambians and for foreigners working with them. She captures the hope and the opportunities, but doesn't hide from the challenges or the painful reality of the lives of ordinary people in one of the world's poorest countries.

Anne writes not as a critical outsider but as a friend, sharing the daily struggles of the lives of colleagues in the Prison Fellowship of Zambia, of prisoners and their families. It is a story that we are all the richer for reading.

I congratulate Anne for her work and VSO for supporting it. She tells a personal story of the sort that has kept me engaged and enthused as President of VSO for the last ten years.

Devon, March 2008

ZAMBIA

200km

NDOLA
CITY CENTRE

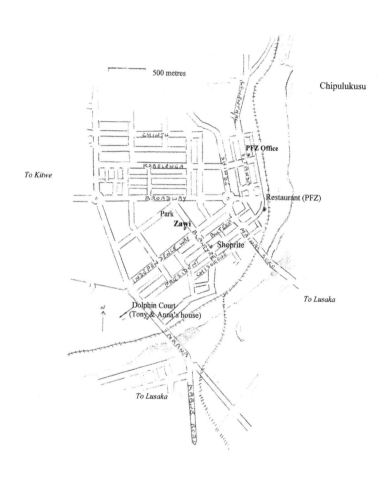

Introduction

Some of my friends thought I was crazy to embark on this venture. For a second or two I stood in the open doorway of the plane, felt the full force of the tropical heat and wondered if they had been correct. Stepping onto the flight of steps I was dazzled by the sunlight and almost stumbled. To steady myself I put my hand on the handrail of the steps but quickly pulled it back. The uncovered metal rail was blisteringly hot. Resisting its support I staggered down the steps, only too pleased after the long overnight flight to get a chance to stretch my legs. It wasn't a long walk to the terminal building but while its shade would be welcome I couldn't resist the temptation to stop and take a first look at the land which was to be my home for the next two years. I stood on the tarmac and glanced around. Everything shimmered in a heat haze, greyish-yellow grass almost burnt away by the sun, dusty trees, terracotta earth and, towards the horizon, the pale lilac of some distant hills, lying hazily in the sultry heat. I knew from my research on Zambia that October was known as the 'suicide month' when temperatures reached their all-year high with the rainy season still some weeks away. As I stood there on the tarmac, the reality of the quest I had begun hit home. This was what months of training had been for, to undertake a two-year Voluntary Service Overseas (VSO) placement in Zambia.

Chapter 1

Good Morning Zambia

It was 10.15 a.m., on Tuesday, October 10, 2000. British Airways Flight No BA255 from London Gatwick via Harare, Zimbabwe, had arrived at Lusaka International Airport. Among the disembarking passengers were ten of us arriving to take up various placements in Zambia on behalf of VSO. Our excitement had grown through our initial application, personal interviews, training and preparation, and now, at last, we were here.

I was aged sixty, a widow since John's death two years earlier, and retired seven years from my job as an Advances Manager with the Royal Bank of Scotland. Until the previous week I lived on my own in a three-bedroomed semi-detached house in Ratho on the outskirts of Edinburgh. It was a very pleasant, very comfortable life, but one which felt flat, unrewarding and unexciting. Doing a little voluntary work in Ratho wasn't fulfilling my need to feel useful and I certainly wasn't ready to settle down with the knitting needles. It felt as if I had been put out to grass too soon but after watching a TV programme on the work done by a 'mature' VSO volunteer in Kenya, I thought I might have found the solution to my restlessness.

I waited anxiously for either acceptance or rejection of my application, and was delighted when acceptance came through. Relatives and friends that I had spoken with about volunteering thought me a bit daft, to say the least, but there I was, recruited and with details of training required in the weeks ahead before any placement could begin. Of the four placements offered, the one of administrator/accountant with Prison Fellowship Zambia (PFZ) in Ndola, a town three hundred kilometres north of Lusaka in Zambia's Copperbelt, struck me as the one which best suited the skills I had to offer. While I waited to hear that PFZ, having been given details of my background and expertise, would be pleased to have me, there was little time to relax. There was training, training, training. Courses covered many subjects ranging from international development to living in a culture where the attitudes regarding the place of women in society differed from ours. Hints on how to keep healthy were important for everyone but particularly so for those going to sub-Saharan Africa where AIDS was rife. At least with my placement in an urban area I was spared the practical training on how to handle a 250cc motor bike, necessary for those going to rural areas to enable them get about, or learn how to dig a latrine. There were visits to doctor, dentist, optician and audiologist and in my case the most time consuming of all, packing up my home so that it could be put in the hands of an estate agent for letting. My younger sister, Marjorie Robertson, took on power of attorney so that she could look after my affairs while I was abroad. I breathed a sigh of relief when the buyer of my car came to pick it up. Eventually on the afternoon of Friday, October 6, 2000, I took one last look round my home before finally I locked it up and handed the keys over to the estate agent.

Now I was standing on the tarmac of Lusaka International Airport, Zambia. Less than twenty-four hours before I had been lunching with my sisters Helen and Marjorie and Helen's husband, Jimmy Tully, at the Stakis Hotel close by Edinburgh Airport. The sky had been grey and overcast and the wind distinctly cool. Now I was in Zambia and the temperature was scorching, the sky a brilliant blue. Whatever happened in the future I was chuffed to have made it this far.

The terminal building was cool, barren and bare and the immigration procedures seemed to take no time at all. Technically I entered Zambia when I walked through the door in the screen of opaque glass squares. The baggage carousel was running and my luggage, one backpack and one large holdall, a total weight of just 35 kilos, were waiting for collection. In these two pieces of luggage was everything I was expected to need in the next two years, from a Swiss Army knife and a multi-tooled Leatherman to a smart dress for special occasions, cotton clothes for comfort in the heat, shoes and sandals, a medical kit, malaria prophylaxis, a dictionary and professional manuals, sun-tan oil, toiletries, a short-wave radio, and even a universal bath plug. Waiting like a mother hen to round up her chicks was Dolores Long, one of VSO's resident staff in Lusaka. Perhaps a bit younger than me, with short, brown curly hair, her long, blue cotton dress matched her twinkling blue eyes. Obviously well-known to the authorities, she shepherded us through customs and past hordes of young men eager to earn a dollar by carrying a bag, towards a waiting minibus and trailer. While we climbed into the bus Dolores supervised the driver and his mate as they packed our luggage into the trailer. Once that was locked she handed out bottles of much needed ice-cold water. The chatter in the bus as we got to know each other was deafening. There had been a great deal of e-mail correspondence between us, and a few of us had met during training weekends at VSO's college in Birmingham, Harborne Hall, but for most of us this was the first opportunity we had had to meet our fellow volunteers.

Leaving the airport there was little grass on the wide roadside verges and what was left had been toasted to a sad, dusty oatmeal colour. Each passing car showered those walking along the unpaved walkway at the roadside with clouds of sandy grit. While some pushed overloaded bicycles, most walked. A family would be strung out in a line, father first, seldom carrying anything, mother and children following behind. The women wore colourful print dresses in reds, blues and greens and most carried a child on her back as well as a basket or bundle tied in bits of material on her head. Many were barefooted. No one appeared to be in a hurry.

Extensive roadworks near the outskirts of the city caused a traffic hold-up and in the delay Dolores took the opportunity to tell us some basic facts about where we were staying and what we would be doing in the next few days. Once in the city centre, people, many in European-style clothes, stood in groups at pavement stalls or strolled along avoiding cracks and holes in the paving slabs. It looked all very shabby and very laid-back. Lusaka is a relatively modern city and its architecture demonstrates this. Apart from two or three tower blocks of around ten storeys, most of the buildings which lined Cairo Road, its wide main thoroughfare, and the small squares which led off it were angular blocks of no more than four storeys high. Hero's Square, a small square off the east side of Cairo Road, was where VSO had its offices on the top floor of a building occupied by the British Council. When we stopped at traffic lights boys and young men worked their way between the vehicles selling newspapers and a variety of other goods including boxes of oranges and children's toys. It was all a far cry from Ratho.

We passed the Fairview Hotel, a three-storeyed pre-war style building with a small car park within high metal railings, where we would start our in-country training the following day. From there we twisted and turned through roads which although still tree-lined became narrower and more potholed. At one corner, a woman was roasting sweetcorn cobs on a small charcoal brazier and at another there was a small stall made from odd pieces of wooden plank, where the goods for sale seemed few. At least traffic drove on the left, a relic of the country's colonial past. Until independence in 1964 Zambia had been Northern Rhodesia, part of the British Empire but now was a member of the British Commonwealth, and one where English was the language used for administration and in business and commerce, and still the language common to all parts of the country.

Our driver sounded his horn as he stopped nose-in towards the large black gates of the Cha Cha Cha Backpackers, whose name had been taken from one of the 'freedom' slogans used during the campaign for independence. When an elderly gateman pulled back both sides of the gate, the minibus drove inside and stopped in a parking area to the side of a low building set in a small garden.

As we piled out of the bus the driver and his mate pulled our luggage out of the trailer. Instructions before we left the UK had been to put the things needed for the first ten days in a holdall there being insufficient space at the Backpackers for all luggage to be stored there. Gradually the melee sorted itself out and what was not immediately required was repacked back into the trailer. Four male members of our party, Dave, Carl, Justin and Will, were shown into a dormitory in the main building while Dolores led the six females to huts at the far end of the garden where we were to be housed. Ruth, Sue and Miriam, a Dutch volunteer and the only non-British member of our group, were in the first of these while I was on my own in a small A-frame next to it. Emily and Vicky had the fourth. The third one was already occupied by Chris and Amanda, the only couple in our group. They had been travelling in various African countries before joining the rest of us in Lusaka but had already encountered some difficulties. When journeying by train from Dar es Salaam in Tanzania to Kapiri Mposhi in Zambia's Copperbelt some of their luggage containing many of the important items they would need in the next two years had been stolen.

I looked round my temporary home, two sloping sheets of thatching which met at the top of the 'A' held together with a bit of tarpaulin. The rear wall was filled in with mosquito netting, as were the areas around the wood and netting door in the front wall. Faded curtains gave some privacy. A mosquito net, pulled together and tied in a knot, dangled over the single bed, beside which were a small set of wicker shelves and a woven floor mat. One single uncovered electric light bulb had been fixed to a spar of the frame. It may have been lacking in home comforts but then it was only for ten days and I had my own space. Dolores had already assured me that the house allotted to me in Ndola, the city in Zambia's Copperbelt where I would be staying and working was comfortable.

After a lunch of chicken stew and rice eaten at a rustic table on the backpackers' veranda, Dolores dished-out some Zambian kwacha notes to each of us, an advance from our VSO quarterly allowance of K1,800,000 approximately £370 sterling, and the going rate for Zambian middle management. I liked the idea of being a millionaire even if the rate was about K4,700 to the pound. With the remainder of the day to ourselves Sue Clay and I set off on a walk round the local streets to see if we could find our way to the Fairview Hotel because the following morning we had to get there on our own. As we walked between the ditches and house walls on what was the pavement, only there was no paving, just red hard-packed earth broken by tree roots, we spoke about what we were trained for. Sue, a trained counsellor who would be working with Kara Counselling, an HIV/AIDS charity, was amused by signs for a health clinic with the unlikely name of 'The Pearl of Hope.'

Back at the Cha Cha Cha, Sue and I collected beers from the bar before joining some of the others sitting round the miniscule swimming pool. The beer, called Mosi-oa-Tunya, the Zambian name for the Victoria Falls, tasted like a very light lager and seemed to be the only alternative to the products of the Coca-Cola Company. I was beginning to work out who was who. I had met Sue, Justin Highstead and Carl Edmonds before arriving in Lusaka. We had all been together at a training day on the HIV/AIDS situation in southern Africa. Carl was a twenty-seven year-old Londoner whose training was in health education. Since his placement was also with PFZ in Ndola we had been in regular contact by telephone and e-mail during the past few weeks. Among the twelve of us we brought a variety of skills to Zambia, including health education and counselling, building and construction, journalism, teaching, fund raising and business expertise. Apart from me at sixty, the others ranged in age between twenty-five and forty. What was important to VSO was not our age but that we each had a skill which we could share with our soon-to-be Zambian colleagues.

Our evening meal was served on the veranda, which after sunset at around 19.00 hours was dimly lit by one low-wattage bulb. Exhausted by travelling I was early to bed. When the mosquito net was unfolded, it had one or two holes which might have stopped bats but certainly not mosquitoes. Too tired to care, I crawled under the blanket and fell asleep as soon as my head hit the pillow. I woke at about one in the morning, chilled. I was shivering. First thought was that I could not have caught a fever after less than twenty-four hours in the country, then I realised that while it was not cold by UK standards the temperature had dropped considerably from its daytime peak and the A-frame gave little protection. I huddled under my thin blanket regretting that I had packed my sleeping-bag among the luggage which had been taken away to be stored at the VSO office. Still shivering, I pulled on trousers, socks and a fleece before cuddling under the blanket. It didn't feel as if I had slept when I heard dogs barking although my watch showed me that it was just after four o'clock. As one dog quietened another two or three started up. It was as if one guard dog had been disturbed and when it started to howl a competition was launched as to which could bark the loudest among all the others. When dawn broke at around six I was glad to take my place in the queue for the showers. Cleaned and dressed, I sewed up the biggest holes in the mosquito net for already I had several bites around my ankles. If they were mosquito bites, I could only hope that the prophylaxis worked.

Breakfast over, we set off for the Fairview. It took us less than ten minutes to wander round to the hotel. The last winding street leading to it was lined with jacaranda trees, the branches of which were covered in hyacinthine-blue flowers. The road surface was rough and rutted but the picturesque trees and the colourful carpet of fallen blooms which surrounded each tree trunk made walking along it a pleasure. Beyond the hotel door was the reception desk and behind it was a row of clocks showing the current time in different cities around the world. While the hour hands allowed for the difference in time zones, the minute hands also showed different times. That each minute hand should have been identical seemed a matter of little concern to the reception staff, who smiled happily when someone remarked on it. We were pointed along a corridor, panelled in dark dingy wood, to the room set aside for

VSO. Kate Greenaway, VSO Programme Manager in Zambia, had joined Dolores for the first morning session. Our group was joined by four more VSOs who had arrived in Zambia in June and two students who were doing a one-year placement in Zambia under VSO's youth scheme. When it came my turn to introduce myself to the company I decided to make my contribution light-hearted by saying that the husband of a friend had thought VSO mad to accept me as a volunteer for I was 'half-blind, half-deaf, asthmatic and a pensioner.' It raised a laugh among those present although Kate wanted to know if the husband was considered a 'friend.' At the coffee break, Dolores said she had some news for me. She had just heard that the house in Ndola which had been identified for me to stay in had gone on fire overnight and had been totally destroyed. As she put it that was the bad news; the good news was that I wasn't in it.

Chapter 2

Wash My Bikini

Our first days in Lusaka were a time of acclimatisation, getting used to the temperature and altitude, as most of Zambia lies on a plateau about five thousand feet above sea level. Our programme was a crash course on being a VSO in Zambia. Many of the problems we would encounter had been covered at our training weekends in the UK but in a general way for VSO has volunteers in thirty-four of the poorest countries around the world. Now we heard specifically about VSO's work in Zambia, the support it gave its volunteers, and the behavioural standards expected from them. There was information on what was culturally acceptable, the importance of greeting people correctly, compliance with local dress codes, even instruction on how to eat Zambian food with our fingers. We were given tips on bargaining for food and goods in local markets and guidance on dealing with corruption which we were warned was an accepted part of daily life. There was advice on personal safety and suggestions on how to keep healthy and how, if we were unsuccessful in that, all volunteers, no matter where they were stationed, were registered to get medical help at the Corpmed Clinic, a well-equipped mini-hospital in Cairo Road.

One of the most interesting talks was by a lecturer from the University of Zambia on the history of the country and how it slid from being the third richest country in Africa to one of the ten poorest countries in the world. His talk on the political and economic history of his country put much of what I had previously read about Zambia into context, helping me understand some of the problems Zambians had suffered in the years from independence in 1964. Among these were how in 1965, just one year after independence, the sanctions placed by the United Nations on its neighbour, Southern Rhodesia, when the government of that country made its declaration of unilateral independence (UDI) had the effect of cutting Zambia off from its traditional trade routes and ports in South Africa and Mozambique; the part Zambia played in supporting dissidents from African nations still ruled by white minority governments; the consequences in the early 1970s of the dramatic drop in the world price of copper, Zambia's main export, at a time when there was a huge rise in the price of oil on the international market. The world economy slumped and when interest rates rose, the payments on Zambia's debt escalated. Despite all their social and economic problems Zambians have remained very proud of being an independent nation.

After four days in the country we had learnt much about Zambia though our living conditions at the Cha Cha Cha were still westernised. All that changed on Friday night when after supper the beat of skin drums reverberated across the backpackers' garden luring us to the poolside where women in long-skirted colourful print dresses, spotlighted by coloured electric bulbs tied in the trees, sang songs of Africa, sweet melodic airs sung without an accompaniment other than the soft pulsating drum-beat. Gradually the tempo changed. The singing fell away as the beat got faster, faster and still faster. When the women began ululating, a high-pitched note vibrated by striking the tongue rapidly against the palate, a shivery, tingling sensation ran down my spine. The drum-beat had reached an ear-splitting crescendo when four grass-skirted male dancers leapt out from behind the trees. Necklaces of bright coloured beads and feathers swung out from their necks as their bare feet kept pace with the rhythm of the drums. Their acrobatic performance was a maelstrom of colour and movement. I was in Africa.

Later many of the younger volunteers went off to sample Lusakan night life. I was happy to seek my bed, much more comfortable now that I had a second blanket, one borrowed from the fourth bed in the hut occupied by Ruth, Sue and Mirriam. They found their hut warm enough but were experiencing mosquito problems. All had been bitten on several occasions. The netting on a small window in their hut was torn making it necessary to burn coils to keep the mosquitoes at bay, though the coils left a smoky, chemical smell.

On Saturday morning we were taken on a tour of the city, driving through the affluent area where among the embassies of various countries including the UK High Commission and the American Embassy were the Anglican Cathedral, the High Court buildings and the Cenotaph. We had a short stop at Kabwata Cultural Village, a compound of traditional rondavels built originally by the colonial government to house Lusaka's black labour force. Since 1974 it has been retained as a centre where local arts and crafts were displayed for sale to visitors. There were toys made from wire, hand carved chairs and stools and African ant-art pictures. Carvings of elephants, hippos, giraffe and many other animals and birds were made from local soapstone, malachite and woods such as ebony and teak. Few of us bought anything, knowing that there would be opportunities in the future to buy souvenirs. Saying 'Shaaleenipo' (Goodbye) to the children who had gathered round we drove off to see a different side of the city, the more industrialised areas where at one site women were breaking stones by hand and men were making bricks by mixing cement in a bucket and pouring it into moulds. We passed through suburban housing areas where houses varied in the degree of need of repair, before skirting a township of mud-brick houses. After lunch we had time to explore on our own. Sue, Ruth, Mirriam and I walked to the Manda Hill shopping complex. While small by most Western equivalents it was modern, neat and tidy and security conscious, obviously the place where white Zambians and ex-pats working in the country as well as the affluent black Zambians chose to shop. There was a super-market, Shoprite, a branch of Game, and various clothes and shoe shops, a hairdresser and a bank with an ATM. One recognisable name was Woolworths but unlike its counterpart in the UK its merchandise was restricted to clothes.

Sunday was a day of rest. Having heard that non-residents could for a small fee use the leisure facilities at the four-star Taz Pamodzi Hotel, just a ten-minute walk from the Cha Cha Cha, Sue, Ruth and I opted to spend the day there. Relaxing by the swimming pool, lying on comfortable loungers while shaded from the sun by large parasols, was indeed luxury. We agreed it was the first opportunity in months that we had had time to read for pleasure rather than books to do with Zambia and our placements. After a short time I put my book down, feeling twitchy and unsettled. The African dancers, the city tour and now beautiful gardens with watered green lawns, exotic flowers and shady trees, a large swimming pool, a nearby bar and restaurant and waiters ready to serve drinks on request suggested being on holiday, something we were not. We were in a Third World country where there were extreme levels of poverty all around us and we were there to work. It helped a little when Ruth and Sue admitted similar confused feelings.

The following morning when we started language training I wished we were back lazing by the swimming pool at the Pamodzi. While English is the official language in Zambia there are seven local languages which are widely spoken and understood in the country, Bemba, Kaonde, Lozi, Lunda, Luvale, Nyanja and Tonga. Which language a volunteer learned depended on which part of the country your placement was in. Early in the twentieth century when the colonial powers carved up Africa they paid little attention to the tribal groups with the result that a country such as Zambia contains many different tribes with members of one tribe split between in two or three different countries. Bemba, the language used by over two millions Zambians in northern Zambia, was the one I was attempting to learn. In three days of tuition with Osman, a local radio presenter, and Brenda, a teacher, I was expected to have a basic knowledge of the language sufficient to enable me greet people, find my way around and buy essential goods. This seemingly simple exercise was not easy and Osman was almost driven to distraction when I failed to pronounce a sound he wanted to hear. I tried very hard but the sound I heard and then tried to reproduce was not often what Osman wanted. I also found it difficult to remember phrases. When walking to the Fairview at the start of our second day I confessed to Ruth, also a Bemba student, that as soon as I thought I had mastered a phrase and went on to the next, I forgot the first one. It was encouraging that she, a teacher and much younger than me, was having the same problems but she was using phrases in English which sounded similar as an *aide-memoire*. For the greeting '*mwashibukeeni*' (Good morning) she used 'wash my bikini.' That helped a little.

The test came on Thursday morning. We walked with our tutors to the City Market, off Cairo Road, a large hangar-style building where a number of stalls were selling everything from household items to food. Using our newly acquired language skills, we had to make a purchase. Ruth, Helen Gosnell, one of the students with VSO youth programme, and I were accompanied by Brenda, who led us past stalls where fish without the protection of ice were set out to attract buyers. Their ghastly glazed eyes stared up as they lay there decomposing in the heat. Butchers' stalls were worse as flies hovered all round and the stench was stomach-turning. At least when we reached the area with household goods there were fewer insects and the smell did not seem quite so bad. Brenda suggested that we each purchase a piece of *chigenge* material, the colourfully printed cotton pieces which local women wore on top of their clothes and wrapped round babies to support them as they carried them on their backs. While we might not be required to carry a baby, chigenges had many uses. Curtains and tablecloths could be made from them. Helen and Ruth had both successfully made a purchase and then it was my turn.

'Mwashibukeeni,' I stammered to a stall-holder.

'Mwashibukeeni,' she replied.

'*Muli shanni, mukwai?*' (How are you?). This was one phrase I was confident with and I remembered to add 'mukwai' a sort of general

13

sir or madam, a polite courtesy. We had learned that in Zambia you did not get straight to the point, but talked through pleasantries such as of how the night had been, how you were that day and about the family.

'*Bwino. Nga iwe, mukwai?*' (Fine, and you?)

'*Nidi bwino, mukwai, naatasha.*' (Very well, thank you)

At this point I should have continued with the courtesies but I gave up. Getting flustered, I pointed to a piece of green material with a pattern in blue and white and stuttered,

'*Ninshinga?*' (How much is it?) Then far too late to do so remembered I should have added "mukwai."

I was so relieved when she replied in English 'Five thousand *kwachas*, madame,' that I forgot all about speaking Bemba or indeed bargaining, which is expected, and said,

'I'll take it, thanks very much.'

She laughed, probably at having made such an easy sale, and wrapped my purchase in a piece of old newspaper before handing it to me saying,

'*Naatasha, mukwai.*'

Reminded that I was supposed to be speaking Bemba I managed to say,

'Naatasha, mukwai, shaaleenipo.' (Thank you, Goodbye).

At great speed she rattled off a long speech in Bemba to Brenda and while her body-language suggested that it was about us not even Ruth and Helen with much more advanced Bemba skills than me could follow any of it. Then in perfect English she thanked us for making our purchases at her stall urging us to come back soon.

A further opportunity to try out one of our newly acquired skills, eating *nshima*, the staple food of most Zambians, came when we went for lunch to a local restaurant in a side street near the market. It was little more than a few wooden tables and some red and blue plastic chairs set out on a concrete platform where a rough wooden roof shaded clients from the fierce noonday African sun. At the back was a wall where painted murals of the items on the menu were peeling with age. The redolent cooking aromas permeating from behind this wall were being overwhelmed by the stink from a nearby open drain. I had eaten nshima before. Friends in Scotland who had lived in Zambia had introduced me to this Zambian dish, a sort of stiff porridge made from maize, but then cutlery had been available. This time there were no knives and forks. Trying to ignore the stench, I surreptitiously took a wet wipe from my handbag and gave my hands a quick rub. Along with the others I then damped my hands in the bowl of water which had been abruptly stuck on the table by a young girl who appeared confused about serving foreign white people with Zambian food in a restaurant principally used by locals. Taking a small portion from the piping hot nshima in the fingers of my right hand, I tried to roll it into a ball with which to scoop up the accompanying chicken stew and then strove to get the lot into my mouth without plastering it all over my face but was not entirely successful. If I was to stay in Zambia for the next two years I had to get used quickly to eating like this. The following evening nshima would be served at the dinner at which we should all meet for the first time with the representatives of the various organisations for which we were going to work.

At this dinner we would be using our newly attained knowledge of Zambian cultural manners. After as much titivating with dress and make-up as I was able to do in the limited facilities of the backpackers' hostel, which lacked a decent mirror, I walked with the other volunteers one last time to the Fairview Hotel. In the high evening temperature we strolled along the tree-lined roads where the jacarandas had dropped their lovely blue flowers into carpets on the dusty surface. At the hotel I would meet some of the people I would be working with for the next two years. In two days' time I would be travelling two hundred miles north with them to Ndola to take up my duties. The mood among the volunteers was one of suppressed excitement. All we had been working towards for many months was about to begin.

Chapter 3

'Journey into a far country'

Approaching the Fairview Hotel, we passed a row of gleaming white 4x4s and at the end of the line one battered fawn Toyoto Hilux. On its dusty door I could just read 'Prison Fellowship Zambia' stencilled in blue. Once inside the hotel Carl and I were introduced to Rev. Francis Mpzeni and Maurice Shakwamba, Chaplain and Health Co-ordinator/Project Manager respectively to PFZ. Maurice stretched out his right hand towards me. As he did so, his left hand supported his right wrist. I carefully did the same and we both bobbed in a slight curtsey. We had greeted each other with respect. I turned to Francis to do the same but he opened his arms and pulled me into what he called a Christian embrace, but which felt more like an uncomfortable bear hug.

The fifth person at our table was Osman, our language instructor. He had previously explained that Osman was his family name but that it was perfectly polite to address someone by surname without the courtesy of the title 'Mr'. After the introductions and Rev. Francis had said grace there was what would have been considered a lack of conversation in the UK. Food took precedence over talk. I had to stifle my impatience as there were a hundred and one questions I wanted to ask, the most urgent one being "Where am I going to stay?" Dolores in her role as my Placement Officer was the contact between VSO Zambia and PFZ. Since hearing about the house fire she had e-mailed PFZ and had been assured that suitable new premises had been identified. The responsibility of arranging housing furnished with such basics as a bed, table and chair and an easy chair is undertaken by the organisation receiving the volunteer. No matter how hard I tried on this subject I could not get information from either Maurice or Francis. I was told that as I was in their care I would be looked after. Carl and I did learn a bit more about PFZ, a Christian mission to prisoners, ex-prisoners, their families, and the victims of crime. In the mid-1990s it had adopted a holistic approach to its work of taking the Christian message into the prisons and now undertook health work, in which Carl would be involved, ran a micro credit scheme and did vocational training. My involvement would be to work with the Director to improve the management and accounting systems in all parts of the organisation and help staff in writing funding proposals. One bit of information I did glean during the evening was that there had been a change of Director. Rev. Ennocent Silwamba, with whom I had expected to be working, had moved to the UK to study theology and had been replaced by the Rev. George Chanda. It was Ennocent's home I was to have occupied. Far away in the UK it must have been upsetting to learn that his home had been destroyed by fire. Maurice and Francis's main concern was that they wished to start back to Ndola the following evening, Friday, rather than on Saturday morning as previously planned. Carl and I could have insisted on waiting until Saturday but thought showing a willingness to co-operate would stand us in good stead with PFZ so we agreed that we would be picked up from the Cha Cha Cha at 17.00 hours on Friday.

Our instructions on cultural differences had made us aware that a Zambian's sense of time differs greatly from that of a European. A European understands time as linear; past, present and future. A Zambian thinks of it as circular, what goes around comes around. 'Mailo' in Bemba means both yesterday and tomorrow. No Zambian gets too worried about being later than planned. So there was surprise when the PFZ Hilux trundled through the Cha Cha Cha's gates at 16.30, half an hour before the appointed time. It didn't take long to load Carl's and my personal luggage together with the water-filters and mosquito nets which VSO provided for each volunteer into the rear of the Hilux. VSO also supplied fridges and cookers and the ones allotted to Carl and I had already been delivered to PFZ in Ndola. They had not been in the house which burnt down.

Farewells taken, we set off through the Lusaka rush-hour traffic. It was soon obvious that it was going to be a very slow, exceedingly hot and dusty journey. The temperature was still over forty degrees Celsius in the shade and showed no sign of lessening. Vehicles of every description jostled for space. There were dilapidated mini-buses crammed to capacity with returning workers, old bangers with cracked windscreens, bright shining white new Mercedes whose smooth suspensions were being tested to the limit on the potholed surface, and powerful 4x4s, all of this throwing up clouds of rust red dust. The speed was that of the slowest overloaded truck, although from time to time an impatient driver would overtake blindly, causing much blasting of horns and screeching of tyres. I kept hoping that Maurice, at the wheel of the Hilux, would not get too close to the lorry in front. Its load of family furniture bore more resemblance to the makings of a Guy Fawkes' bonfire than a household on the move. That a young lad was sitting on top trying to keep things from falling off only increased that impression.

Approaching the outskirts of Lusaka, we bounced down the Great North Road, the main road leaving the city for travellers not only to the north of Zambia but also to Tanzania and the Democratic Republic of the Congo (DR Congo). A pall of smoke drifted from refuse being burnt in ditches at the side of the road. A market area near the city boundary, a few stalls made from old planks of wood, was strewn with rubbish. Grubby children often competing with goats and hens scavenged through the dirt for anything of use or played among the litter using the outflow from a waste pipe to make mud-pies. Into all of this ancient minibuses disgorged their passengers. We drove under an arch, where I could see sufficient letters still in place that made me realise it was proclaiming the country's independence in 1964. After being waved though a police checkpoint, a series of oil drums, painted with black and white bands and set in a line along the middle of the road, Maurice casually explained that we had been mistaken for a government vehicle so had not been stopped. As I watched the driver of the 'Guy Fawkes' lorry being directed to the side of the road for questioning it dawned on me that the police at these checkpoints were armed with machine guns.

Once out of the city and into open countryside the traffic, now considerably reduced, speeded up a little. The sun still beat down mercilessly from a seemingly endless blue sky. Occasionally we passed through villages where the road was lined with a few little shacks which served as shops. I wondered where small businesses such as Mallindu's Grocery, The Honest Butchery, Njombe's Investment and General Dealers, and Joe's International Café got their custom, for from the little I could see the villages were very small with little apparent hinterland. Mostly it was miles of open savannah, dotted here and there with the odd dusty tree and occasional columns of smoke, a land which probably had changed little in centuries. It would have looked much like this when David Livingstone made his explorative African journeys almost one hundred and fifty years before. Everything, including us, was parched dry and covered with a film of red dust. After months of drought those who lived there must have been eagerly anticipating the welcome relief the rainy season would soon bring. An hour or so into the journey the brilliant sun became a fiery red ball in the western sky. For just a few minutes, as it dropped rapidly over the horizon, it cast a deep pink luminosity, a brilliant glow over everything. The sky, streaked with orange and saffron, swiftly darkened to leave only thick, inky, darkness. The heat remained just as intense. I still peered eagerly out of the windows but now could see little but the elephant grass at the roadside swaying in the headlights of the occasional passing car and an odd pinprick of light flickering in the darkness.

After about 120 kilometres of bumping between the crater-sized potholes we reached our first town, Kabwe. We pulled up in front of The Hungry Lion, Zambia's answer to McDonalds; all that seemed to be on offer was chicken and chips. Any worries I might have had about food hygiene disappeared for surely anything coming out of that boiling hot fat had to be reasonably free from lurking bacteria.

Kabwe appeared to be one long street. The high-raised covered pavements lined with shops were reminiscent of scenes from countless cowboy films. Originally known as Broken Hill, its claim to fame was the discovery in 1921 of an almost complete human skull and a few other human bones estimated to be over 125,000 years old, the oldest human remains yet found in southern central Africa.

Maurice's warning that the next bit of road was the worst was truly vindicated. The Hilux bounced and swerved, jumped and skewed. With no seat belts in the back, I held on to anything which stopped me being thrown about. The suspension had long since accepted defeat. The rest of the vehicle did not seem far behind from going the same way and my body was beginning to empathise.

Our luck at police checkpoints did not hold. At one stop an overweight policewoman eyed us suspiciously and was extremely curious about the *musungos* (whites) in the rear seat. She suddenly grabbed the door nearest me, causing me to almost fall out on top of her. When she gabbled something unintelligible at me, I could only think to try out a local greeting, fleetingly and incorrectly remembered from my language tuition. My Scottish accent together with a greeting more suitable for morning than night-time, 'Mwashib-keeni mukwai'and my poor pronunciation of it, sent her into gales of laughter which suggested any crisis there might have been was over. Any remaining danger came from her already strained blouse buttons. My face was in the firing line if they exploded off, a very likely scenario as her massive bosom heaved in merriment, stretching the material to bursting point.

After a further thirty miles the road improved slightly. We passed through Kapiri Moshi, the only other town en route to Ndola and the site of the only major road junction. It is here that the road to the east branches off, leading onto Dar es Salaam, almost two thousand kilometres away on the Indian Ocean. The only other incident of note was at yet another police post. This time the officer knew of PFZ's Christian Mission. He was reluctant to let us pass unless we gave him a Bible. Maurice convinced him we did not have any and eventually we did get on our way. For the remainder of our journey Carl and I were left to discuss all the things we would have to do when we eventually reached our houses.

It was well past 22.00 hours, when we at last reached the outskirts of Ndola, after an exhausting, hot, dusty journey from Lusaka of over five hours. I felt the jolt when we crossed the railway line and Maurice said we had crossed a river but I did not see even a glint of water. We passed the hospital with its many darkened windows, circled a roundabout, and took a quick turn right before pulling in at black gates set in high walls covered in broken glass and barbed wire. Dead-beat and almost completely drained, I tried to focus on what was happening. I heard the name 'George' being spoken and prayed 'Please may we not be taken to meet the new Executive Director at this time of night.' Maurice and Francis got out of the car. Eventually I learned we were at a guesthouse and a check was being made to ensure that George had remembered to book us in. I had arrived at my second abode in Zambia, thirsty, dirty, and desperately tired.

But sleep was still a long way off. Maurice and Francis were in conversation with the guesthouse managers, a Canadian couple. Everything was discussed between them in English, as if Carl and I were not there. I heard the lady-of-the-guesthouse say, 'I've put Anne in the flat but Carl will have to share a room in the main building.' Our luggage, water filters, etc., were being hauled from the Hilux and dumped on the ground.

The whole area of the guesthouse was fenced off with interior fences behind which dogs could be heard barking fiercely, not something destined to make me, severely bitten by a dog when a child, feel at ease. The first building was the managers' house with its own small garden. Across a modest courtyard was a low single-storey building with yet another building to the side. I was told this was the flat. Here was my first lesson but not my last in 'same word, different meaning' between standard English and Zambian English, for I had been looking for a building with more than one storey. A helper was busy moving my luggage and I went with him to the flat. It consisted of one fairly large room separated into seating, dining and cooking areas with two separate bedrooms leading off but no toilet or bathroom. These were across a small covered walkway and were to be shared with other guests. By the time I had had a quick look round and rejoined the others, Carl's luggage was being dragged towards the main building. When I asked why Carl could not have one of the two bedrooms in the flat, there were looks of shock and horror. Exhausted, I blurted out, 'Good heavens, I'm old enough to be his mother if not his grandmother.'

That brought further hurried discussions and then his luggage was dragged towards the flat and after mutterings about some food supplies that had been left and that someone would come and collect us the following day we were left in peace to make ourselves comfortable for the night. The bedrooms were clean but fairly basic, a single bed and a wicker dressing table, and the one I chose had a mosquito net already in place.

Exhaustion, dehydration, and a lack of food, for there had been only the chips in Kabwe since a sandwich at lunchtime, together with all the tension of the unknown, had given me an almighty headache. On my own I might well have just fallen into bed but Carl had started to look for food. His six-foot frame needed sustenance and certainly I needed water. I had started the journey north with a supply of bottled water but in the heat had drunk it so was relieved to find in the fridge a container of clean, filtered water. There were also milk, tea, a chicory mixture which served as coffee, sugar, margarine, bread, rice and spaghetti, and my first cockroach. It got thrown out. While I made tea, Carl cooked our supper, spaghetti in marge, seasoned with some black pepper, left by a previous occupant.

Chapter 4

Ndola

Tired as I was, I did not sleep well. When dawn broke just after six, I gave up trying and got up. The cement-floored shower across the passage was Spartan which didn't encourage loitering. Back in the flat I made a cup of tea and settled down on the rather hard settee with a novel, one of six books borrowed from the British Council Library in Lusaka on an 'out of town' membership. They had to be returned sometime during the next four months.

Carl had still not put in an appearance. Breakfast was beginning to seem like a good idea when there was a loud knock on the door. The odd-job man who had brought my luggage to the flat the previous evening had come to guide Carl and me to the guesthouse lounge where he said visitors were waiting for us. Assuming Carl still to be in the land of nod I went alone. A young couple sat nervously on the edge of a sofa. The man, tall and slim, rose as I entered. He introduced himself and his wife as Robam and Mary Mukubwa. He said that he was the accountant at PFZ and Mary and he had come to invite Carl and me to go to church with them. Suddenly I could not think what day of the week it was. Could it be Sunday? Seeing my confusion Robam explained that they went to church on Saturdays and he thought we might like to join them. Still a bit nonplussed by his offer I said how tired I was and of how as far as I knew Carl was still asleep so perhaps we could forgo this unexpected but kind invitation. They were obviously being friendly but I thought we still needed time to adjust to our new surroundings. He looked disappointed but said he had one of the PFZ vehicles so would come after church to take us shopping for food. They would have to leave the service early as the only supermarket in the town, Shoprite, closed at 13.00 hours. Not sure whether I had heard him correctly I hesitantly enquired:

'Leave early, if you are en route for church now?'

'Oh yes. Don't worry. We will be here in plenty of time for shopping.'

Church services in Zambia seemed to last much longer than those in the UK.

Back in the flat and with Carl up and about we gave a lot of thought to the shopping list. What did we need? How long were we shopping for? Were we moving into our houses that day and what else did we need besides food? We were ready and waiting when Robam reappeared with a Toyota Venture which looked a bit more reliable than the Hilux of the previous evening. On being asked about our housing, he was no more informative than Maurice and Francis had been.

Having visited a branch of the Shoprite chain in Lusaka I had some idea what to expect. There was plenty fruit and vegetables, oranges, apples, grapes, tomatoes, sweet potatoes and ordinary 'Irish' potatoes but many shelves had large empty spaces. You certainly did not choose by brand but by what you could get. The beef looked good and there were chicken and pork. Having decided to pool our resources for this first shop, Carl and I worked our way round getting what we felt would see us over the weekend. Knowing that the following Monday and Tuesday were holidays celebrating the anniversary of independence, and unsure when we would have the next opportunity to shop, made it difficult to judge what we would need. When Carl saw some beer on a shelf, it seemed a good idea to add a few bottles to our shopping basket. Checking-out took time for with no barcode scanners the check-out staff had to look for the sticky price label on the goods and key it in. Before being allowed to leave the store we had to display our till receipt to the security guard standing at the exit. He had to have proof that all goods in our bag had been paid for.

Robam dropped us back at the guesthouse and said he would pick us up again at 18.00 hours. There was to be a welcome dinner for us at a restaurant. That evening I dressed with care in a matching cotton skirt and blouse of pale blue check. In keeping with local custom, my skirt was at least four inches below the knee. I wondered about wearing make-up. I was not sure how that would be viewed now I was at my placement but decided in favour of it, feeling that a personal statement had to be made at some point and that it might as well be sooner rather than later.

It was almost dark when we stopped in front of a row of darkened shops. Only one street light appeared to be working and that was some distance away. The paving stones were neither level nor secure. It was almost an obstacle course to reach the one door where a single light showed but I made it skipping over holes left by missing slabs. Through the door was a dimly lit long room with one large table. Carl and I were seated in the centre of one side while the Executive Director of PFZ, George Chanda, and what seemed to be the more senior members of staff sat facing us. Rev. Francis Mpzeni, the chaplain and one of the few members of staff I had already met, led the company in prayer and read a short passage from the Bible before grace was said and Carl and I were invited, as guests, to lead the way to the buffet table at the far end of the room. A lot of trouble had been taken to prepare this reception for us. There were dishes of meat stew, rice, nshima, chicken legs, baked potatoes, various vegetables and salads and bottles of Coke and Sprite. Aware of how precious food was in Zambia, I appreciated we were being offered a great compliment. I chose a small amount from each dish. Carl did the same while whispering to me that he could always go back for seconds. He quickly found out that that was a mistake. Zambians don't leave food. They don't always know when they will get their next meal so when there is food they eat it. Poor Carl, he even had to remember that it is polite in Zambian society to leave a little food on your plate indicating to your host that you have eaten sufficient to satisfy your hunger. A chicken bone did the needful for him. Water was brought for hand washing. We were invited to tell the company something about ourselves. There were more prayers and then with hardly any time even to say 'Hello' to everyone, we were returned to the guest house. I still did not know the names of most of my new colleagues.

How my life was changing. A meal out on a Saturday night and back home by eight. Our good manners in choosing to eat little at the reception had left Carl ravenous and even I felt peckish. Thankfully, not knowing about the dinner, we had bought food for Saturday so we ate a pasta supper, split evenly between two plates. The amount of food on my plate would have kept me going for a week. Agreement was reached; in future when we ate together two-thirds to Carl, one-third to me. As we spent the evening talking we learned a lot more about each other. Carl, tall, slim, with broad shoulders and dark hair, was twenty-seven. He had a degree in psychology and a Masters in Health Education. His family stayed in East Finchley, London, but he had been working in Leeds. As a student, he had spent some weeks in Nigeria and it was then that the idea of working with VSO had appealed. He felt that if he was to achieve this, the right time to do it was now, before he probably settled down with a wife, family and mortgage. At the opposite end of the scale, he learned that I was sixty, five feet two in height and just a little rounded. I had a home in Ratho on the outskirts of Edinburgh, and how having spent thirty-six years in banking the opportunity to take early retirement in 1993 had been timely for John's health problems had taken a turn for the worse. Both of us accepted that our reasons for being here were varied and not completely altruistic. Being useful and sharing skills with our Zambian colleagues was mixed in with the chance to travel, stay in and learn of a different culture, and meet new people.

We both declined the offer of being taken to church the following day. It wasn't just the length of the service. It had more to do with a feeling that we had to be our own person even as we appreciated the kindnesses our Zambian hosts were showing us. We used the time growing acquainted with Ndola, Zambia's second city and the commercial capital of the Copperbelt region. The city centre, laid out on a grid system, included most of the government, adding vocal flourishes in between the lines. Prayers, including a request for divine help for Carl and me as we started our new duties, were followed by a Bible reading and a brief homily given by George. Devotion completed, George held a staff meeting when the business of the week was discussed, much of which revolved round our arrival. When everyone else was dismissed, Carl and I were asked to remain. We heard of how Prison Fellowship had come to be formed, of how Charles Colville, one of Richard Nixon's staff caught in the Watergate break-in, had founded Prison Fellowship International after serving his sentence in prison and of how there were now affiliated organisations in over eighty countries, including the United Kingdom. George handed out lots of papers on the organisation as well as information giving the terms and conditions local staff had to adhere to. Although they did not affect us directly, as we were volunteers and not paid Prison Fellowship staff, he expected us to respect these terms. He went on to explain that he knew that in our culture certain things were seen in a very different light from how they were viewed in Zambia. He understood that there would be certain aspects we might have difficulty adhering to and that for example he could not force us to abstain from drinking alcohol. However, he did not want to hear that either of us had been found drunk in the gutter. Obviously, our purchase of four bottles of beer, unthinkingly done on Saturday, had been noted and reported back. At the end of the interview, we still did not know what was expected of us in the way of work, but I had learned two valuable lessons: one, because I came from a different background, people would pay close attention to what I did, and two, my preparations had proved to have been less thorough than I had thought. I had never anticipated that something as innocuous as having a bottle of beer would cause a problem. I thought of the horror there would be in the office if George knew of the empty beer bottles lying in my bag, which sat on the floor by my feet.

Chapter 5

'Getting to Know You'

George informed us that until clearance arrived from the office of the Commandant in Chief of the Prison Service which would allow Carl and me to visit prisons, we were restricted to working at the PFZ offices. Since this was where I had expected to be working either with the director or the accountant I didn't see that as a problem. Most of those early days, I spent my time watching and listening. George, whose promotion from Manager of the PFZ Micro-Credit Project to Acting Executive Director had been so recent that it had still to be confirmed by the PFZ Board of Management, was settling in to his new duties. With so many demands on his time he had little to spare for me. Robam was obviously unhappy with the title of "accountant/administrator" which had been given to my placement. He was protecting his position and was reluctant to let me have sight of the accounts. While we never had a face-to-face confrontation about it, that would not have been the Zambian way, he made it clear that he thought I should take on the menial tasks which in his opinion were more suitable for a woman. While letting him know I hadn't come six thousand miles to be his clerkess, I played for time watching, listening and learning about office procedures while letting the staff get used to me being around.

In the absence of the Chairman of PFZ, Dr Mathani, an international businessman, George had driven us to meet Bishop Chikwamba, the Vice-Chairman, who had welcomed our being there and the skills we each brought to PFZ. But both Carl and I were meeting unexpected hurdles despite our presence having been given the blessing of the Board of Management. Carl's problems began after he started training the PFZ health volunteers who visited the bookkeeping but I still had much to learn about how things were done here and Mark appeared satisfied that it worked.

Gradually I became more aware of the variety of work and the problems faced by PFZ. There always appeared to be someone sitting on the blue settee in reception waiting to see George or looking for help of some kind. When prisoners' wives called bringing with them a string of children and a variety of problems it was often Regina and Mutinta who dealt with them. Newly released prisoners came looking for clothes and money to pay their fares home. Chama, the office gofer, looked after a supply of cast-offs from which he could usually provide something, although the style and quality of these was often not appreciated. Through all of this Mutinta ran a secretarial service for anyone needing letters typed as a fund-raising venture, a bit like a modern day scribe.

The days passed with no developments on the house front. What was increasingly obvious was that PFZ had never identified a house for Carl. Despite the looks of horror from Maurice and Francis when I suggested that he move into the second bedroom at the guesthouse, they must have been hoping that I would agree to Carl sharing my house. And then one Thursday afternoon I was told that I was being taken to see a house. First impressions were excellent. It was in the city centre, a small compound off a road leading from Broadway with some signs saying 'Blantyre Road' though others named it 'Blantyre Avenue.' Whichever it was, it was a wide, tree-lined road near the centre of town, named after the small town in Scotland where David Livingstone, respected here for his stance against the slave trade as well as his missionary work, had been born and lived as a child. The compound, called Zawi, was sandwiched between the High Court building on the south and an overgrown park on the north, the site of burgeoning bougainvilleas I saw on my first Sunday walk round Ndola. There was a high wire fence all round, except where an eight-foot wall divided the compound from the park. That afternoon the wire gates in the fence stood open, showing the central garden of grass and trees with five blocks of red roofed single storey houses; two blocks of four terraced houses on each side; and a single block to the west surrounding the grass covered area. A little guard hut stood just inside the gates. Although the people I saw were mostly young or children, the general appearance of the compound reminded me of sheltered housing for the elderly.

It looked good so I was optimistic when George parked in front of the third house on the left. Two steps led up to a flat area in front of a wooden door in which a window had been cut. The covering was of torn mosquito netting but could easily be repaired. The cracked glass panels on the inner door were a bit more dis-heartening but my spirits were truly dashed when I walked into a room thick with dust then stumbled over a pile of rubble, bricks, broken plasterboard, lime and dirt, which lay in the middle of the floor. Though the haze I could see that bare electric wires were dangling from the ceiling and an electric plug was hanging off the wall. The metal window frame was twisted and a handle was missing. With a sinking heart and trying not to breathe in the dust, I skirted the debris, and looked through one of the internal doors. It led to a kitchen where the fittings were circa 1940s. Bolted to one wall was a hot-water tank which had bits of wire sticking out the bottom making it look like some piece of Gaudi art.

Going through the second internal door I saw where the rubble had come from. A wall built to partition this bedroom in two had been knocked down. The window here was in only a slightly better state than the one in the living-room one and the metal curtain rail above it reminded me of those used at home when I was a child. The bathroom which opened off the bedroom also looked circa 1940. The bath had dark stains under the tap area and the bottom of the toilet bowl looked filthy. The seat was grubby and only half attached as the area around the hinges was broken. Now I knew why Claire Welch, the returned volunteer I had met in Edinburgh, had warned me about needing cleaning materials. While I was thinking about this, George was saying something about my moving in on Monday or Tuesday. Panicking, I tried to say it would take me some days to make it ready, but he did not see any problems.

'Keep calm,' I told myself. 'Explain what the problem is in clear terms.'

When I tried to speak of the rubble, dirt, electrics, security, mosquito netting, I got the standard answer, I was in PFZ's care and was not to worry. Back in the office, George was not available so I spoke to the other staff, but again felt I was not listened to. On Friday, there was no one in the office I could speak to about the house. As the day wore on, I got more and more worried. If I could have got access to the house during the weekend I could have started cleaning, but this now seemed unlikely. Eventually, I decided that the only thing I could do was to express my concerns in writing so I made a list of the problems and gave it to Robam when he arrived in the office late that afternoon.

Carl, who still had not had any information on his house, went with me on Saturday morning on a shopping trip to Shoprite to buy food for the weekend as well as things I would need, such as a kettle, a plastic basin, a blanket and a pillow. Completely over-laden, we decided it was too far to walk back to the guesthouse so would try travelling on one of the dilapidated blue and cream minibuses which ran around the town. There were no destination boards or bus numbers to help identify the one we wanted and it took a little while for the bus boys to accept that we musungos were serious when we asked which one passed near the road the guesthouse was on.

A door in the side slid open to let passengers climb in. Four seats were squashed together on a bench, backing on to the driver's cab. Of the three rows of seats which faced them, the first had three seats, the second had three fixed seats and one which folded up to allow access to the back row of four seats. The only empty seats were in the back row. Leaving my pillow with the bus boy but still clutching my other purchases, I hitched up my skirt and to the

37

great amusement of the other passengers clambered clumsily past the folded seat and over the wheel casing. Once seated, the window at my side was opened and the bus boy pushed the pillow in on top of me. The bus took off with the bus boy standing, balanced in the door space. Still like this, he collected the fares. Passengers passed kwacha notes forward to the people in front who in turn passed them on to the bus boy. Change was returned in the same way. Getting out was even more awkward than getting in. Attempting to scramble back over the wheel arch, while clutching the pillow and two polybags, I stood on the hem of my skirt and almost nose-dived out the door.

Pleased to have successfully managed that trip, we decided on a second one. This time our purchases included a few bottles of beer. Having passed the Shoprite security guard, we stopped to load our purchases into backpacks. The last beer bottle had just disappeared, when the PFZ Venture drew up beside us. Robam was driving with Francis beside him. Thinking we were going to get a lift back to the guesthouse, I climbed into the back-seat but one look at Francis's face told me he was annoyed. Had he seen the beer bottles and were we in for another lecture on alcohol? I got a lecture all right, but not on alcohol. He ranted and raved at me for a good three to four minutes before stopping for breath. I was still not sure exactly what my error had been, only that it seemed to have something to do with the note I had written regarding my worries about the house. He kept going on about communication. When I tried to say that what I had been trying to do was communicate because no one would talk to me about the house, he started all over again. Through it all, Robam sat with his back to us, looking steadily out of the front window. Shocked at being harangued like this although I could not understand why such umbrage had been taken to a simple note, I wondered what had happened to the Christian welcome given just a few weeks before. There was no suggestion of a lift to the guesthouse and by then I didn't even want one. Holding back tears with difficulty, I struggled out the vehicle before they spilled over. Carl followed. He seemed to be as astounded as I was. Even as Robam drove off, I was still aware of Francis venting his anger.

Apart from some words of comfort from Carl, we hardly spoke as we walked the mile back to the guesthouse. I think we were both trying to make some sense out of what had happened. I was exhausted. Later we talked it through and came to the conclusion that I had, in ignorance, made a cultural error. I decided that I had to speak to George immediately after prayers on Monday morning.

The devotion on Monday morning was taken by Maurice but I did not absorb much of it. I was concentrating on what I wanted to say to George. He agreed to my request for a meeting, but Francis remained in the room. He positioned a chair to the side of George's desk and sat with his long legs crossed. The top one swung back and forth non-stop. I sat in a chair facing George. Still feeling emotional, I explained that I had not intended any discourtesy when I wrote regarding my worries about the state of the house. It appeared, however, unwittingly I had done this. That being the case, I offered him and PFZ my apologies. I did, however, think that it was time that the situation regarding the house was discussed, in case I made another such mistake, particularly as I understood that after the fire in the house designated for me PFZ had promised VSO that they would have accommodation ready for both Carl and me. As I felt my meeting with George should have been private, I refused to look at Francis but was aware that the swinging of his leg was getting faster, a sign of irritation. While George was obviously embarrassed by the whole situation, he took the wind out of my sails by announcing that over the weekend the house had been painted and I would be taken there later in the morning. But I still did not know if I was supposed to move in that day.

Robam drove me to Zawi. On the way we stopped to get light fittings and bulbs. The house had improved. Debris had been removed and the walls given a coat of cream paint, which smelled very strongly of metal. Judging by the number of spots and splashes on the floor, the work had been done at speed with little preparation, just a quick brush over with paint. Chama was there with a mop and pail wiping the floors. As I thanked Chama for his help, I began to see how different cultural thinking had led to the problem. I had expected to have to personally clean the house. PFZ staff did not think a white woman could or would do this. I had worried because no one would tell me what was happening; the Zambians thought I would not worry if they said they would look after me.

My neighbours in the compound were curious about the white woman who was coming to stay there. Children pressed their noses against the windows to see what their strange new neighbour looked like, then ran away giggling when chased by Robam or Chama. It was not only the neighbours who were curious. Gradually over the morning different members of staff and my landlord, Allan Keppeso, arrived to see what was happening. If I was to have any privacy, curtains were immediate necessities. Mellbin Simingola suggested where material could be purchased and that the tailoring department of PFZ would make the curtains. No one actually said that I would not be moving in that day, but gradually I realised that no one was expecting me to.

Mellbin got great pleasure in looking at different materials until we agreed on a heavy green cotton brocade for the bedroom, a patterned dark blue with green print for the living room, and two lots of chigenges for the kitchen and bathroom. He checked all the material from end to end to ensure there were no flaws before allowing the assistant to make out an invoice. When I took this to the cashier, it was carefully checked before my cash was accepted and a rubber-stamped receipt issued. Only then were instructions given to the assistant to cut the required lengths. A second assistant wrapped my purchases in an old piece of material. Then this and my receipt were carefully scrutinised by the security guard before Mellbin and I were allowed to leave the premises. I had spent almost all of my VSO household goods allocation on curtains but felt it was money well spent.

Chapter 6

Zawi

I had a further reprieve on Tuesday. Allan Keppeso, who as well as being my landlord worked for the Zambian Electricity Company, called at the office to take me to the house. He had brought glass to replace the broken panes in the door and wanted to repair the hot water tank in the kitchen. George Chanda brought two joiners, some strips of wood and a roll of mosquito netting but no tools. They used my scissors to cut netting to fit the outside door and hammered in the nails to secure it with a large stone. Planning how they were going to make wooden frames to fit inside the metal window frames took much thought on their part and a lot of input from Allan and me. The end result was nowhere near perfect but better than it might have been had Allan not persuaded them to use a book as a set square. The screens would at least stop the less enterprising mosquitoes from getting in. Allan, unfortunately, was not successful in repairing the hot water tank.

The bedroom curtains were too long and hanging them presented problems for Chama, but by Thursday the bedroom was habitable if sparsely furnished. The wooden bed frame had a new six-inch deep foam mattress. By making use of some nails, hammered into the walls by a previous occupant and which like every thing else were covered in cream paint, I erected a mosquito net over the bed which was even quite colourful for the only cotton sheets I had been able to buy were fuchsia pink, covered with a sky blue blanket. There was a fitted cupboard with shelves and hanging space which would take my clothes.

My VSO fridge and cooker were brought from storage. The cooker which had two solid heating plates on the top and a small oven/grill was new and the box it came in was an unlooked-for benefit. Covered with a strip of material it served as either dining table or bedside table. The fridge appeared to have provided food storage for a number of other volunteers but a good clean would make it serviceable. There was a working surface at one end of the kitchen, with a cupboard below it while at the other end a fitment had been designed on the old dresser idea. Beside the back door a large cupboard would originally have been the larder, but time (and the fridge) had made it more suitable for storing cleaning materials. One look at the cupboard under the sink decided me that it would be best left unused.

I moved in on Thursday. Feeling rather lonely I ate my meal of scrambled eggs, all my meagre supplies could manage, sitting on one of the two dining room chairs which now adorned my living room and tried to ignore the annoying metallic smell of paint but which was not strong enough to get rid of the cockroaches. My table was the second chair, for apart from the fridge and cooker meant for Carl's house that was the only other piece of furniture in the room. There was still no definite news on PFZ's move to find another house in the same compound for him. As children from the compound kept peering through the window I had pulled the curtains shut even before the failing light made it necessary. While one had a straight hem, the other had a very uneven scallop and the pattern in the material was running in different directions. For all Mellbin's enthusiastic help, I think it was the first time the tailoring department had made curtains. I began to have some sympathy for PFZ whose plans for installing me in an already furnished house had disappeared quite literally in a puff of smoke.

Meal over, I planned to get down to some serious cleaning but when I turned on the tap no water came out. I tried the bathroom taps but the result was the same. I heard a neighbour pass by my back door and as there was light from the security lamp above the bathroom window I introduced myself. She said that water came from a borehole in the garden and the pump attached to it was turned on only at specific times, early in the morning, midday, and around tea time. I should get some containers and fill them during the times the pump was switched on. I did not have many vessels large enough to store water but those I did have were under the tap early the following morning, catching the trickle of water which dribbled out.

Up early on Saturday morning, I got to work before it grew too hot. All Zambians seem to rise at dawn, around six o'clock, but while I was not quite that early I was early enough to get water to wash in. My quick shower involved boiling a kettle of water and mixing the hot water from that in a pail with some cold. Standing in the bath, I soaped myself all over, then rinsed by using a plastic mug to scoop up water from the pail and pour it over myself. After a quick breakfast of tea and toast, I got the elbow grease going. I scrubbed out cupboards and swept floors. I scoured the bath and toilet. They weren't as dirty as I had first thought. This area is known as the Copperbelt because of the minerals in the earth. Water with a large metal content had over the years had left deposits, making everything look grimy. As the windows in the kitchen and bathroom where I was working were higher off the ground than those in the living room, I had some privacy from the children but every time I walked into the living room there seemed to be at least two little black noses pressed against the glass, trying to see what I was doing. If I went outside, they ran away, giggling. Eventually one boy, maybe nine or ten years old, dressed in a torn, red T-shirt and fawn shorts, became a little bolder than the rest and stayed within speaking distance. I told him my name was Anne and asked in English what his was. He took two barefooted steps backwards in horror, and turned as if to run and join the others. They had stopped a short distance away and were watching to see what happened. Slowly he changed his mind and turned back towards me. He obviously understood English for while studying his feet he said,

'Kawata,'

'Hello, Kawata.' I held out my hand.

Head still down, he watched me through eyelashes long enough to have made even a giraffe envious. He thought for a while, and then his grubby right hand, supported at the wrist by his left in the correct respectful manner, was placed in mine, but then mine wasn't particularly clean either. His pals crept a bit closer to see what was happening, and then a bit closer still. Kawata's back straightened. He'd been brave. He had spoken to this strange white woman, who came from a far-away country. He called the others over. They came, slowly, only one or two at first. Kawata introduced Chilomba, his younger brother, who was possibly five or six. Philippa, their little sister, came next. The beads on the end of her short hair plaits swung as she edged forward. She looked for Chilomba's hand and held on to it tightly. Still clutching that hand, Philippa pulled her friend, Judy, nearer. Judy's brother, George, who looked to be about eight, and had somehow managed to remain much cleaner than his pals, obviously felt that he could not be outdone by his little sister, so he joined our little group. It was George who told me that they were taught English at school. Suddenly there were about a dozen of them, dancing barefootedly round me, all trying at the same time to shake my hand and speak to me. They chanted my name, pronouncing it 'An-knee, An-knee.' I was aware that one or two of the parents were watching, but no one interfered. I felt this was the start to making friends at Zawi. However, I had made a big mistake if I thought that speaking to the children would make them less curious. For them, friendship meant they now had permission to stand at the window and look in. I definitely needed net curtains.

I was greeted with their chant and their unremitting curiosity about what I had bought each time I walked back from the shops, a journey made on three different occasions that morning to President Avenue, where Shoprite and some other shops were. Purchases included towels, plates and cutlery, a bread knife and a frying pan as well as food to get me through the weekend and the first few days of the following week. Buying bottled drinking water was no longer a necessity. The water filter system was now up and running. But I did buy glue and spent some time sticking the broken part of the toilet back in place, in the hope that the seat would stop slipping around every time I sat on it.

Carl and I had been invited that evening to a *braii*, (southern African for barbecue.) Mark knew Tony Tompkins and Anna Hovells, who taught at Simba, the International School in Ndola. They had originally come to Zambia as VSOs. Prison Fellowship had given permission for Mark to use the Venture for this occasion and it had been arranged that he would pick Carl up from the guesthouse, and then come to Zawi for me at around 18.00 hours. With some time to spare before changing to go out, and in an effort to get some quiet, I pulled the bedroom curtains shut and lay down on my bed, the only comfortable place to relax. Tired with all the day's exertions I nodded off.

Loud knocking woke me. Ignoring it, I turned over. It would be the kids. It kept on getting louder and louder and I kept ignoring it. When it got too persistent and with feelings of anything but friendship in mind I got up to chase the children, but when I opened the bedroom door I found out why the knocking had been so insistent – there was a river running through my living room. It came from the kitchen. Water was streaming through the door and was running on what must have been a slight slope towards the front door. Only a little was escaping under the door. Horrified, I kicked off my sandals and waded to the door through three or four inches of water. Having opened the door to let water run out, I turned back to the kitchen to see where it was coming from. As I did so, my neighbours, who had seen the water seeping through the front door, swarmed into the house. They followed me into the kitchen. It was like being in a London tube train during the rush hour. The place was full of bodies, large and small, fat and thin, some armed with mops and brushes, others just being nosy, but all giggling. The back door was opened. That let some water out, but let more people pile in. Water was streaming through the ceiling, down the walls, through the fuse box, over the cooker switch, into a lake about six inches deep on the concrete floor. It looked as if a water-pipe in the attic

45

had burst. Someone lifted a child up to the fuse box to switch off the electricity. I froze in alarm. No one else seemed worried. Thankfully all that happened was that the electricity was switched off. Another child was sent off with instructions to find my landlord, Allan Keppeso. The fridge was opened and food removed. It just disappeared out the back door. I felt completely helpless, as everyone else seemed to be busy, sweeping and mopping up water. I stumbled back into the living room and stood helplessly by the bedroom door. My camera, radio, and laptop were in the bedroom cupboard and I did not want them to disappear with the flood water. Eventually, when there was no water left in the pipe above my kitchen, only drips came from the ceiling. Gaily informing me that Allan Keppeso would come shortly, my small army of mops and brooms went off to prepare their evening meals leaving me with nothing to do but watch as the floors dried. In the heat, that didn't take long but the wooden kitchen cupboards were still wet and giving off a bit of a stink. My trouser legs had dried but were caked with mud and my T-shirt was damp and dirty. I was sticky, sweaty and altogether filthy but there was no water left to wash with. I would have given almost anything for a hot bath.

Before I had time to change my clothes, Carl and Mark arrived to take me to the braii. As I told the tale of the afternoon's happenings, and explained that Allan Keppeso was on his way to fix the electrics, I knew exactly how Cinderella felt when she couldn't go to the ball.

Allan wasn't long in arriving, maybe just another ten minutes after the Venture left, but by then it was quite dark. Using a torch, he took a quick look in the kitchen before saying nothing could be done that night. He promised to come back in the morning. My emergency supplies consisted of one torch, four tea-lights, and a small packet of matches. When I lit two little tea-lights they didn't give off much light, just a flicker in the otherwise pitch black. I couldn't afford to use up all four at once. I had to try and make them last and also I wanted to save my torch battery in case there was an even greater crisis. The feebleness of the light was the last straw. Completely shattered, I sank down on the edge of the bed, put my head in my hands, and let the tears flow. I had been so looking forward to going out. Most Zambians I had met had been very kind but it would have been nice to relax and make new friends without having continually to think about cultural etiquette. Instead, I had to get through a night without light or food, for even the bread in the fridge had gone. 'Come on,' I told myself, 'You have only twelve hours of darkness to survive. You can sleep and then shop for bread in the morning. Many people including those who mopped and brushed have to survive in much worse conditions.' But twelve hours seemed such an unbearably long time and I didn't feel at all sleepy. I just wanted to be home in Ratho, with my family, in my own comfortable house. Why had I ever had the stupid idea of becoming a VSO?

I began to worry that the house was a potential fire hazard. The house I should have stayed in had been destroyed by fire because of an electrical fault and I was staying in one where all the wiring was wet. With burglar bars on all the windows, the only escape routes were through the doors. Could I find the doors in the dark? The tea lights were moved away from the mosquito netting, just in case.

But just as in the old western film when the hour is darkest and the US cavalry arrives to save the day, my cavalry arrived, not on galloping steeds, but in the PFZ Venture. Anna Hovells, when she heard of my tribulations, had sent Mark and Carl back to collect me. It didn't take me long to get ready to go with them. I had made up my mind that I was not sleeping at Zawi. I checked with Carl that my room at the guesthouse was still available. The managers did not know it but they were having another guest for the night. My torch batteries no longer seemed so precious, so I used the torch-light to grab some clean clothes, a tooth brush, my camera, laptop and radio. I blew out the tea-lights and locked the door behind me as I left, thankful to be gone. It was only a short drive to Dolphin Court, where Tony and Anna lived. As I walked through their door, Anna took one look at me, saw the exhaustion beneath the dirt, and said the magic word 'Bath.' Hot water and fluffy towels, a dream come true.

Washed, refreshed, and in clean trousers and shirt, I came downstairs to meet Tony who was English, and Anna, who was Dutch. Both were tall but Anna seemed to have the edge. At the rear of their house was a small balcony with steps leading down into a garden. As this backed onto Nkana Road, the main road going north through Ndola, there was some traffic noise but not enough to disturb the peace of the evening. Coils and citron candles were burning to ward off the mosquitoes. The floral scents from the garden did not quite drown the smell of chemicals given off by the coils, but once the braii got going, the mouth-watering cooking aromas from the sizzling steaks and sausages took over. I settled down in a comfortable basket chair and gratefully accepted the offered cold beer. Life with VSO was not so bad after all.

Chapter 7

Settling In

The basket chair at Tony and Anna's home was comfy, the food was tasty and the conversation chatty. It was a pity that such a lovely evening had to be cut short, but Carl and I had to be back at the guesthouse before the gates closed at 21.00 hours. The managers at the guesthouse were sympathetic to my plight when they heard the tale of the flood at my house and I rented my old room for one night for US $6, less than £4.

When Alan Keppeso met me at Zawi the following morning, he climbed into the attic, wound some waterproof tape round the break in the pipe, mopped up the water which still lay in the fuse box with some rags and switched the power back on. The fridge motor coughed into life with none of the display of flashes and sparks I had anticipated. As far as Allan was concerned the house might still be damp but the problem was fixed.

What surprised me even more than the way the house dried out was that there were no children peering in the window and no neighbours sitting inside their doors, but then it was Sunday and in Zambia nearly everyone goes to church on Sundays. My neighbours, dressed in their Sunday best, began to return. They came in twos and threes or a family at a time. Those who had a Bible carried it very carefully. Often it was wrapped in a protective piece of cotton. Most of the men and boys were dressed in western-type clothes, trousers, shirts with creases pressed into the sleeves and colourful ties. A few had traditional shirts made from brightly patterned cottons. Cut to be worn over trousers, these shirts had short sleeves and rows of cream embroidery round the neck. Traditional dress for the women was an ankle length straight skirt made up in the same vibrant cottons as the men's shirts, topped with a matching, fitted blouse which showed a slim waist to advantage while the short sleeves were in a variety of complicated bouffant designs. Turbans made from the same material were equally convoluted. While many of the women wore traditional dresses there were some dressed in western-styled clothes reminiscent of those seen at Marks and Spencer and British Home Stores in the 1980s and 90s. Philippa and Judy came to visit me wearing pink organza dresses with short, puffed sleeves and sashes tied in bows at the back reminding me of dresses I had worn to parties some 50 years ago.

The Sunday clothes were soon replaced by those more practical for playing in the Zawi garden. During the afternoon inquisitive children visited me. Their parents were also curious about me but were not so open about it though I was sure they knew everything I did, for the children ran a very effective news service. My neighbour from number six knew my fridge was working when she called in the afternoon to return the food which had been taken from it during the flood. Following local custom I offered her a cup of water and thanked her gratefully for looking after the food. But I got the feeling that she thought I had bought more food than one person needed, saying it would have been dreadful if all that food had been wasted.

My days gradually acquired a routine. On weekdays I got up about six-thirty. My first job, even before warming water in the kettle for my plastic-mug shower, was to fill the containers in the fridge with drinking water from the water filter. It was important to keep the supply going so I put two pots of water on the cooker to boil. Once they had boiled for five minutes, they were put aside to cool until lunch time when I poured the contents into the top part of the water filter. The water was purified as it slowly dripped through ceramic cones into the lower container. Another important morning ritual was taking my malaria prophylaxis. Two tablets of Paludrine had to be taken daily and one of Nivaquine weekly on Sundays. The Venture, with either Mark or Mutinta at the wheel, arrived at around seven-thirty to collect me. I began to get to know different streets as we drove this way and that collecting various members of staff en route to the office. Still only slightly involved in the day to day work of PFZ, I found the days long. The lunch-time trip home was a welcome diversion. It also meant I seldom had to use the smelly, non-flushing, ladies toilet at the office. After Carl moved into No.13 Zawi, across the grass from my home at No.3, we shared meals again, taking it in turn to provide the food. Lunch was usually a sandwich made from freshly baked bread bought on the way home and filled with rather rubbery textured cheese and slices of tomato. A piece of fruit and a cup of coffee completed the meal. Getting the fruit was easy. There were always street vendors selling whatever fruit was in season. It was a bit more difficult getting the means to make a reasonable cup of coffee. Sometimes Shoprite would have Nescafe instant coffee on its shelves but it sold out quickly, so I had to be lucky to get a jar. People with vehicles could buy a number of jars but I was restricted by how many I could carry. Nescafe was a huge improvement in flavour but a lot more expensive than the local easily-obtainable chicory/coffee mixture.

One day at lunchtime Carl arrived back angry and annoyed. He had been subjected to one of Francis' bullying outbursts. He had disagreed with Francis in a discussion about Christian beliefs. Francis did not think that anyone who held views different to his should be involved with PFZ. He declared that in his role of chaplain he had jurisdiction over the beliefs of all who worked there. Carl had tried to point out that the information provided to him by PFZ prior to his accepting the placement had been that it was an ecumenical organisation. As such it accepted that all Christians did not have exactly the same beliefs. That had not saved him from Francis's harangue. Indeed he thought his response about PFZ's ecumenical stance had inflamed Francis even further.

When we returned after lunch it was obvious that George knew about the row and was trying to pour oil on troubled waters. Long discussions in Bemba between George, Maurice and Robam took place in the accountancy department. A few days later, a room across the grass from the main office and one not previously used by PFZ became the chaplain's office. The health department remained in the room in the corner of the complex. After Francis's desk and filing cabinet had been moved to his new office, the health department had extra space in which to work and that made life easier for the six PFZ local health volunteers who worked from there, as well as Maurice and Carl. My perception of Francis eroded even further two or three days later. When a call of nature forced me to use the office toilet, I found a very upset Marjorie Fwolishi taking refuge there. Marjorie was the only woman health volunteer. She had had a severe dressing-down from Francis and it must have caused her great distress for only desperation would have caused someone to seek shelter in that toilet. Francis, in one of his intimidating moods, had lectured her because she had taken part in the health department's sex education programme to prisoners about HIV/ AIDS. He said that as a woman she should not have been involved in this.

George wanted to introduce a more open management style, but knew there would be difficulties with certain members of staff who only understood a dictatorial regime. We discussed the possibility of the senior staff, George, Maurice, Francis, Robam, Mark and me, having weekly management meetings. No names were mentioned but we both knew that the most obvious source of dissension was Francis. My impression was that Francis felt that he, not George, should have been the one promoted to the post of Executive Director. George's plan was to hold such meetings each Monday after devotion. He would take the chair. As he wanted proper minutes kept, he asked if I would take on that charge. I agreed on the understanding that once a pattern had been established responsibility for the minutes would be passed on to someone else. I hoped to demonstrate how they should be taken, yet not be seen as a secretary.

Gradually I got involved in the work of PFZ. Maurice held the title of Projects Co-ordinator as well as Health Department Manager. He started to involve me in writing funding proposals for the tailoring and restaurant programmes. It soon became obvious that not only did he have great experience in networking and seeking funding, he had an incredible energy and commitment. He had a degree in economics from The University of Zambia and also an insatiable desire for further knowledge. I was not surprised to find that the health department was the best funded part of the organisation. I started to experience the 'Sharing Skills' part of VSO's motto for I had to draw on Maurice's experience before I could begin to write serious funding proposals. He was delighted when I used my contacts at home to get books sent from the UK on writing such proposals. To be effective I not only had to find out more about these departments, I had to be able to identify suitable sources of funding. I spent time with Mellbin and Idah, listening to their plans, trying to work out which were viable and which were just impossible dreams. It also let me see how the programmes were run for neither of these managers had had any management training, formal or otherwise. When I discussed this with George, we agreed that an afternoon a week should be set aside as a training session for programme managers for which I would be responsible.

But there was a cash-flow problem. It had become so serious that we were all involved in an effort to get the local churches to support PFZ's work financially. Every member of the PFZ staff had to attend church services throughout Ndola when we spoke of the work of PFZ before collecting donations towards it. On one such visit, Carl and I went with Francis to the Pentecostal Apostolic Assemblies which held its services in the gym at Kansenji High School. As there was a prison nearby the people of this area knew a little of PFZ's work. As usual the hymn singing was superb. There were three different choirs all taking part in the service. I loved it when the ladies of one choir, all dressed in colourful traditional dress, progressed down the centre aisle in a slow, stately dance. They came in two-by-two moving in unison, three steps forward, two back, swaying in time to the rhythm of their song. Carl and I were both invited to tell a little about ourselves and about our part in the work of PFZ. When Francis rose to speak, he told his own story. He was an expert orator, who knew exactly how to work an audience, when to make his point and where he had to bring in a joke to relieve the tension. He was very impressive, as was his story. He had been a policeman, in his own words, a bad policeman. He had taken part in an armed jewel robbery but had been caught. He never disclosed if anyone had been hurt in the raid but it seemed there might have been for when he was found guilty he was sentenced to death. He spent thirteen years on death row in Mukabekoh Maximum Prison in Kabwe, never knowing if each day was his last. While in prison, he became a Christian, or as he described it, 'He found the Lord.' After his conversion his request to President Kaunda asking for his sentence to be reduced to life imprisonment was successful. When Frederick Chiluba became President, Francis petitioned for a pardon, which was granted. Someone in Australia, who had heard his story, supported him by paying his expenses and upkeep for the two years he spent at the pastors' training school. After graduating, he joined the staff of Prison Fellowship Zambia. Listening to this I saw how his experiences must have affected him. During his time in both the police force and in prison he had been accustomed to being ordered about and to bullying and he knew no other way of behaving. What the effect on him had been of not knowing from day to day whether that day was going to be his last is something I could not even guess at.

Chapter 8

The Funeral of Bishop Chikwamba, PFZ's Vice-President

The news that Bishop Chikwamba, PFZ's Vice-Chairman, had died suddenly of cerebral malaria shocked everyone. Just two days before he had been undertaking a heavy workload. His death was a double blow to many at PFZ, for not only was he the link between the PFZ board and their day-to-day lives but as bishop of the evangelical churches he had been their spiritual leader.

As a mark of respect, the office was closed that day but the staff were instructed to gather at the office the following morning when we would go to the funeral service together. Mutinta asked if I would like to go to the funeral house with her. I didn't know what she meant by the 'funeral house' but she said this was the house of the deceased where friends gathered to commiserate with the bereaved family. I wasn't sure what to do. I declined the invitation as I didn't want to be seen as intruding on private grief but asked her advice about what to wear at the funeral. She said that while she and Regina would cover their legs with chigenges my blue checked skirt and blouse would be appropriate, saying my skirt was sufficiently long to be respectful. She also advised that I take a bottle of water with me.

The following morning, George's room was packed as we gathered together for prayers and instructions. The funeral was scheduled for 11.00 and was to be held in a building described on the map in my guide book as Broadway Cinema. Situated back off Broadway in a small square which also served as a car park and bus terminal for the Lusaka coaches it was no longer used as a cinema and had been taken over by one of the evangelical churches. Seats had been reserved for the PFZ staff but we had to be in these seats before ten o'clock as there would be a huge crowd struggling to get inside. We

55

travelled the short distance to Broadway in the three PFZ vehicles, which were then parked in the square. Instructions were given that when the service finished we were to return to the vehicles, but no vehicle was to be opened before every member of staff was present, otherwise the cars would be filled by members of the public struggling to get into or even onto any transport going to the cemetery. Roses had been bought and each member of staff would lay a rose at the graveside when called to do so.

We had to push our way through the large crowd which had gathered for the service. Many of the women were wearing chigenges with colourful patterns which identified them with certain churches or groups. All wanted to be part of this farewell to an obviously well-loved man. Many were weeping, some quietly while others were tearing at their hair and wailing. Some raised their beautiful voices in hymn singing. Inside, I sat with Mutinta and Regina in our reserved seats in the balcony. The place filled up fast with a colourful, noisy, chattering crowd who drowned out the singing filtering in from outside. The fittings and décor were still those of the 1930's style cinema. Seats and a lectern stood where once a screen had shown Hollywood idols such as Gregory Peck and Audrey Hepburn. Great bunches of coloured balloons were tied at each side of the platform and a table, draped in green, had been placed in front of it. The fire door to the left stood open letting in some much needed air.

Shortly after 11.00 hours the platform party of various pastors and local dignitaries arrived. They were followed by Mrs Chikwamba and her four children, one of whom was just a toddler. She was dressed in European style, in a simple black dress with a large white collar. We were all requested to stand when the coffin was brought in through the fire door and laid on the table in front of the platform. The lid was unscrewed and laid to the side. We were told to sit but Mrs Chikwamba remained standing throughout the service, although a chair had been set out for her.

Hymns were sung, prayers said, and one after another various speakers told of their associations with the late Bishop. His brother spoke on behalf of his family, a speech which referred only to his parents and siblings. His wife and children were not mentioned. One pastor after another preached, each louder and longer than the previous one. Coming from a Presbyterian background where a prospective minister can be asked to preach when applying for a vacancy, I began to wonder if that was what was happening. Mutinta had warned me that it would be a long affair. It was. In my short time in Zambia I had already realised that most Zambians will use ten words when one would do. At one church service, I had listened to a fifty-minute sermon on the brevity of the Lord's Prayer. By 16.00 hours, just as I was beginning to feel a desperate need to move, the service was brought to a close. One by one every member of that large congregation and all the people who had stood outside while the service was relayed to them filed through the front of the building and past the open coffin before leaving by the fire door. This opened into a small courtyard surrounded with a wire fence.

Along with some of my colleagues I pushed my way through the crowd back to the PFZ vehicles. We were jostled and squashed against the cars by people desperate to secure a lift to the cemetery but it was almost another hour before all the other members of staff eventually arrived. George, who had been trying to shelter me from the pushing and shoving of the crowd, called Carl over to where we were being squeezed against the door of his car. I expected him to tell us to get in, for he had been worried about me being elbowed and knocked by the swarming crowd and only fear of the numbers who would force their way into his car had stopped him taking the car keys from his pocket and thrusting me inside. Instead he instructed Carl to use his height to force a passage through the crowd for both of us. We were to go home. Darkness would have fallen long before the interment ceremony was complete and George was worried that it might be difficult and dangerous for us if in that huge grieving and unsettled crowd we became detached from the PFZ group. I would have liked to have experienced the remainder of the day's ceremonies, but as I was exhausted by the heat and the crowd going home seemed a great idea.

Chapter 9

'Friendships begin with liking...'

W hen Justin Highstead arrived unexpectedly in the office one Thursday, Carl and I agreed to meet him for a drink that evening. Justin's placement was with a newspaper which aimed at making teenagers more aware of the HIV/AIDS risks. He was in Ndola with Rachel, a Zambian colleague, to make arrangements regarding its circulation.

It was the first time Carl and I had been out in Ndola after dark on our own and we were a little apprehensive. George had impressed on us that people who went out after 20.00 hours were up to no good so it was not safe. Apart from the lack of working street lights, the only problem we had found in Lusaka when walking at night was that many cars drove without headlights. But in Lusaka there had been a group of us. We decided that a taxi might be a good idea as we weren't exactly sure where our agreed meeting place, Danny's Restaurant, was. Carl negotiated a deal with the driver of a battered banger. It was only when we had both climbed into the rear of the car and the driver took off with such acceleration that a shower of dirt and stones was thrown from his wheels that he turned round to ask where he would find the restaurant. He didn't appear to see the absurdity in agreeing a price without knowing where he was going. When I said I thought it was on President Avenue, he spun round in a U-turn forcing the one other vehicle on the road to do an emergency stop and his luck held for he missed every other obstacle that came his way including most of the potholes before pulling up in front of Danny's neon-lit entrance in another shower of dust and stones.

Danny's turned out to be an Indian restaurant. The outside was decorated with coloured lights while inside the walls were hung with sequinned tapestries depicting stories from eastern legends. The largest percentage of diners came from Zambia's Indian community with a few white Zambians and South Africans, some of whom would be involved in the mining industry. The cost of a meal here would exclude many black Zambians but there were a few present. Rachel and Justin were finishing their meal at a table near the rear. She knew of a nightclub nearby called Circles which they wanted to go to and sampling Ndola nightlife seemed a good idea.

Circles was dimly lit apart from where the bright disco lights lit up the few dancers gyrating on the small dance floor. A glass ball circling above them reflected the colours and threw off rainbow flashes. The music was not African. It was what I would have expected in any such night spot in the UK and similarly the decibels were high and hard on the ears. A bar was squeezed in one corner and as our eyes got used to the poor light we found some empty bench-style seats near a table. It would be busier at the weekends. Looking at the clientele, I realised that some Zambians do go out after 20.00 hours. It was fun to watch the dancers for Zambians have a fantastic sense of rhythm. When a young Zambian approached Carl and asked if he could dance with *Ba Mama*, i.e., me (*ba* is a form of respect), Carl said he could not answer for me. The request would have to be put to me personally so a rather embarrassed young man looked at me, not at all sure of what to do. With a smile, I joined him on the dance floor. After that I was never short of dance partners. I even got an offer of marriage but I think my British passport held more attraction to my suitor than me. To save any embarrassment to my partner I pointed to my wedding ring, the only piece of jewellery I had with me in Zambia, and we shared a laugh.

We didn't stay late. Carl and I had to be at work by 08.00 hours the following morning and Rachel was returning to Lusaka the following day. When Justin heard about our plans of travelling to Kitwe for the weekend he decided to stay on and join us. For all of us it was a chance to see a bit more of Zambia. Kitwe, about sixty-five kilometres west of Ndola, is the nearest town to it. Helen Gosnell, whom we met during our in-country training in Lusaka, had e-mailed an invitation to stay with her. She was working with CETZAM, a micro-finance project, and would meet us in a hotel bar in central Kitwe. I had never done a sleep-over before but armed with sleeping bag and sheet of foam was prepared to give it a try.

We met Justin after work and walked to the bus terminal on Chisokene. Again when we asked which bus went to Kitwe, we found disbelief that white people would wish to travel on a bus but eventually one was pointed out and we clambered on and sat patiently until all the seats were taken, for a bus in Zambia does not leave at a specific time. It goes when it has a full complement of passengers. What I had not realised was that full meant that folding seats over the aisle also had to have passengers on them. A tinned sardine would have had just a little more squiggle room for everyone on the bus had some sort of baggage. One woman even had a couple of live hens that protested about being tied up in a polybag. They clucked and crowed until they got the message from her well aimed kick. When someone wanted out at a stop en route, almost everyone on the bus had to move to let the passenger past.

Kitwe, a mining town similar in size to Ndola, relied for its prosperity on the nearby Nkana Mine. At the time of independence in 1964, copper was Zambia's main industry and wealth provider, accounting for 90 per cent of the country's exports by value. President Kaunda chose to spend the large revenues from the mines on badly needed education and social policies instead of using these monies to reduce the country's national debt, much of which was a legacy left from the colonial period. As the country fell deeper into debt there was little or no reinvestment in the mines and in an effort to direct their operations the government bought a share in each mine. But in the early 1970s the price of copper on the world market plummeted. The rise in oil prices in 1973 on global markets fuelled by the actions of the oil-producing states in the Middle East caused the world economy in general to slump. Zambia's debt grew and grew. Efforts to stabilise the price of copper failed. The government borrowed further funds from the International

Monetary Fund (IMF) banking on an expected rise in the copper price as the world economic situation improved. This never materialised and Zambia's economy deteriorated even further despite various programmes involving the IMF. The mines came under the control of the parastatal Zambia Consolidated Copper Mines (ZCCM.) In the late 1990s, as part of President Chiluba's government privatisation programme, ZCCM was to be sold off but the government, unhappy with the value put on the parastatal by the proposed purchasers, controversially turned the offer down. In 2000 there was expectation that full privatisation of the Nkana Mine would soon take place so even in the dark I could sense that Kitwe had a buzz about it lacking in Ndola.

Helen met us as planned and seemed pleased to discover she had an unexpected third guest. Another minibus took us to where she stayed in rooms attached to the CETZAM offices. A leisurely meal and tales of the new experiences we were all having made for a pleasant evening. The following day we headed by car first for Kalulushi, a small mining town about sixteen kilometres south of Kitwe where Mike Bird stayed. He was someone else we had met in Lusaka and was one of only two other VSOs in the Copperbelt at that time.

We had no problems finding Mike's house. He was obviously well known for when we stopped to ask for directions we were shown straight to it, a small bungalow, surrounded by a garden and a wall. Water was also a problem here and he had to use a tin bath for washing. After he proudly showed us the groundnuts and chillies he was growing in his garden, we set off for the Chembe Bird Reserve in the Chilyongoli Hills

We didn't see lots of unusual birds but it was fun. At the end of the hot dry season, the water in the small lake was low but still carried a 'Beware of Crocodiles' warning. We sheltered in a thatched cabin together with children and their leaders from a church outing during a short but fierce rain storm. Afterwards we joined them in a game of rounders. Back in Kalulushi, there was a slight panic when the petrol station had no fuel for sale. Mike saved the day. He found someone at the local market who sold us some black market petrol, enough to get us back to Kitwe.

By 21.00 hours, I would have been quite happy for another quiet evening but everyone else wanted to go to a night club. The whole ambience in Cinderella's was busier and more up-market than that in Circles. We found a table in the garden under a pergola draped with coloured lights. After a night of dancing and a lazy breakfast on Sunday morning Justin, Carl and I retraced our bus journey to Ndola arriving back in time for Justin to catch a coach to Lusaka.

The one disturbing part of the weekend was when the Zawi children, pleased that we had returned, told us that someone had been checking on our houses. This man had contented himself with looking in my windows but had been in Carl's house, saying that the back door had been unlocked, something which left Carl wondering if he had gone away for the weekend without checking the door. With the all-seeing eyes of children, Kawata and George could give a very good description clear enough for Carl to ask Francis the following morning if it had been him. Francis unconcernedly admitted it was he, saying he had only been concerned for our safety. No other member of the PFZ staff appeared upset by the knowledge that Francis had entered one of our homes unasked but I decided that I needed a stronger padlock on my back door.

One Wednesday Tony and Anna arrived by car to take Carl and me to a bar for a drink. They had arranged for two Irish volunteers from the Society of Missions to Africa (SMA,) Brian Higgins and Kevin McDonagh, to meet us there. Falcon's Bar was a small pub at the end of Independence Way with three chip-shop style benches and tables and blaring music. Sitting outside in the warm evening temperature relaxing while we waited for Brian and Kevin I wondered if anyone from PFZ would notice. A couple of beers were not going to incapacitate either Carl or me but the weekly devotion taken by Francis that Monday had included veiled threats about the eternal damnation which awaited those who drank alcohol.

Brian and Kevin took so long to arrive that we began to think they were not coming but just when we were deciding to go they turned up. Both were in their early twenties and had completed degree courses in Ireland before coming to Zambia the previous month. They were opposites, Brian fair and tall, Kevin dark and stocky. Their placement involved working with orphaned street children, mainly boys, left without homes. Getting these children into shelters at night would be something similar to the work done by Dr Barnardo in London one hundred years before. They said that they had been held up by something to do with work but I guessed from Tony's teasing that already they were noted for poor time-keeping.

Over the next few weeks a pattern began to emerge in my social life. Wednesdays meant meeting for a drink, usually at the Falcon, with Saturdays a night at Circles. Mike often joined us for the weekend, sleeping on Carl's floor. Brian and Kevin introduced a Norwegian volunteer, Torunn Wilk, who was more in my age group. Although Torunn had a vehicle to enable her get to one of the local townships where she taught crafts to women, she used it only during the day, realising that both she and the vehicle were at risk if the vehicle broke down after dark. Brian and Kevin also had a vehicle for their work but being male had fewer worries about this. While we enjoyed these sorties to a local bar sometimes we met at one or other of our homes and had a meal together. Anna's crepes were voted a scrumptious treat.

One Sunday, Torunn and I set off for a small recently opened lodge near Kitwe, where the walking trails near the higher reaches of the Kafue River carried notices saying 'Beware of crocodiles and hippo.' Neither crocodiles nor hippos upset us by putting in an appearance as we walked in the shade of trees, along paths lit with dappled sunlight. The jacaranda trees were still sprouting their pale lilac blossoms, complementing the whites, lilacs and blues of the Yesterday, Today and Tomorrow plants whose flowers last only three days, deepening from white, through lilac to blue before dying.

The 'Mountain Trail' turned out to be well named. A mountain-goat would have loved it but the view from the top of the very steep hill was worth the effort, even if it had taken scraped hands and broken finger nails to get there. Kitwe to the west was unmistakable because of the grey slag-hills, the tailings left from the copper-mining from which cobalt was extracted. Ochre mud-brick houses, some painted white or pink, and sun-bleached straw thatched rondavels were scattered among small cultivated areas, developed in ground where once there had been well-watered market gardens which in colonial times grew produce to meet the demand of the white miners and their families. From our lofty position we looked down on an open panorama of lands which stretched miles in every direction. Six months since the last serious rain, everything was tinder dry. Patches of dark smoke and orange flame showed where the bush was on fire, sometimes sparked off by the sun's rays, but more often purposely done to keep the bush from encroaching on tiny cultivated fields and also to chase out the small mammals living there which were captured for food. Villagers stood by the roadside with dead rats and mice hanging from a pole, encouraging passers-by to stop and buy.

Torunn and I did stop on our return drive to Ndola, not to buy dead rodents but to look at the Chichele Mofu Tree. In local Bemba tradition it is an Ngulu, a house of spirits in which the spirit of a long-dead chief lives. The tree had been left where it grew when the road was improved. It now stood, protected by metal railings, in the central reservation of the dual-carriageway. In 1976, it was declared a National Monument to commemorate World Forestry Day. Had superstition meant that the tree had not been moved as that would have upset the spirit?

We also stopped at the end of a tree-lined avenue which led to the memorial to Dag Hammarskjold, Secretary General of the United Nations from 1953 until his death on September, 17, 1961. Trees encircled the monument, a plinth topped with a world globe, which had been placed at the actual site of the aeroplane crash in which he was killed. Nearby was a small museum displaying details of Hammarskjold's life and career with the United Nations and telling of how he had been trying to negotiate a way out of the troubles in Katanga, the mining province of the DR Congo, when his plane crashed here. Although the crash happened not far from Ndola, there was a twelve-hour delay before the search party found the site. Forty years on it was difficult at first to understand why it had taken the authorities so long but when looking at aerial photographs taken at the time of the crash it was surprising to see that in 1961 this land had been a forest.

What I had taken to be trees planted to enhance the memorial site turned out to be the few which had been left when vast forested areas in the Copperbelt were felled to fuel the electricity generators for the copper mines. The deforestation began after World War II when the supply of coal imported from Southern Rhodesia had been insufficient to meet the demand of the power stations. Felling trees had continued until hydro-electric power became available from the Kariba Dam on the Zambezi. Between that and the slash and burn tactics used by small-holders to keep their land clear, by 2002 there were so few trees left in the Copperbelt that each day charcoal-sellers crossed the border from the DR Congo pushing bicycles laden with sacks of charcoal to sell in Ndola's markets.

Chapter 10

Go to Prison

When George announced that the prison authorities had forwarded the necessary clearance documents for Carl and me to be included in the prison visits, I was not sure if I was pleased or not. I knew it was important that I was aware of the conditions in the prisons but I expected visiting them would be a very unpleasant experience. George arranged for us to visit two local prisons, Kansenshi and Ndola Remand. The prisoners held at Kansenshi were serving short to medium term sentences and many of them had been convicted of theft. People held in custody while awaiting trial were held at Ndola Remand Prison where it was possible for the accused to have to wait up to five years before his case came to trial.

Kansenshi Prison was in the north-west part of town. We drove through the first set of gates towards a barrack square of hard packed earth where the Zambian flag hung limply from its flag-pole as if it too was suffering from the intolerable heat. The massive prison gates stood on one side. Opposite them were the administration buildings, one storey high with a long, covered veranda in front. George parked his car in the square. Seeking shelter from the blazing sun, we climbed the steps onto the veranda and waited in its shade until the officer-in-charge was ready to see us.

He was dressed in a smartly pressed uniform which consisted of a green jacket with shining brass buttons, one of which was missing, a Sam Browne belt, fawn trousers and highly polished ox-blood red leather shoes. I looked around while George and he went through our accreditation. The windows at both ends of the room were curtained in a bright green material patterned with orange palm trees. Together with the red settees and the chipped black filing cabinet which stood in the corner, the curtains made up the national colours.

Formalities over, we were shown the other offices and the medical room which occupied the rest of the administration building. When we crossed the square to the actual prison we were joined by two armed prison guards as protocol demanded that the officer-in-charge had to have a guard. Entry was through a small door which opened in one of the large gates. Coming from the bright sunshine into the shade my eyes took a little while to adjust before I saw that we were in a large entrance hall sparsely furnished with one small table on which was the visitors' signing-in book. Light filtered through the grill at the opposite side showing walls which were almost rubbed bare of the green and cream paint which had once brightened this cheerless place. A few charts and papers were pinned to the walls. One woman, a visitor who was waiting for her husband to be brought to the grill when she would give him a little food she had brought, sat curled up in a corner. As I entered my name in the visitors' registrar I caught the quite distinct smell of disinfectant.

The disinfectant smell was drowned immediately we passed through the grill door into the prison yard where the brick-red earth was baked solid by the sun which blazed directly overhead. In the stifling heat, nothing could overcome the stench of humanity which hit us as we walked between compounds divided by high wire fences. Gagging, I tried to breathe through my mouth in the hope that would help. Around us the guards on duty saluted and the prisoners froze into statues. Most were dressed in shirts and shorts of off-white rough cotton, something like flour-bag material. A few were in rags. All appeared to be about the same height and build, with stick-thin limbs. They seemed like clones of each other.

Our little procession consisted of the officer-in-charge and me, followed by George and Carl, who in turn were followed by our two armed guards. A guard unlocked a gate in one compound and we walked through. The prisoners stood silent, watching. It seemed that most had been sitting in whatever shade they could find. The cell building was about half the size of a tennis court and was made of concrete. It had a few small windows with metal bars set high in the walls. There was a suggestion that once the walls had been painted cream and green but what remained was now a drab colour-lessness. Some prisoners had tied their few personal possessions in supermarket bags and hung them from the window bars. The bags were pathetically small but their bright yellow plastic was the only touch of colour in that dreary room. At one end was a short stack of mattresses. When I asked a guard how many prisoners were accommodated in this cell, he looked around before saying quite casually 86 or 87, depending on the size of the prisoners. Each prisoner must have had just enough room to lie down. Later I found out that the mattresses were used by the cell captains, the men with most influence in the cell, and one of them might use four or five mattresses for himself while the ordinary prisoners slept on the concrete floor with no space to turn unless everyone else turned at the same time.

With those conditions, one toilet which no longer flushed and with no protection against mosquitoes these cells were breeding grounds for diseases such as TB, cholera and malaria. HIV/AIDS was a huge problem in the prisons. The miracle to me was that anyone survived. We saw where the prisoners washed both themselves and their clothes. There was water with a piece of soap which was more valuable than any precious metal. At another part of the prison, a large pot of nshima was being cooked over a fire made from the branch of a tree. The guards' comments suggested that a prisoner got one portion of nshima each day. This would be supplemented with vegetables from the prison gardens and occasionally there would be a little meat. We saw the gardens and the vegetable plots where prisoners were watering their crops very carefully for what was produced here provided some nutrients in their diet. On these rations hunger would only be alleviated, never satisfied, but the vitamins and minerals from the vegetables would stave off complete malnutrition.

There were a few women prisoners enclosed in a completely separate part of the prison. The crime many had been found guilty of was theft but if a mother has no food to feed her children or money with which to buy food the temptation to steal must be overwhelming. Some young children were with their mothers. A mother who had no one to look after her children outside prison could keep them with her, but she was allowed only one ration of food. Often these children were still being breast-fed. Possibly because of the shortage of money for food, mothers in Zambia breast-feed a child long after a western child would have been introduced to a diet of solids. The trauma of being in prison must have increased terribly for a mother who had older children with no family to look after them, for these children would have to fend for themselves on the streets. PFZ's practical help to the women came in three ways. It tried to ensure that food was available for the children in prison, that children left at home were looked after, and they sought donations of sanitary towels.

The conditions in both parts of the prison were awful but with almost no resources staff were trying very hard to improve them. It was clear that they valued Prison Fellowship's assistance with the prisoners in practical matters such as health education and vocational training and also in spiritual guidance.

I was even more impressed by the staff at Kansenshi after I had been to Ndola Remand Prison. This time the stench met me long before I was inside the green painted building where the crenulated walls reminded me of Fort Zinderneuf in Beau Geste films. Here we were kept waiting in a small, dark office for some considerable time before the officer-in-charge was ready to meet us. A chair was set out for me. The men stood. When I saw the chair, which looked as if it would fall apart, I would have preferred to stand but that would have offended the secretary who was being polite. It possibly was her chair. There were holes where the missing arms should have fitted and the horse hair stuffing was pushing out from under the dirty cover. I felt it wobble as I sat on it very gingerly. Eventually we were shown in to the officer-in-charge's room. The greeting was much more restrained than the one offered at Kansenshi. His room was small, poorly lit, overcrowded and untidy with curtains of the same design as at Kansenshi pulled over the windows. My view of the prison was restricted to a look through a door into a central open quadrangle. Cells opened onto this area but we were discouraged from going into the prison.

By the time we got back to the office I felt filthy and exhausted and was only too pleased when 17.00 hours came and I could get home to wash. My make-do shower using a plastic beaker now seemed like a luxury. I had expected these visits to be grim and was not disappointed. People can with time reconcile themselves to living in awful conditions and the prisoners had no alternative but to do so. The respect I had for my PFZ colleagues, especially the volunteers who were paid expenses only for their weekly prisons visits, had been raised considerably. Personally, I was promising myself that I would be very careful and law-abiding during my stay in Zambia. The last person I ever wanted to be, was a prisoner in one of those prisons. Visiting them had been a very disturbing experience.

Chapter 11

'Water, water everywhere' – but not a trickle from the tap

When I first arrived in Zambia, I was told that the hot wet season could start anytime after Independence Day, October 24. Although we had had two or three heavy showers the actual rains did not begin until well into the last days of November. I had seen people carrying large golf-style umbrellas. I had even seen a great number of these for sale in Shoprite. Each week I promised myself I would buy one but I kept putting that particular purchase off for another week. I left it too long for when the real downpour began and the dirt pavements and roads became ankle deep with dirty-orange slimy mud and the trees dripped long after the rain had stopped there were no umbrellas left in Shoprite or in any other shop. Even wearing a nylon mackintosh, I was soaked to the skin. The water went straight through the seams.

It did not rain non-stop. Although there were some overcast grey days when the rain was a steady drizzle, called London weather by the locals, most days the mornings started bright, sunny and oven-hot. Some days stayed that way. On others the energy-sapping humidity would build up until I felt like a wet rag, wrung-out and unable to concentrate on anything. Relief from the humidity came at last in the form of a light breeze but when that gentle breeze began to rustle the leaves of the mango tree in the PFZ office garden I learned to take cover as rain would follow soon after. Often as the sky darkened with rain clouds, there were electrical storms, sometimes two or three rolling around simultaneously. Again and again lightning, like some expensive fireworks display, would force its forked spikes across the dingy sky illuminating everything for a second or two. As one clap of thunder burst overhead there would be echoes of it from other storms some distance away. Rain, great sheets of water, pounded down. The noise of it battering against the corrugated-iron roof reverberated throughout the office making concentration on work almost impossible. All electrical equipment had to be switched off to protect against power surges. That meant the electric fan which made working conditions just bearable had to be unplugged. Frequently there was a power failure. The staff sat and sweated in the half-dark, wincing at some of the loudest bangs of the storm. Nothing could be done until the storm had passed. Deaths from lightning strikes were not uncommon during these storms which normally did not last long, thirty minutes at the most, ending as quickly as they started. The relief to the ears was soothing, the reduction in the humidity levels refreshing, and the bright sunshine cheering even if everything outside was flattened and covered in water.

If caught in a vehicle when the rains came caution was required, for although a travelling vehicle ran any lightning strike safely into the ground, the windscreen wipers were useless against the deluge. Responsible drivers, and there were not too many of them, drove very carefully even after the rain had stopped for the roads became quite dangerous. The force of the rain washed loose gravel out from potholes making them much deeper. It found any weakness in the road surface and roughed it up until a new small crater was formed. The next storm would make it bigger and even deeper. Often the potholes were hidden by flood water because the drainage ditches, blocked by rubbish could not clear the torrent. Sometimes a pot-hole was found only when a wheel sank axle deep into it, causing damage to the suspension. Accidents were common. I could under-stand why 4x4s were popular. Not only were they higher off the ground so less damage was done if a wheel went into a deep pothole but the four-wheel drive was needed to give grip on the dirt-roads. These had been baked so hard during the dry season that the rain water reached the top layers only, turning the surfaces into greasy glutinous sludge, quite as slippery as any icy road.

I realised immediately why Zambians longed for the rainy season. Their land was transformed. Much of the dust was washed away. The leaves on the trees changed from dusty grey to shining green. Everything looked and smelt fresher. The blue jacarandas had finished flowering but red and yellow flowering trees brightened the streets. There were flame trees in the garden surrounding the High Court, immediately behind Carl's house. In the early morning light when I pulled back my bedroom curtains, I could see why they got their name. Their orange-red blossoms rose high above the leaves making them look on fire. Within a day or two un-trodden areas of brick coloured earth began to take on a green film, as dormant grass seeds started to sprout. Orange and brown French marigolds grew in clusters where the PFZ vehicles parked outside the office. Tall red, yellow and orange iris-type flowers shot up in the damp drainage ditches. The brilliant colours, the freshness in the air, the broad smiles on the Zambian faces all joined together in giving the town, poverty stricken though it was, an air of cheerfulness. I was getting used to this country. People were certainly getting used to me. To begin with they stared at me as I walked past, sometimes alone, sometimes with Carl or one of my other work colleagues, for it was very unusual for a white woman to walk, especially if elderly. Many people began to smile shyly at me. Some of the bolder ones shouted, 'Muli shaani, madam?' They pronounced it 'ma-dam'. While I did not know who they were, they knew exactly who I was and where I worked. They assumed I was a missionary for that seemed to them the logical explanation for a white woman living among them. One Zambian actually told me I was 'a strange type of missionary.'

With no street lights many houses had outside security lights. At Zawi, all houses had one light over the bathroom window at the rear of the house and one over the front door. I had no control over the light at the rear but there was a switch for the one at the front door. When I got up in the morning, I put the light off and Carl knew I was fine and vice versa. Most nights we still shared our evening meal, taking it in turn to make it. It was not easy to buy quantities of food suitable for one and there was no freezer storage. So quite apart from the social advantages of sharing a meal it was also more convenient to cook for two every second night rather than cook for one every night. In the fierce heat great care had to be taken about storing any remaining food safely. We got back from the office around 17.30/18.00 hours when we each went to our own homes. That gave time to wash and freshen up, particularly important as mosquitoes are attracted by sweat. While it was cooler to wear a skirt during the day, I changed into trousers and a long sleeved shirt in the evening as a further prevention against being bitten. Any areas left uncovered were treated with an insect repellent. Sometimes there was work to be prepared for the following day, especially if one of us was doing formal training or coaching. About 19.30 we met for supper, possibly a pasta or rice with chicken or pork and some fruit. Having cleared up we usually spent an hour or so listening to music, talking or doing a crossword puzzle. One night when I left Carl's house to cross back to my own, a distance of about twenty metres, I found one or two flying ants buzzing around. At certain times of year, deep within an ant hill, changes take place so that the new ants are hatched with wings. This enables them to fly off and form new colonies thus ensuring the survival of the species. They weren't dangerous, just a nuisance, until I got to my own door, where the light had attracted them in thousands. While I tried to get my key in the lock, they got in all round my face, in my ears, my hair, under my specs, so I couldn't see, against my nose, so I had difficulty breathing. I felt as if I was in Alfred Hitchcock horror film 'The Birds.' I pushed the ants away and struggled to get through the door without opening it too far, only to discover that inside was as bad as outside. They had got under the door. I slammed the door shut and ran through the living room. The bedroom was not quite so bad but still they were buzzing round my face, down the neck of my shirt, in my hair. Without waiting even to take my shoes off, I dived below my mosquito net and onto my bed. The net was already tucked in under the mattress on three sides and I pushed the fourth side in as quickly as I could. Some ants did get inside but as they flew against the net its impregnation against mosquitoes killed them. I removed my shoes but that was one night I went to sleep without washing. In the morning there were only a very few ants still alive. The floor was covered with a layer of tiny black bodies and miniature transparent wings. I swept them up and threw them outside. Later I got a telling-off from the children. The ants were considered an edible delicacy. I had thrown away a treat. The children were disappointed in me and told me so in no uncertain terms.

Once the rains had started, Zambians dug over pieces of ground and planted seeds. Mostly it was the women who did the back-breaking work of gouging out the concrete-hard ground with mattocks, a type of pickaxe/spade in the shape of an adze. Many were planting maize, not a good move in town for rain water lay in the leaves of the plants attracting mosquitoes. If the choice was going hungry against the risk of malaria, I suppose everyone was going to choose planting maize. I decided to plant some seeds in my small garden so I asked Knox, the office gardener, if he would come and dig it over for me. He was delighted for that meant some extra cash for him and a meal while he was doing this. As I watched him make small seed beds with little raised earth-walls all round them, I remembered reading about this type of gardening in Barbara Kingsolver's book *The Poisonwood Bible.* It was set in the Belgium Congo (later the DR Congo) in the late 1950s. The American missionary would not accept the local custom of making raised beds. He stamped the walls down with his feet because 'he did not do things that way' and lost all his precious seeds when they were washed away the first time it rained. I didn't think that I would have broken the walls round the seed-beds but at least because of the book I knew why they were built. Knox carefully planted my tomato, lettuce, onion and leek seeds and I was given instructions on watering them on the days when there was no rain.

When I washed clothes and sheets getting them dry became a real problem. When I first moved into Zawi I had bought a nylon clothes rope and strung it between the security bars on my kitchen window and a branch of the lemon tree which grew in my small area of garden. Almost immediately my neighbours to whom everything was communal began using it. I didn't mind that except when I wanted to use it myself and I had on various occasions pushed their clothes along until they were a bundle at one end so that I had room for my own clothes. I suspected that as soon as I went to work that process was reversed, but the clothes dried anyway. After the rains came, that no longer worked. Sometimes even when it was dry the humidity in the air stopped clothes drying. On more than one occasion, it was sunny when I left for work and by mid-morning my clothes would be dry but then storm clouds began to gather and by the time I got home at lunchtime everything was not only wet but dirty as well. The rain came down with such force that dirty red-brown mud was splashed over everything. That meant boiling kettles to get enough hot water in the bath with which to do not just a re-wash but a scrub. I got used to having dripping clothes dangling from a piece of rope tied above the bath.

Although no water came out of the taps, plenty came through the roof. Water streamed through the ceiling and down walls. Allan Keppeso did his best to block the worst of the holes in the roof but could not do a proper repair until the dry season. He did replace the defunct hot water tank with a new one. It was twice the size of the original and with only a trickle of water making its way through the pipes to my house never became sufficiently full of water for us to find out if it worked.

When Anna said that one of her neighbours was leaving and their maid, Harriet, was looking for a new job Carl and I decided to employ Harriet between us. She arrived at around 07.15 each weekday morning and left in the evening when we returned from work. During the day she cleaned our houses, and washed and ironed for both of us. Her wage was K100,000 (about £20) per month plus the cost of a bag of mealie meal, K17,000 (£3.50). Her arrival was a great improvement for us although the cockroaches were not so happy. Their numbers dropped rapidly after her scrubbing brush worked its way into all the small dark corners.

Chapter 12

A Woman's Place

One afternoon Mutinta Mudenda and I drove in the Venture to one of the local townships to check on the welfare of a prisoner's family. People seeking help normally came to the office but this family was in a particularly bad way. The wife was disabled and the children very young. They were really struggling to cope. Mutinta suggested that I wait outside their mud-brick hut until she had seen what the situation was. Later she called me in. The mother was lying on one worn blanket with another draped over her legs. Three children, two girls about four and six and a small boy, cowered near their mother as if seeking her protection. As a white woman I represented authority and that scared them. The only possessions I could see were a chipped enamel basin and a few plastic mugs. While I could not see into what appeared to be the only other room in the house, I got the impression that it was just as poorly furnished. Maybe they had sold their few possessions to get money for food. In a country where a large percentage of the population live below the poverty line of US$1 a day, this was extreme poverty. I had never seen such poverty and deprivation and yet the hard-packed earth floor was swept clean and tidy. With the husband in prison, they had no source of income other than begging and they welcomed PFZ's help of some mealie meal to make nshima, with a few medicines for the mother and clothes for the children. Mutinta said the medicines were nothing more than painkillers. Once outside, I asked Mutinta if I should leave some money. She said 'No.' If I wanted to give something, give it to Prison Fellowship, who would pass it on. If I was seen to give to one family it would be expected by others.

On our return journey I was still thinking about what I had

seen when we stopped at Kansenshi Prison to pick up Regina Kangwa, George's PA. She had been there to make arrangements with the officer-in-charge for a church service to be held at the prison. Shortly after we left, true to form, the petrol tank ran dry. On the evening staff-run, the first stop would be at the petrol station in Vitanda Street across from the office when the pump attendant would be instructed to put five thousand kwacha's worth of petrol, just less than two litres, into the tank. It was so normal for the Venture to run out of petrol that it carried a cut-off top of a plastic water bottle for use as a substitute filter when petrol was poured into the tank from a can.

As Mutinta knew someone who stayed quite near where we stopped, she went off on foot to try to beg or buy sufficient petrol to get us back to the office. Regina and I stayed to guard the vehicle from any enterprising locals who saw it as a free supply of spare parts. Thankfully it had come to rest under the shade of a large tree so we had some shelter from the heat of the sun. We passed the time chatting. Regina wanted to know about my family. When had my husband passed on (Zambians seldom use the word 'died') and did I have any sons or daughters? I told her John had died almost three years before in December 1997 and that I had no sons and daughters of my own. John, who was divorced from his first wife, had had three sons from that marriage, one of whom had been killed in a car crash. Allowing for the conservative nature of society in Zambia, I wondered what reaction I would get to the word 'divorced' but got none at all. Regina was much more interested to know if my husband's family had been annoyed with me because I had not given birth to a child. I laughingly replied that no doubt I had annoyed them often but not because of that before realising that she had a reason for asking that particular question. When I asked why she was so interested, she admitted that although she had been happily married for some years she and her husband Jackie had, in her words, 'not been blessed with a child.' It was not unknown for a family to pressurise a husband to divorce his wife because she was 'barren.' This was causing her many anxious moments. It did not seem to have occurred to any of them that the problem of not conceiving might not be the wife's. We discussed the possibilities of that and I think I helped cheer her up for she laughed heartily when I told her that some months after John and I were married an elderly friend kept embarrassing me by asking why I was not pregnant. Fed up with his constant questioning I followed John's advice and told him 'We were having great fun trying.' I was never asked again.

I found the hierarchical and dictatorial attitudes in the office hard to deal with. While everyone went through the ritual of the morning greetings with each other, the words 'please' and 'thank you' seemed to be used only if the person to whom they were addressed was considered in the same peer group or a higher one. Marjorie Fwolishi and the other local health volunteers who worked with Maurice in the health department were considered to be on the lowest rung of the social ladder along with Knox, the gardener, and Chama, the messenger. It was not considered necessary to be polite to them. If someone wanted Chama to do an errand, he or she would stand in the door and bawl 'CHA-MA'. I could understand the need to shout for there was no internal telephone system but having watched some whites in the supermarket speak disparagingly to the check-out staff I wondered if this was a legacy of the colonial era which had been absorbed into Zambian lifestyle. It seemed so at odds with the Christian message which was extolled at the Monday morning devotions at Prison Fellowship. I always said 'please' and 'thank you' to Chama when he either took letters to or brought mail for me back from the post office or did some other errand for me. Doing so confused him to begin with but gradually he got used to it and I always got a lovely smile from him when he came into the accountancy department.

Each member of staff had to take a turn of conducting the Monday service, and when it was my turn I took my Bible reading from Luke Chapter 12, verses 41 to 44, 'The story of the widow's mite' and tried to bring out that not only was her gift more important than that of the rich man because it was a greater proportion of her means, but that she, a poor widow, was due respect because she was a person equal in the sight of God to all others no matter what their means or place in society. In the discussion afterwards this point was conceded but Mark and Carl were the only ones who saw where I was coming from. They tried to reinforce my point but I still did not think that anyone related it to his or her own attitude to those they considered social inferiors.

Mark, Robam and I continued our discussion in the accountancy department afterwards when Robam said he was unhappy with the Bible I was using. It was a small lightweight copy of a recent translation, The New International Bible, which had been given to me by a friend before I left for Zambia When I asked what the problem was, Robam laid his own Bible, a heavy, black leather-bound King James edition on his desk. He said that it was the real Bible for it gave Jesus's actual words. My Bible was wrong. Mark and I exchanged glances. I knew I had to consider my words carefully. I asked Robam if he thought Jesus spoke English. He did not answer that directly but stated adamantly that the words in his Bible were the exact words Jesus had spoken two thousand years before. He was really quite shocked and unbelieving when both Mark and I explained about the different languages, Aramaic, Hebrew, Greek and Latin, used in Palestine in Biblical times. We tried to explain that many different translations had been made by scholars of different traditions throughout the centuries, only one of which was the King James edition, which dated from four hundred years before and was written in the language used in Britain at that time. I don't think he believed us because everything in his education had taught him to believe in the authenticity of his Bible.

The story of the widow's mite came home to me when, after spending one morning at the restaurant doing book-keeping training with Idah, I left just before she became busy with lunchtime customers. Chama, who had brought a message for Idah from the office, left at the same time. As we walked back to the office a child-beggar dressed in rags, rose from the dusty pavement and stood in front of us. He put his hand out asking for money. I was continually being asked for money and as we had been told that it was government policy that the beggars were not to be encouraged, I walked past but Chama, who earned very little, stopped and slipped a note into the child's hand. I felt very embarrassed.

At Ratho in December, I would have been busy with preparation for Christmas. In Zambia my Christmas preparations were few. When an ex-prisoner called at the office, I bought some of his hand-painted cards and posted them off to my family. Chama was delighted when I began to receive Christmas cards. He was so happy when he brought back lots of mail from the Post Office for me that I felt the cards should have been for him. When more than one calendar arrived he was in raptures when I gave one to him. It took pride of place on the office wall. With nowhere to lay the cards I stuck them to the wall of my living room. The neighbourhood children began a nightly ritual of coming to look at them. Never having seen snow they were curious about it, liked the penguins, and asked what presents Santa Claus brought. They wanted to be told stories about the pictures. Arguments arose about who was getting which card when I was finished with them. Chilomba and his friend, Twesa told Phillipa and Judy that they could have the ones with angels for they were suitable only for little girls. The boys calculated that that left the pictures of animals, birds, snow scenes and Santa for them.

Shoprite played some rather scratched records of seasonal music on the public address system. *I'm Dreaming of a White Christmas* did seem inappropriate when the temperatures were in the nineties and rain was pounding down on the corrugated-iron roof. I wondered what Zambians made of Good King Wenceslas trudging through snow 'deep and crisp and even.' There appeared little awareness at Prison Fellowship of the approaching Christmas season. I knew that most of the staff had little or no spare cash to spend on the commercial side of it. There was never going to be a shopping frenzy as in the west, but I had expected religious anticipation yet there had been no reference to it at all. In the information packs Carl and I had been given prior to coming to Zambia we had been told that December 25 and 26 were official holidays and while still in Lusaka during our in-country training our group of volunteers had agreed that we would spend Christmas together. An e-mail had arrived from Vicky Mulgatroyd in Mongu in Zambia's Western Province saying that she had booked all of us into The Zambezi Waterfront, a campsite on the banks of the Zambezi River near Livingstone, from Saturday, December 23, to Tuesday, December 26. Carl and I decided that it would be preferable if we could travel to Lusaka on December 22, for Ndola to Lusaka was a four-hour journey by coach and Lusaka to Livingstone another six hours. We planned to ask George for permission to leave early on the Friday afternoon.

On Monday morning, after a devotion led by Mutinta, but before we had a chance to speak to him, George announced that all the PFZ staff would be travelling to the Maximum Prison in Kabwe on Christmas Day when we would all spend the day with the prisoners in the Condemned Section, a prison within a prison for those on Death Row. He was not pleased when Carl and I told him that we had made other plans because we had been unaware that we were expected to work over Christmas. Reluctantly he agreed that we had been told these dates were holidays and that he could not force us to go to Kabwe with the rest of the staff. When he declared that he expected us to be back at our desks on Wednesday, December 27, we thought better of requesting an early finish on the Friday. It was going to be a very long journey to Livingstone and back for a two-day break.

Chapter 13

Zambian Advent

Anna invited Brian, Carl, Kevin and me for supper on December 5 for the Dutch celebration of Sinterklaas Nacht (St Nicholas Eve.) According to Dutch tradition St Nicholas along with his helper, Zwarte Pieten (Black Pete), comes during the night and fills children's shoes with small gifts, sweets and short poems about the owner of the shoes. We talked about our Christmas plans. Tony and Anna were going to a small game reserve. Brian and Kevin had not arranged anything special and jumped at the chance when Carl suggested they might like to join our group of VSOs at Livingstone. Both he and I were sure the others would say 'the more, the merrier.' When Brian spoke of using their vehicle to travel in, I was delighted. That would not only be so much more comfortable than the inter-city coaches, it would save considerable journey time during our few precious days. Sometime during the evening Sinterklaas had left gifts in the shoes which we had kicked off at the door when we first arrived. A ballpoint pen and a tube of lemon sweets had been thrust into my sandal but it was the poems we all had to read out loud to the company that raised howls of laughter. They gave a good summing up of each of our abilities, including my dancing skills (or lack of) at the local nightspot, Circles.

The following Sunday I joined the packed congregation at St Andrew's Church where the choirs gave wholehearted renditions of traditional carols such as *Silent Night* and *Once in Royal David's City*. The church, built in the pre-independence era, had been designed with a high vaulted roof and unglazed windows to provide some relief from the blistering heat but even that and the pulpit punching of the preacher did not prevent my eyes from drooping during his almost one-hour long sermon. What seemed incredibly sad was the children's address when the youngsters in the church were warned that while Christmas brought presents for some, the only present many of them would get was the knowledge that Jesus, who loved them, was born on that day. I thought of the younger members of my family and all the toys and books they would receive. For most of these Zambian children Christmas morning would be just the same as every other morning. There would be no filled stocking, no cheerfully wrapped gifts. Some would not even have food for breakfast.

The Zawi children were becoming my friends. Kawata, Chilomba, Phillipa and Judy, all dressed in smart navy and white school uniforms, knocked on my door each morning to say 'Muli shaani' before they left for school and me for work. Kawata, because he was the first to speak to me, would always be a bit special. His father had died earlier that year and at ten years old he took his responsibilities as the man of the family very seriously, being protective of his younger siblings. This was not always appreciated by his brother Chilomba, who was sharp as a needle. Phillipa was inclined to follow Chilomba's lead and she like him showed promise of doing well at school. George and Judy were quieter but both were interested in everything, asking lots of questions which I did my best to answer. It did not matter how carefully I replied. The response was invariably 'why', 'what' or 'how'. These children helped me feel comfortable and at home in the compound. It would have been fun to try and find Christmas presents for them but I hadn't seen toys or books in Shoprite or any other shop and then had I bought for these children others who were around now and then would also have looked for presents. The list would have been endless.

After devotion on Monday, December 18, George announced that the office would be closed from lunchtime on Friday, December 22, until Monday, January 8. As PFZ had a serious cash shortage I suspected the change of dates had something to do with money or rather the lack of it. Limited cash reserves could be saved if the office was closed. No contingency plans for emergency help for the focus groups were mentioned but in that close networking community someone would know where to find either George or Francis. The Christmas Day visit to the Condemned Section in Kabwe would still take place with PFZ providing the food, including beef, for the Christmas dinner. All this meant Carl and I could now leave for Lusaka much earlier on the Friday and we did not have to rush back on the 26th but if this information had been available sooner I would have used the two-week Christmas break to see other parts of Zambia. As it was, our little group in Ndola had made arrangements to have a Hogmanay party at Tony and Anna's house and I had promised to help Anna prepare the food. She and I had been planning the menu for days, seeking out places where items like cream, crusty breads and real cheese, unlike Shoprite's rubbery version, were accessible with a vehicle.

Before my Christmas break, I had to help with food of a different kind. Robam asked me to accompany him to Chipulukusu to look at some cows, one of which was to be purchased by Prison Fellowship. The animal would be butchered and the meat sent to Kabwe Prison. On Christmas Day, after conducting a service for approximately two hundred prisoners held under sentence of death in the Condemned Section at that prison, the PFZ staff and the prison officers would join together with the prisoners for a meal at which the meat would be served. A great fuss was being made about this gift, probably one of a few times in the year when the prisoners were given meat. I had never bought an animal for butchering before so was not at all sure how many meals one cow could produce. In fact, all the cows looked so skinny that I did not think any one of them would feed fifty people never mind the actual figure of around two hundred and fifty. Eventually we chose what looked like the fattest, and Robam made the necessary arrangements to have it turned into butcher meat. Back at the office, we reported on our purchase and when George said it was a pity PFZ could not afford to add a goat I decided that as I was not going to Kabwe on Christmas Day I would pay for the goat. It cost me K15,000, about £3. The butchered cow and goat meat was sent packed in the back of the Hilux, in the blistering heat, about two hundred kilometres south to Kabwe. No one other than me seemed worried about the lack of refrigeration. I was told later that the prisoners enjoyed their dinner.

I should have been grateful that the water tank in my kitchen did not work immediately as the water supply was still very sporadic with insufficient water to fill it, for while making a telephone call to wish my sister Marjorie in Edinburgh 'A Happy Christmas' there was a tremendous bang. It carried seven thousand miles over the phone and Marjorie, hearing the crash, was extremely alarmed. I think I knew at once what had happened but after taking a quick look round the kitchen door reassured her that it was only the hot water tank jumping off the wall. It did bring down quite a bit of the wall with it but because it was empty I did not for once have a flood. There was just plaster and dust to clear away.

On Thursday evening, I relaxed European style. Carl and I were the guests of Brian and Kevin at a party given by the Irish priests attached to the Catholic Diocese. After ten weeks in Zambia, sandwiches and savouries which might have seemed conventional at a party at home were now delicacies and tasted absolutely delicious when enjoyed with plenty of liquid refreshment. It was well after midnight when I watched Brian and Kevin collect the leftover sandwiches. Curious, I asked why. They were going to take the food to some street children and Carl, Marco, an Italian volunteer, and I went with them. We went to the police station where Brian and Kevin lodged a note of their intent and then lit only by the light of a last quarter moon and one torch we walked up a dark alleyway off Blantyre Avenue, not far from my own house. The sour smell of urine was not disguised by a lingering trace of wood-smoke and a rustle in the rubbish strewn scrub at the side of the path suggested that rats or snakes might be lurking there. Nine boys, possibly between eight and twelve years old, were huddled together against the back of a building, the overhanging roof of which provided a little shelter. It was difficult to guess their ages. Living on the streets without proper nourishment they might have been older than their sizes suggested. Even with them there was an obvious hierarchy, for the oldest and biggest were in the centre getting the most shelter and warmth while the youngest and smallest were on the outside of the huddle. Their bed was some bits of cardboard laid out on a concrete ledge and their covers were a few pathetic pieces of dirty torn cloth which might once have been sheets. In the gloom I could see that one or two had tied supermarket plastic bags over their bare feet. Some were awake but others grumbled at being disturbed until they discovered Brian was offering them food. What really shook me was the quiet way they waited to get their allotted share of the sandwiches and how they passed round the container of orange juice.

Brian explained that Carl, Marco and I were friends, not police. One of the older boys spoke excellent English and the others appeared to understand at least part of what was being said. Most must have been at school at some time in their short hard lives. Gradually they relaxed and became like kids anywhere, laughing and joking with us. When we asked what they needed most, they said sheets to cover them so that they had some protection from mosquito bites and also soap to wash with. They told us where another three smaller children were sheltering but not until after all the food had been gobbled up. We gathered that the three had been expelled from the larger group. They had been given some money which they had not shared with the full group. They had used it to buy pyjamas from a shop which sold charity clothes.

I had replaced my original purchase of single bed size sheets with ones large enough to fit my three-quarter size bed but the original fuchsia pink ones were still in my cupboard. I whispered to Kevin that I could get these and give them to the children. He went back to Zawi with me and we picked up all the old newspapers I had in the house together with two bars of Lifebuoy soap. Back with the children, Brian made them all stand up and encouraged them to lay the newspapers down on top of the cardboard. The boys were reluctant to do this. In the shadowy moonlight, they were trying to read bits of news. After bargaining with them for the old bits of sheet for the three smaller children, we stretched the vivid pink sheets over the boys, making sure that as much as possible of their skin was covered. It the shadowy moonlight the fuchsia pink did not look so bright and the boys certainly weren't worried about it. They settled back down to sleep for the rest of the night. They could wash in the morning. Brian was quite sure that they would find somewhere to wash, for they knew their best chance of staying healthy was to try and keep clean.

When we checked on the three younger children from the smaller group, we found them curled up together in a small space between buildings. They were cuddled so tightly together that at first I thought there were only two boys. Where they were had no sheltering overhang so if it rained they did not even have the limited protection available to the other group. One child was very hot and feverish. There was nothing we could do for him at that time of night other than cover him and the others with the dirty bits of sheet and make sure they had clean water. Brian and Kevin would come back in the morning and check on all the children, but in particular on the sick child. They hoped that it would not be too long before the night shelter, a sort of unofficial orphanage, was open. Children like these could then get safe shelter at night, have a meal, have the opportunity to wash and have access to medical help when it was needed. The next step on from the night shelter would be a day shelter followed by a return to schooling. Primary schooling was free but children had to wear uniform and shoes and many parents could not afford those. Some new Open Community Schools where uniforms were not necessary were being introduced by charities and NGOs. For Zambia to be able to develop, it needed its children to be educated. Since independence a lack of educated people had been one of Zambia's greatest problems. In 1964 there were only about one thousand people with a secondary education and less than one hundred with a university degree. The programme set up in the early years of Kaunda's presidency to address this had suffered when the economy took a severe downturn in the early 70s.

When I did get to bed it was a long time before I went to sleep. I couldn't stop thinking about those street children. It was a struggle in the morning to make the office on time but I did do so even if I spent the morning yawning. I had just a few bits of tidying up to do before I could leave for my Christmas holiday. I gave Chama and Knox small gifts of money as a thank you for their services and wished everyone else the compliments of the season before dashing home to eat a quick lunch. Brian and Kevin had said they would pick Carl and me up at about 14.00 hours but true to their reputation it was fully two hours after that before we eventually piled our bags into their vehicle and set off for Lusaka. The sick child we had seen during the night had needed medical attention and a guard at the shop behind which the boys had spent the night had taken the sheets from the children saying he knew they were stolen. Once Kevin had rescued the sheets he had established a safe place in which the boys could leave them during the day.

I was looking forward to travelling south and seeing the countryside. Most of my journey to Ndola had been undertaken in the dark and apart from visiting Kitwe I had not been out of the Ndola district since I arrived. As we left the city area, we passed the oil refinery where a recent fire had caused disruption in Zambia's oil supplies. The refinery stood at the end of the oil pipeline which allowed oil to be pumped from Dar es Salaam on the Indian Ocean to Ndola. The pipeline was opened in 1968 after sanctions applied to Ian Smith's Southern Rhodesian government on its Unilateral Declaration of Independence in 1965 meant that Zambia was cut off from its traditional trade routes through to South Africa and Mozambique.

The small villages near the road became fewer as we drove further from the city. We passed groups of women walking in single file along the edge of the road. From the twigs sticking out from the chigenge-tied bundles carried on some of their heads I guessed they had been gathering firewood. No one appeared to hurry. They all seemed to walk at the same pace and often a woman or even a young girl carried a baby on her back as well as her bundle of sticks. In each of the small settlements there was lots of colourful activity as evening approached. Outside the mud-brick or wooden huts women in their rainbow coloured chigenges were lighting cooking fires from which spirals of smoke rose through the air. As we got even further south there was often little to see but burnt-orange earth with scrub and small trees and if it had not been for the little stalls at the side of the road where people were selling lots of home-produced items the countryside would have seemed deserted. Sometimes we would pass a lay-by where some planks had been laid over stones to make an improvised shop. Tomatoes and peppers were assembled in little stacks on the planks with a woman or sometimes even a child waiting patiently in the hope of a sale. Stallholders would lift their produce up as cars passed, hoping to entice people to buy. That Friday there were lots of live hens being offered for sale. As we drove past, a woman or child would lift a hen in their stretched out arms so we could see how big the bird was. Before I left Ndola my neighbour at No.4 had three live hens in her garden – presumably destined to be someone's Christmas lunch.

The road was in reasonably good condition until just north of Kapiri Moshi. After we passed the junction where transport for north-eastern Zambia and Tanzania turned off it deteriorated rapidly. The town itself was busy with people, trucks and buses. The petrol station did a brisk trade as drivers heading north-east on the Tanzanian highway liked to leave with a full tank. They might be lucky to get fuel at one of the few small towns en route but they were not taking that chance. Trains to Dar es Salaam left from the TAZARA terminus on Tuesdays and Fridays which increased the amount of activity on these days. Although many miles from any recognised border with either Tanzania or the DR Congo, Kapiri Mposhi exuded all the excitement and danger of a frontier town.

We dodged people, trucks and the water-filled potholes before we reached the brightly-painted, old railway engine which stood in a siding near the road on the south side of the town, a cheery, suitable monument in a town where the one claim to fame is that it stands at one end of the TAZARA railway. It seemed to signify that we were through the town and all its hazards. Because we were later in leaving than planned and we wanted to get the largest part of the journey completed before it grew dark, our only stops were at the police checkpoints. South of Kabwe (a major town, not the one-street township I thought when we stopped on my first journey north) we were driving in the dark and at one checkpoint it was noticed that a bulb in a sidelight had failed. Kevin worked at replacing it for some time but couldn't get the spare bulb to light. We could not go on until we had paid the fine of K65,000 for driving without this light. No one seemed worried that we would still be driving without it so we guessed that this might be a little bit of private enterprise. A little negotiation and a suggestion that it was a Christmas gift and certainly not a bribe brought the sum down to K30,000 and we got a letter which got us through the remaining two checkpoints.

Our destination in Lusaka was Dave Clinton's house. When we arrived a party was in full swing. Everyone in our group who was travelling to Livingstone the following day was there. Brian and Kevin quickly became part of that group. Will, whose placement had finished prematurely and who was moving to a new placement in Ghana, marked the occasion by producing a local delicacy, fried caterpillars, for us to try. I discreetly dropped mine down the back of Dave's settee. Less than enthusiastic looks on the faces of others suggested my caterpillar was not going to be lonely. About 23.00 hours everyone except Vicky Murgatroyd, Sue and I decided they were going clubbing which seemed daft to me as those going for the coach to Livingstone would have to be on their way by 06.00.

Justin, Mark Calder, a gap-year student staying with him, Ruth and her Canadian friend, Sheila, caught the bus but some of the others didn't waken until around 10.00, long after the coach had left for Livingstone. Eventually, at midday, we set out with eight in a vehicle designed for five, six at a push. Kevin drove with Vicky, recently recovered from dysentery, in the front. Sue, Emily and I were packed in the next row with luggage pushed on top of us, with Brian, Carl and Dave squeezed on a seat meant for two. Not surprisingly, our vehicle decided that it had had enough of being overloaded and started to overheat before we had gone very far. The climb out of the Kafue River valley proved too much for it and we had to stop to let the engine cool down. We had completed only about one quarter of the journey to Livingstone when we limped into the tree-lined streets of Mazabuka, the centre of Zambia's sugar-cane industry and the most developed town between Lusaka and Livingstone, seeking a garage for some emergency repairs. It was after 16.00 hours when we limped off again with as many spare water bottles as we could lay our hands on.

The journey was in some ways a bit of a nightmare though actually much of it was quite good fun. We sang Christmas carols but often the first verse only because no one appeared to know the rest of the words. Singing was better with Christmas songs, such as *Jingle Bells* but here too there was lots of la-la-ing. We had to stop often to let the engine cool. Because there were so many of us, we were not afraid of being stranded or maybe attacked. There was concern about the vehicle getting us to Livingstone but the stops in the middle of nowhere, especially after dark, were an opportunity to just breathe in the African air, hot, sultry and very slightly spicy. With no light pollution, the millions of stars glittered brightly.

With about one hundred kilometres still to go, we did begin to worry. The map showed that there were no towns until we reached Livingstone and we were running short of water. When we saw the lights of a farm up on a hill, we decided we had to get help. That meant leaving the main road and travelling about three/four kilometres up a dirt road towards the lights of the farm. We were unsure what sort of reception we would get. People who stay in such remote places do not welcome strangers approaching in the dark. The farmhouse was surrounded by a high fence topped with razor wire and with many guard dogs charging at the fence and barking loudly. Brian, who was driving, turned the vehicle so that the security lights lit up the words 'Friends of Africa' painted on its side and Sue, Emily and I used our higher pitched voices to say that we had run out of water and needed assistance. When the farmer and his son came out they were armed but soon realised we were genuine travellers in need of assistance. They were knowledgeable about cars and helped with a makeshift repair, filled our water bottles, and gave Brian the name of a garage in Livingstone where he could be sure of getting a good mechanic.

There was only half an hour to midnight when we arrived at last at The Waterfront, exhausted and hungry. I thought there was some hysteria in the laugh which was raised when Sue read the notice which greeted us, 'Beware of Crocodiles and Do Not Feed the Monkeys,' and Kevin growled 'Never mind the fucking monkeys, we need food.' But The Waterfront had stopped serving meals hours before so it was back four kilometres to Livingstone for chicken and chips. Returning to the campsite, we were given details of the names of the tents we had each been allotted to. All were called after birds. Ruth and Sheila, who had arrived earlier in the day were in 'Kestrel', about ten metres from mine and led me over a small bridge and along a path laid out through well watered grass to my tent 'Eagle'. Like all the others it had been erected on a raised platform, probably to keep the base dry in the rainy season when the grass could become very muddy. Another path, lit by lights set in the ground, led to showers where the water was welcomingly hot. It was the first proper shower I had had for ten weeks but I didn't waste any time on it. The white sheets and fleecy blue blanket looked much too inviting. I was soon tucked up in bed in my own tent with the door carefully zipped and locked. The canvas would not have kept a crocodile out but guards were on patrol, presumably to keep at bay all predators, both human and animal.

Chapter 14

Christmas by the Zambezi

It was the monkeys which woke me. In the early morning light, two vervet monkeys chose the roof of my tent as the setting for an altercation. It got rather noisy and agitated and going by the shadows being thrown against the tent walls I guessed they had been joined by others. Eventually they moved off and peace was restored. Breakfast was served at tables set on decking which stretched out over the Zambezi. Looking towards the Victoria Falls, I could see the spray, the *Mosi-oa-Tunya*, 'the smoke that thunders,' about five kilometres away. The shimmer of sunlight reflected on the river. As it rolled gently towards the Falls it passed Siloka Island where branches of trees swept the water. The main current, which acted as the border with Zimbabwe, and which was much fiercer, flowed past the other side of the island. I knew of how in 1855 David Livingstone, the first white man to see the Falls and who named them Victoria after the Queen, had stopped on an island near the escarpment. What I had not realised was that there were other islands in the river above the Falls. My appreciation of the hazards faced by Livingstone increased immensely. Five kilometres upstream I could hear the dull roar of water surging and scrambling down over the precipice into the gorge, pounding the rocks below.

Mirriam and her friend Gerrard roared in on Mirriam's motorcycle. Noise, she informed us did not equal performance. In her placement at Chisekesi she had to travel over ten kilometres to be able to buy food and as there was no reliable public transport VSO supplied her with a 100cc motor cycle. Gerrard did not look as if the journey as her pillion passenger had been an enjoyable experience but they had arrived safely. Last to arrive were Chris and Amanda. They had travelled from Mongu but had a sorry tale to tell. Chris had found his placement impossible and had resigned from VSO. He had been working as a building superintendent on a construction site attached to a convent. The building was to be an orphanage but Chris had found working with the nuns difficult. He and Amanda hoped to stay in Zambia and Chris was looking for work. The song *Ten Green Bottles* adjusted to twelve struck a chord because of the original twelve in our group now there were only nine still working for VSO in Zambia.

We had to see the famous Victoria Falls. The Waterfront organised taxis to take us as far as the Zambian customs post. Once at the Falls we started our sightseeing by walking across the Zambezi on the bridge which formed part of Cecil Rhodes' uncompleted design for a railway link from Cape Town to Cairo. Rhodes, a British born South African businessman and politician, was responsible for forming the British South Africa Company in 1889. When it occupied Mashonaland and Matabeleland (now Zambia and Zimbabwe) the area was named Rhodesia after him. The bridge takes both trains and cars and, as Rhodes planned, they are near enough to the Falls for both to get wet from the spray as they cross. There were lots of formalities at the customs on both sides and when we did eventually get into Zimbabwe there was horror among us when it was discovered that the entry fee to see the Falls from that side was US $20. Everything in the tourist area around the Falls was priced in US dollars. Maybe $20 was not a lot in UK terms but when your monthly volunteer allowance is around £110, it's a fortune. Some of us decided to go anyway. Others were disappointed because they felt they could not afford it. I knew I was having a visit from my sister Marjorie in April and expected we would return to Livingstone so decided to wait until then when the rains would have raised the water level in the river and the Falls would be even more spectacular. I had seen Livingstone only in the dark but as we walked through the town of Victoria Falls I got the impression that the Zimbabwean side of the Falls was in a good state of repair with carefully tended pavements, street lights and hanging flower-baskets. Those who had missed out on the Falls were obviously disappointed, but cheered up when I suggested that cocktails were on me. Attracted by the fancy pineapple statutes which topped the massive gates of the Kingdom Hotel, a building designed in the form of a paramount chief's palace, we found a table in the shade near the swimming pool and began to relax. When the waitress came with the cocktail menu most chose a long drink but Carl thought it would be fun to order 'A Blow Job.' The waitress never even blinked as she took the order but after she had brought all the other drinks she returned with a silver salver held at shoulder height. On it was a small sherry schooner glass filled with a brown liquid topped with white cream which, with great solemnity, she presented to him. The rest of us enjoyed the joke as we sipped our long drinks.

Later we met up with the group who had gone to the Falls. They judged their $20 had been well spent but had had to avoid a black mamba snake on the path. Back through Zimbabwe customs we walked back over the bridge, dodging the curio sellers with their copper bracelets and carved animals, before stopping to look through the 30-metre gorge towards the escarpment, a little of which could be seen through the gorge and spray. Rainbows gleamed through the spray. The escarpment is 1,700 metres wide, approximately the same length as Princes Street in Edinburgh. Water which has just dropped 120 metres over the length of the escarpment boils and bubbles, races and tumbles to force its way through the narrow gorge and under the bridge on which we were standing. Cameras clicking, we watched mesmerised for some time before daring to cross road and rail to watch the mad, intrepid bungee jumpers leaping off the edge. When we reached the Zambian customs post, it was overrun by baboons which climbed over cars and lorries stopped at the frontier. As we waited for clearance I watched them steal anything which was not tied down. One even snatched a paper bag out of a man's hand. Another one fished a potato crisp packet from the rubbish bin but after eating what was left of the contents had to look for water to drink which it got by putting its paw under the radiator of a car.

The Zambian side of the Falls was and is spectacular. Awesome can be an overused word, but here it was appropriate. The gorge, gouged out over millions of years, is deep and winds back and forwards. There are seven different areas of falls along the total escarpment, all coloured with rainbows created by the spray. Cameras have to be protected for the spray, thicker in places than a haar, makes everything wet. When we arrived at the start of the Knife Edge Bridge, a rickety affair which took people over to an island in the gorge created over many years by the force of the water, a choir, dressed in blue gowns, was being filmed as they sang. Their voices rose clear and true over the noise of the water pounding into the gorge. Rainbows played against the backdrop of cascading water. I sat for ages enjoying the fantastic sight, a film set seen live, while taking pleasure in the wonderful music of Africa. That I was soaked through from the spray didn't matter.

The following morning, Christmas Day, we were up very early. The Waterfront had organised a game drive for us in the Mosi-oa-Tunya National Park. Two specially constructed buses each having three tiered levels of seats behind the driver were waiting for us. It was a short distance to the entrance to the part of the park where the animals inhabit a protected zone. It was a fantastic morning. We came upon a family of elephants. I saw only one to begin with, and then gradually eight or nine came into sight. It was difficult at first to see just how many there were. When the driver took the bus nearer I was almost frantic with excitement when a very young baby came out from behind its mother. Our driver said that the baby was about one year old. It still had a fuzz of brown hair over its skin. He was also very careful. The bus was nearly always in reverse gear when we were near animals so he could back away very quickly from any imminent danger. There were zebra, impala and a herd of buffaloes. We saw four of the five white rhino, the only ones left in Zambia. The Zambian government realised how important it was that these animals were protected from poachers and they had their own special team of armed guards. Sadly, our guide said there were

99

no longer any black rhino in Zambia. He told of how there is little actual colour difference between them but as the white rhino eat grass, they have a different shape of mouth and keep their heads to the ground. One passed within three metres of the bus and it was huge yet it did not appear to be upset by our presence. (Despite the government's attempts to protect the white rhino some died naturally and poachers killed the remaining ones in 2007.) We came across a family of three giraffes. They looked magnificent, so stately and elegant. The male one was almost arrogant as he turned his head to inspect us through eyes fringed with elongated lashes. They very slowly wandered off and I realised just how perfect a camouflage their colouring is in the bush. Round nearly every corner, there was something new to see until we became quite blasé; it was just another herd of antelope. We were shown where elephants cross the Zambezi onto Siloka Island, choosing the deepest part of the river as there are less likely to be crocodiles there. The females go first, followed by the young ones with the bulls bringing up the rear, so that if a crocodile attacks a calf, the bulls can rescue the baby. It showed just how dangerous crocodiles are when they will attack something as large as an elephant, even a baby one.

Back at The Waterfront we held a Christmas service singing carols to the accompaniment of Mark's guitar. At 17.30 hours, it was a happy, cheerful group who climbed on board a river-steamer for a sunset cruise on the Zambezi. There were hippos, or at least we saw their open mouths before they sank out of sight, and many crocodiles, all looking positively evil. The colours as the sun dipped in the sky were almost impossible to describe; turquoise into bright ultra-marine tinged with gold. The water gave a mirror reflection while the sun itself became a startling red globe sliding slowly below the horizon. As it fell out of sight, sky and water became apricot orange, deepening slowly at first to red-orange before all colour faded and darkness swiftly took over. The complete silence, for even the paddles on the steamer had stopped, and the magnificent colourings of an African nightfall left me speechless. The music which had been silenced as nature provided the spectacle burst once more into life and we danced and joked. There was food and drink and it was a very merry party which landed back at The Waterfront where an African band were pounding away on their skin drums while tree frogs croaked and cicadas chirped away like an accompaniment of wind chimes. Later on my way back to my tent, I stood on the little bridge and listened to the music, a harmonious cacophony of many different sounds. Lights placed high in the trees twinkled in reflection on the dark water below. I thought of the memories I had of Christmas at home in Ratho. This Christmas Day had been so different but it had been a wonderfully happy one.

Now that there was no urgency to get back to Ndola for work on Wednesday, we stayed on at the Waterfront for another two days. The men and a very brave Sheila went white-water rafting on the Zambezi. The rest of us lazed around, reading, sitting by the pool, having a swim although three strokes completed a length, or just dozing in the shade. When Kevin and Brian took the vehicle into Livingstone to get it repaired, I went with them and visited the museum. Many exhibits showed evidence of prehistoric life in this region, information on tribal customs and dress and a display on the life of Livingstone. In the evenings dinner was served under the stars. Afterwards we sat around with beers while Brian entertained us with jokes and stories. I was quite convinced that his ancestors in Ireland must have been bards because his gift for story-telling kept us entertained for hours.

We had one other expedition to the Falls. Just north of the Zambian customs post we hired a guide, a student with a good knowledge of conditions on the river. He led us about half a mile upstream to where a small weir had been built between the bank and a small island in the river. In December the water from the rains up-country had still not worked their way down river as far as Livingstone. Later when the river was in spate it would be covered completely but at the start of the rainy season, the top, just inches wide, showed above the water. From there we jumped between and over rocks and onto small bits of land too tiny to justify being called islands. Gradually we made our way back to a rock-pool almost on the edge of the waterfall. Those who were brave enough to look over saw that the Falls were just below us. Just before sunset we worked our way back when our youthful guide, probably seeing me as ancient, solicitously chose the easiest route for me.

It had been a great break but on Thursday we were on the road back to Lusaka. The garage in Livingstone reckoned that the temporary repair would hold until the vehicle was back in Ndola provided it was driven at a speed of under eighty kilometres an hour and we had lots of stops to let the engine cool down. This time I got the front passenger seat. Age has its compensations although I did have the supply of water bottles under my feet. That was still better than being squashed in the back with five others. While Vicky and Sue had joined Ruth and Sheila on the bus to Lusaka, Justin and Mark had missed it so once again there were eight packed in the back of the vehicle. With Mark's guitar and a drum as well as our luggage there was even less space than on the journey south but we were prepared for many stops so we made them fun. A Scrabble game was ongoing as long as there was light by which to see the letters on the tiles. Later, after dark, we hit very poor driving conditions. The road was under repair for over fifty kilometres and we were detoured onto a temporary dirt tract running along side the main roadway. By that Thursday night, with maintenance work stopped for the holiday period, the surface had been torn apart by earlier traffic. Rain also had taken its toll. Kevin, at the wheel, had to twist and turn, swerve this way and that to miss the worst potholes and bumps and by the time we got back onto the tarmac road both engine and driver were in danger of over-heating. He took the first opportunity to pull off the road and we all piled out, grateful for the opportunity to stretch our cramped limbs. There was not a light in any direction. We appeared to be alone in a land which stretched forever into the darkness of an African night. Someone said 'Look up' and we all stood still. The

Milky Way cut a swathe across the blackness. We stood gazing heavenwards at the fantastic display of stars. With little competition from a new moon they sparkled like diamonds. I could identify Orion, the hunter, by the three stars at his belt and looked for the Southern Cross. The stillness was so intense, it seemed almost tangible. We stayed quietly by the side of the road, feeling its spell, afraid to make a sound until the elephant grass swaying in the warm air gave a faint rustle and somewhere in the distance a train rumbled past on its overnight journey south. Mark brought out his guitar. His first few chords were soft and low and carried gently on the evening air. His music blended with the backdrop and when Brian began to keep the rhythm on the drum, the magic of Africa held us in its spell. Our impromptu concert was watched by millions of stars and one very new moon. It was a pity about the mosquitoes which arrived in force but you can't have everything. They did remind us that we could not stay there all night so once more we packed ourselves in and ambled on our way. We did eventually make Lusaka safely.

The next day I had some time in the morning to shop at Manda Hill, Lusaka's one shopping mall with twenty-five well stocked shops located round three sides of a square. I bought some kitchen tools and a mirror for my house and some nibbles for the Hogmanay party before walking to the very last unit in the complex, O'Hagan's Irish Pub, to meet the other volunteers. Brian and Carl decided to stay on in Lusaka for a further night. Kevin and I set off in the vehicle which seemed strangely empty but we made Ndola without incident. As we approached the town I found myself thinking 'nearly home' and realised that I thought of my little house at Zawi as 'home.'

Settled back in Ndola, preparation for the Hogmanay party began. I began to understand how the ex-pats who stayed here lived. If you had transport there were several places where different foods could be purchased. We got cream and some homemade cheese at a small farm shop, we found an Indian shop which sold lots of different spices and groceries not available at Shoprite such as root ginger and ground almonds, and we visited a Greek bakery where they made European continental breads. We bargained with the street-sellers for vegetables. We scoured the shelves at Shoprite for ingredients and found some tins of meat, salmon, and fruit not normally on the shelves. With transport available I took the opportunity to stock up on tins of food. There was even some Scottish smoked salmon in the very small freezer section. Loaded up, we headed back to Tony and Anna's home at Dolphin Court. The house provided by the Simba International School as part of their contract was in a pleasant complex situated between the main road north from Lusaka and the golf course, the playground of a few ex-pats, where the greens and fairways were kept watered and green all year by a large, inexpensive work-force. The cricket ground, patronised jointly by the white and Indian communities, was nearby. When Anna parked in the square outside her home we carried our purchases into her kitchen. It had been equipped with fridge, freezer and cooker when she moved in and she had added dishes, cutlery and cooking equipment she had gathered during four years in Zambia. She and I cut and peeled, cooked and baked, laughed and giggled, as we produced and garnished our party fare of quiches and mousses, jellies and tarts.

It was a very international gathering, with Anna from Holland, Tony, Mike and Carl from England, Torunn from Norway, Brian and Kevin from Ireland, Julian, (a friend of Tony and Anna's from their days as VSOs who now stayed in Burundi), their next door neighbours, three doctors from Cuba who worked at the hospital in Ndola, and myself from Scotland. The acknowledgement of Anna and my efforts in preparation of the food came with the speed with which it was enjoyed. We sat in candlelight on the patio and at midnight waved the sparklers Tony produced and sang Auld Lang Syne as we toasted the New Year of 2001.

Chapter 15

Travelling Zambian Style

I started the new year knowing that PFZ's cash flow problems had not been improved by the office closure. George, keen to ensure that such a situation did not reoccur, asked me to do an exercise on budgeting. He wanted me to spend time individually with each of the senior staff, explaining what a budget was, how to produce one and how to monitor actual expenditure against it. While the exercise went well with most of the managers, there was one huge problem in producing reasonably accurate budgets. They couldn't accurately predict when most of their income would be received. Idah might have an idea of her daily takings at the restaurant and Mellbin could estimate when fees would be paid to the tailoring school, but when donations might be received was an imponderable. Despite this the managers had faith that things would work out and carried on with their existing work to the best of their financially restricted abilities as PFZ took on another project. The lease for the over-grown park near my home at Zawi had been obtained from the town council and PFZ planned to employ ex-prisoners on restoring the park to some of its former glory. The project had three objectives, a badly needed recreation area for the people of Ndola, a training project for ex-prisoners in gardening and other skills, and an income generator for PFZ from payments to be made for the use of the facility for church conventions, weddings and family reunions.

Before anything could happen the site had to be cleared and prisoners from Kensenshi Prison were hired to do that. Each day a file of forty prisoners walked the five kilometres from the prison. They were under the supervision of two armed officers and two blue bands (trusties) who carried long canes which they used indiscriminately to check someone who looked like slacking. Part of their cost to PFZ was that it provided food and it was surprising how generous local businesses were when George and I sought their help. We obtained mealie meal and butcher meat and the promise of a daily supply of bread. A cooking pot was set up over an open fire in the park and work started. It was important that grass, a type known as Simba, was well established before the end of the rainy season. Grass in Zambia was planted in a similar way to that used by gardeners in the UK when making a new bed of strawberry plants. Suckers were removed from the original plants and transplanted in prepared ground.

At the end of January VSO arranged a seminar in Lusaka for volunteers and their opposite numbers at the organisations where they worked. The theme was on the problems we faced while working together. Maurice Shakwamba was attending with Carl but George, busy preparing for a meeting of the PFZ Board, his first as director, felt he could not take the time to accompany me proposing that Francis Mpzeni, the chaplain, deputise for him. I felt that Robam Mukubwa would have been a better choice. Robam needed to understand that my presence at PFZ was an opportunity for him to learn, that I was not there to criticise him or undermine his authority. He was always polite to me but as he saw things, it was not appropriate for a woman to be instructing a man. I hoped that if he saw how other Zambians worked with their volunteers, irrespective of gender, it might help him overcome that prejudice. I telephoned Dolores Long, my Placement Officer in Lusaka, and explained the situation. A third invitation arrived at PFZ allowing Robam to attend. As VSO were paying a travelling, meals and overnight allowance, all three Zambians were keen to go. For them it was a paid-for opportunity to visit relatives in the capital. For Carl and me, it was an opportunity to meet up not only with our own group of volunteers but also to meet for the first time some of the other fifty or so other VSOs in Zambia.

We had been allowed a full day off in which to travel but it was my first inter-city coach trip and as I had been told that the most convenient coach to catch was the first one which left in the morning I made sure I was at the coach departure point in the square off Broadway just after first light, around 06.45 hours. The coach was already almost full. There was the usual jostling crowd around the bus and the small wooden booth which served as a ticket office. Some people were stowing luggage in the hold, some were waving off their relatives or shouting advice to the lad tying boxes on the roof, while still others were just watching the melee. Dirty, smelly, ragged beggars and some curious children mingled among the crowd waiting hopefully in case someone felt charitable. Boys selling newspapers and drinks pushed their way through the moving throng of massing folk, conditions ripe for to anyone wanting some pickpocketing experience. Before leaving Zawi I had carefully fastened K25,000 into the zipped breast pocket on my bush-shirt so that I didn't have to hunt for money in my purse to pay for my fare while being pressed and crushed against the booth. My identification papers and other money were in a travel pouch hidden under my shirt and some US dollars, my emergency funds, were carefully folded into a zipped pocket in my belt.

After one ticket-seller had carefully checked the proffered notes twice, the other, painstakingly inserting two sheets of overused carbon paper between the pages of a receipt/ticket book, wrote out my pass for Lusaka. Clutching it and my small backpack, I climbed up the four steps into the coach and set about finding a seat. All the blocks of two seats on the pavement side of the aisle had been filled by the early birds. Those that were still empty were in the centre of a group of three. I passed by one vacant place where I would have been squeezed between two ladies of somewhat ample form and settled eventually for a seat near the rear between a middle-aged lady in the aisle seat and a young father with two children, a little boy held tightly on his knee and a girl of maybe five or six tucked in between him and the window. Children travelled free but were not entitled to a seat. The adults responded politely to my 'Muli shaani' but the children were shy. I felt quite Zambian when I leaned over my fellow travellers and called through one of the open windows to buy a copy of *The Times of Zambia*. Reading it kept me occupied for the twenty or so minutes until the remaining seats were filled. Then with every seat sold, the mood became excited and noisy as passengers shouted their last messages to the waiting crowd. Orange curtains were pulled over the windows to reduce the heat and glare from the rising sun and with a great trumpet blast of its musical horn which warned other traffic of its intended progress the coach swept out the car park and on to Maina Soko Road. Accelerating quickly, it sped through non-functioning traffic lights at the busy junction with President Avenue, indifferent to any other vehicle on the road.

Once the coach was moving most passengers settled down to catch up on some sleep and all was very quiet for the first hour or so. Bumping over the level crossing on the main north-bound railway line, just before reaching Kapiri Moshi, appeared to be the trigger for people to start stretching their cramped limbs and chatting to one another. I offered my newspaper around. Zambians love newspapers and read them avidly. During the American presidential elections the previous November the PFZ staff had read and discussed every piece of print they could get hold of on the controversial recounts in Florida after which George W. Bush became the American president. The journalism in the local papers was very different from that of the UK. As *The Times* was a government sponsored publication, the editorials were carefully written to avoid any confrontation but sometimes still managed to include a slight censure. The feature story was the moves being made by President Chiluba to have a change made to the country's constitution which would enable him stand for a third term. As with the American constitution a Zambian president can serve only two terms. Such stories were reported but lacked informed critical analysis. What little international news there was, was usually a straight crib from the BBC World Service or Reuters. A very restricted publishing budget meant there were few photographs unless the event being

covered took place in the capital, Lusaka, or Ndola, where the paper
was printed, or the subject of the article provided his/her own photographs. The cost of paying for a vehicle to transport a reporter and
a photographer was considered too high. The style and phraseology
of English used by the columnists would be considered old-fashioned
in the UK. An obituary would speak of the deceased 'having
answered the call of God' and while it was considered risqué to
mention the word 'sex' and certain pages from a red-top British
tabloid would have been considered porn, there was usually some
obliquely told story about the priest or pastor who had been caught
in a compromising situation or the details of a court case covering
a particularly nasty divorce. Perhaps the biggest dissimilarity to the
British press was in the sports section where a reporter might exhort
the members of his favoured football team to attack opponents
with 'extreme viciousness.'

After accepting my offer of the paper, the lady in the aisle seat
dug into the depths of the huge Gladstone bag she was balancing
on her knees and produced a rather bashed-up pair of spectacles
with a crack in one lens. She propped the paper against the bag
which bulged at one end in a most curious fashion. It looked heavy
but whatever was in it must have been very valuable to her for
when the man in the seat opposite offered to put it in the overhead
rack she declined his offer and held it in her lap for the four-hour
journey. From time to time she opened it as if to check on the
contents. I wondered if she had a small animal or bird in the bag
and if so how it was getting air. At least the contents did not smell.
I had heard a story from one volunteer, who complained that after
one journey her olefactory senses had taken weeks to recover.
When about to make a ten-hour journey from Mongu in the west
of Zambia to Lusaka she was horrified when she watched an open
crate containing two goats being tied onto the coach roof. Her
remonstrations that this was cruel to the animals were ignored
until she changed her plea that the animals were unlikely to survive
the journey. Then the owner, horrified that his goats might die,

tried to put the crate into the hold. They probably were his only capital asset. He became somewhat hysterical when he was told that that would not do either, so the hard-pressed bus boy put the crate with the goats in it in the bus with the passengers. After a ten-hour journey on a bus full to capacity with passengers, but including also two rancid goats, it was hardly any wonder her sense of smell was gone.

When my fellow-passenger, still clutching her Gladstone bag, returned the carefully folded paper, she called me 'sister.' She was keen to be helpful and told me that when the bus stopped briefly at Kabwe you had to move quickly if you wanted to go to the toilet for there was always a long queue at the ladies. It cost K200 (4p). When you paid you were given one piece of toilet paper.

The children's father also read my paper. His family were beginning to get used to me. When the young boy decided that my lap might be more comfortable than his father's knees and moved over, the little girl took the opportunity to climb up on to her brother's place. At the start of the journey she seemed to be asleep on her feet, propped between her father's legs and the bus side, although at one point I had watched her pull the corner of the window curtain aside so that she could look out. Her legs must have been very tired from standing squashed in her tiny corner. Her father gave her a lovely reassuring smile and a gentle hug. She looked so pleased with herself that we all laughed. Emboldened by her success, she stretched up and ran her hands over my hair. Her father was shocked but I was getting used to how curious children were about 'musungo' hair which feels so different from their own wiry hair which in her case was pulled tight into tiny plaits. At the ten-minute comfort stop in Kabwe, the father left the children in my care for a short time. When he came back he brought them a treat, a bag of chips. I felt quite one of the family when they offered me one of their sauce-covered greasy chips. When the bag was empty, it went the way of all other rubbish collected on the bus. It was pushed out a window on to the road.

We arrived safely in Lusaka and having called 'Goodbye' to my fellow travellers, I crossed Hero's Square to the British Council building where the VSO offices were on the fourth floor. There I picked up mail which had been left for me, had a coffee and a chat with Dolores about how my placement was progressing before going for a sandwich and a soft drink in one of the fast-food outlets in Cairo Road. The front of the cafe was open onto the hustle and bustle of the pavement where among the dust street sellers had laid out their wares, including books which looked as if they had spent many weeks on the ground, leather belts, baseball caps and shoes. Pedestrians wove their way between the goods-for-sale, beggars, and the holes caused by broken or missing paving slabs. Sandwich finished, I joined the throng, taking the opportunity to do a little exploration and some shopping before finding my way to Dave Clinton's house where I had been offered a bed for the night.

The following morning those attending the seminar settled down in a comfortable conference room to deal with subjects which affected us all. The forty or so people there were a mixture of volunteers and Zambians. Robam and Francis were there on time but Maurice failed to put in an appearance until later in the morning. Francis answered any queries on behalf of Prison Fellowship. Robam sat quietly, saying nothing unless a question was specifically addressed to him but his eyes scanned the room taking in every detail. We discussed the problems common to the organisations represented; it was AIDS which created the greatest problem for the PFZ representatives. VSO had invited two ladies from the government sponsored organisation, National HIVAIDS/STD/TB Council (NAC), to address the seminar and speak about their work which was trying to increase AIDS awareness and prevention. The ABC of prevention was spoken of, Abstention, Be faithful, use Condoms. Francis was on his feet objecting. It was not right to advocate the use of condoms. They were an abomination in the sight of God. Robam was nodding in agreement as were representatives from other organisations. I saw that Maurice had again left the hall. As his stance on advocating the use of condoms was the exact opposite to that of Francis, this could have been a shrewd move on his part. If not present he could not be accused later of siding with the 'pro-condom' lobby. Francis proclaimed loudly that the use of condoms was a sin, wickedness in the sight of the Lord, quoting passages from the Bible in support of his claims but was rapidly disabused of his arguments by one of the speakers. The ladies were obviously experienced in dealing with interruptions and complaints like his. He was asked if it was Christian to allow someone already affected with the disease to continue to have unprotected sex which led to another person becoming infected. The statistics of new infections showed that the abstention Francis was advocating was clearly not being adhered to. Why were the churches not addressing that rather than objecting to the use of condoms? The ladies went on about the disastrous problems Zambia was facing and how drastic action was required if the epidemic was to be controlled. Suddenly the other heads stopped nodding in agreement with Francis and he slid back into his chair, rather like a balloon with a slow puncture. At the afternoon tea break, Francis still had a small group of like-minded followers, but not as large as he might have expected. Some of those who had been nodding in agreement earlier were now actively discussing subjects other than this. Like Maurice, they were using their discretion. Their background traditions and training had taught them that they should agree with Francis but obviously a few of them were reconsidering their stance on the use of condoms. For myself, I was all in favour of 'abstinence' and 'be faithful' but statistics showed that as a total stratagem for dealing with the AIDS epidemic they were completely inadequate.

While it had been annoying to see Maurice spend such a short time actually at the seminar, I found out later that he had been using the time to good effect on behalf of Prison Fellowship. A Zambian Television crew arrived to film part of the seminar for their news programme. Maurice had been arranging that Carl be interviewed on the work PFZ's Health Department was doing in the prisons.

Although the production lacked the smooth sophistication of the BBC it was good PR for both PFZ and VSO.

Like most of the other VSOs from out-of-town placements, Carl and I stayed on in Lusaka for the weekend. Friday night's celebrations included a farewell party for two homeward-bound volunteers which took place at one of Lusaka's well-known meeting places, the terrace bar at the InterContinental Hotel. The contrast of its cosmopolitan ambience – white wrought-iron tables and chairs spaciously set round a flower decked swimming pool – to the cement yard and plastic chairs of Circles was laughable, yet I found myself missing the friendlier atmosphere of our Ndola nightspot. Later when I accepted a lift from the VSOs whose farewell party we had just attended I had not realised that the offer of transport meant climbing into the back of a truck. With a helping hand from our driver's son, possibly five or six years old and already standing on the back, I made it by putting one foot on top of a tyre and swinging myself in over the sideboards. Emily, Dave, and Carl, all much taller than me, easily scaled the sides. When the driver took off, I used fingers, elbows, heels, toes and every other part of my body which could be brought into service to stop myself from rolling all over the place. As we flew round one corner, Emily fell against Dave who slid rearwards towards the point of no return. We lunged, grabbed and held him until the opposite gravitational pull on the next corner threw him back on top of us. What would have happened if we had turned right instead of left did not bear thinking about.

Carl and I accepted another lift the following morning. On the last Saturday of each month the Dutch Reform Church on Kabulonga Road held a market in its grounds and we wanted to visit it. Although the market opened about eight-thirty, it was nearer ten before we were picked up but the journey to it was much more relaxed than the previous evening's dash across town. The market was obviously a popular place as vehicles of every sort were parked at quite some distance on either side of the market gates. Entrance cost K2,000 (40p) with the proceeds going to church funds. Stallholders were selling everything from craft goods to coffee and cheese. In the shade of a large open barn, tables displayed clothing, some of which was hand-made, household goods, jewellery and home baking as well as the coffee, cheese and craft items which included stone and wood carvings, paintings and metal-work. Bamboo mats laid on the ground were the background for toys made from wire, large garden pots and wickerwork baskets. Business everywhere was brisk. One stallholder travelled each month from Chipata, almost 600 kilometres away on the Malawian border, to sell her embroidery. Food such as hot dogs and pies was on hand as were much needed cold drinks. I was put off from buying too much by the knowledge that anything I bought had to be carried when I caught the coach to Ndola the following day. But I did buy a dark-green wall hanging which had been hand painted with colourful African depictions of an elephant, an antelope, and a woman carrying a water jug on her head. It would help brighten my house in Ndola and later could be taken back to the UK as a memento. Over two years later when I returned home the hanging came with me and it now decorates a wall in my study. A more practical purchase at the time was a cane lampshade for my living room at Zawi.

By the time we queued for the Ndola coach the following day, the rolled up hanging was the least of my worries. Saturday evening had found a group of us in The Brown Frog on Kabelenga Road. The clientele pushing in at the bar to collect a supply of glasses and buy large jugs of beer were of mixed age, colour and race. It had been a good evening, perhaps too good for Carl who spent much of the following morning in the toilet and when we left around eleven-thirty to go to the bus station he asked Dave for a polybag in case of emergencies. The bus station was busy. Jill Slevin, the fourth Copperbelt VSO who worked in Kalulushi, queued with Carl and me to get tickets only to find that we would be on the second bus to leave for Ndola. From the crowds of people milling around, there appeared to be more than enough to fill at least two and possibly three buses. Many were crowded on the one small bench provided for waiting passengers while others stood around in groups guarding large bundles and packages as children played until they got tired then curled up on top of a bundle and went to sleep. Excitement rose as one coach arrived from an unknown town and deposited its passengers. Without any information to the expectant crowd, its doors were shut and it drove out the gates. The buzz fizzled out and the company went back into its semi-somnolent state, awakened only when it started to rain. We huddled under my recently purchased umbrella except when Carl had to make a dash for the bushes. Thankfully the rain did not last long and around thirteen hundred hours another coach arrived. I knew this one had come from Ndola. I recognised it from the large picture of Christ it had stuck to its windscreen. I often wondered if the driver thought that the divine protection gained from the picture compensated for his loss of a clear sight of the road. Passengers unloaded, this bus also took off but this time to refuel. Watching its return and the scramble of passengers to get on kept us occupied but at last laden both inside and out it trundled off on its journey north. Those of us waiting for the next coach settled back down to a patient wait. Standing in one place had made my back, legs and feet ache so I was thoroughly fed up by the time the next coach arrived. Having watched what happened when the passengers rushed to get on the first coach, I was in the melee with all the other women pushing and shoving to get on this one. As the crowd forced their way towards the bus steps, I used every ounce of my strength to get to that door. If there was a tiny space I burrowed through it using my elbows and knees to good effect. There was no quarter given as I got to the door of the bus and got my foot on the step. Propelling myself past someone else I showed the bus boy my ticket and climbed up the four steps into the coach, and sank into the outside seat of the first bank of three seats behind the driver. As on the journey down, once I had identified these three seats as being for my party no one else tried to claim them.

Eventually, at nearly 15.00 hours, the coach was loaded. I had stopped worrying about time. I was on the coach and there were enough people to fill it so as soon as everyone had settled down and the luggage was stowed it would be on its way. Carl was at the window, still clutching his polybag, Jill in the middle with me in the aisle seat. I had a clear view of the road over the driver's head and the height of the bus meant I could see more of the land than if I had been in a car. There were large areas of commercial arable farming, particularly between Lusaka and Kabwe but even that brought little change in the variety of scenery so I dozed. As we left Kabwe a video, a third-rate horror film filled with blood and guts, was fed into the coach's video system. The noise from it ensured all snoozing was at an end. The sun was beginning to dip towards the horizon when the sighting of an aerial showed that we were getting close to Ndola. I began to relax and think of food. Meanwhile the film was building to a hair-raising climax. The ghastly blood-covered images which filled the screen were bringing gasps of horror from the passengers when suddenly a loud bang reverberated through the coach. It started swaying and pulling off to one side. The gasps of horror became terrified screams as people realised a tyre had burst and the bus was out of control. The driver struggled to hold the coach straight. Sweat was running off his face as he gripped the wheel. People began to panic and shout to God to save them. Many were out of their seats pushing past others in the aisle in an effort to get to a door. I don't know how the driver remained calm, but he did. There are not many hills on that part of the road but as luck would have it we were travelling downhill into a valley just as the tyre went. The driver fought the pull on the wheel and as the coach gathered speed resisted the temptation to stamp hard on the brake. The panic in the bus was not helping him as he strove to keep the coach from swaying off the road. We made the foot of the hill and somehow he managed to guide it round a slight bend and into the upslope on the other side of the valley. Gradually the gradient slowed the coach and shaking with strain the driver at last used both hand and foot-brakes. The bus stopped at the side of the road.

As soon as the door was open passengers were scrambling to get out. Once out, some sank to their knees and thanked God for a safe deliverance. Carl, Jill and I were the only ones to say thanks to the driver as he sat shaking at the wheel. Emergency over, he was suffering from shock. There was even more danger for those kneeling in the road. Drivers of passing cars were too interested in finding out what had happened to pay attention to the road and one car was swerving towards those who prayed before the inattentive driver realised what was happening and dragged his steering wheel round. I could not see a village or houses nearby but people arrived from somewhere, standing around eager to find out what had happened with the lack of casualties a disappointment to some.

The feeling of relief did not last long. A few passengers began to grumble about this unscheduled stop asking how long it would be before we were on the road again. They complained that they had paid the fare and it was up to the coach company to get them to their destination. We were in the Ndola district but were still some distance from the town itself, too far to walk unless that became absolutely necessary. Some passengers started to pester the driver and the bus boy about getting the wheel changed but that was not going to be easy. The bus did not have a jack without which it was impossible to raise the side of the bus high enough to remove the damaged tyre. Various plans were put forward including one in which the men tried to heave the bus up far enough to enable the bus boy to release the wheel, a ludicrous idea. The driver of a lorry which had stopped was reluctant to lend his jack. Worried that he would not get it back, he drove on. The appeal to a second lorry driver met with the same response. After about twenty minutes, another coach from the same company as ours pulled in and its bus boy dragged its jack from the luggage compartment and handed it over. When our boy crawled under the chassis to hold the jack in place while others used it to raise the bus I decided it was time to take a walk up the road, away from the scene of possibly one very squashed boy. Thankfully the spare wheel was locked in place, the burst tyre was packed away for repair, and the passengers were loaded on once more. We reached Ndola without further incident, exhausted but safe, almost nine hours after leaving Dave's house in Lusaka.

Chapter 16

Pies and Birthday Pickles

Whatever Francis felt in private about the seminar and the items discussed, his report to the staff after Monday's devotion was positive on the benefits of attending such an event. HIV/AIDS was not mentioned by either him or Robam. Maurice, however, did refer to the actions being recommended which if taken could reduce the levels of stigma attached to victims of the disease, possibly a gentle reminder to Francis of what had happened, a little bit of 'I won't tell what happened at the seminar, but I am remembering.'

February brought no lessening in PFZ's financial problems so I was surprised to learn that George, Francis and I were to make a trip to visit the PFZ care group in Mansa. The journey would have been about two hundred kilometres if it had been safe to travel north across the DR Congo pedicle, but was about three times that long when using roads through Zambia to journey round that part of the DR Congo which encroaches into Zambia. At the start of the twentieth century when the European powers were carving up Africa, Britain and Belgium agreed to split the mineral rich area now known as the Copperbelt. Belgium took control over the eastern part and it remained part of the DR Congo after that country achieved independence from Belgium in 1960. Our trip would involve going south to Kapiri Moshi, then east for about forty kilometres before turning north again for Samfya and Mansa, a return journey of over 1,100 kilometres and this during the rainy season, a trip which would cost a minimum of K500,000 at a time when PFZ had severe cash-flow problems.

The weekend when I should have been preparing for the journey to Mansa, I spent most of my time in the toilet. Occasional trips to the kitchen allowed me to make up a rehydration fluid, a mixture of filtered water, salt and sugar to a recipe given in a prior-to-leaving health briefing. Since Christmas I had suffered diarrhoea on two or three occasions. That February weekend I realised that what was upsetting me was more serious than a slight bout of diarrhoea perhaps brought on by eating food which had gone off. Out came my well-thumbed traveller's health book and I realised that I could have dysentery. Thankfully, the telephone was on one of its short working spells and Maurice came in response to my call for help bringing suitable medication from the PFZ supplies and the dysentery was caught before it became too serious. It certainly stopped me from going on the Mansa trip. I was just so glad that we had not left on the previous Friday, as had been proposed at one time, for I felt tired, miserable and shivery, which seemed absurd in temperatures of over 30 degrees C. Trying to get warm I wrapped up in every piece of clothing I possessed and must have looked like the Michelin man. Sitting up in bed was not an option as there was no headboard on the bed and if I leaned against the wall the bed moved away from it, letting my pillows slip down onto the floor. I cushioned my deckchair, a Christmas present from Tony and Anna, with my sleeping bag to try and make it more comfortable but when George paid a surprise visit to check on how I was it too was wrapped round me for warmth. Once he knew I was too ill to travel to Mansa, he had also dropped out of the visit although Francis had gone. For the first time since I arrived I moaned about the lack of a comfortable seat and George did promise that I would get one as soon as funds were available. Both Francis and George had a roomful of comfortable chairs and sofas. Perhaps they had thought of lending a chair but were worried that if a chair ever left either of their houses, it would never be returned.

Maurice and Carl had been invited to attend a conference VSO was organising in Windhoek, Namibia, on AIDS. They prepared a paper giving details of the HIV situation in Zambian prisons and the programmes which PFZ were encouraging to inform male and female inmates of how the disease was spread. Some research had indicated that the infection rate in the prisons was above 40 per cent. Many inmates, both heterosexual and homosexual, were already victims of the disease prior to being sentenced. In Zambia, haunted as it was by superstition, one belief common among male prisoners was that a non-active sex life meant that the penis shrivelled up until it became non-existent. Heterosexual men often saw homosexual sex as a way to prevent that even though the homosexual act was illegal. The punishment for being caught in such an act was a custodial sentence. This caused unacknowledged problems in the prisons. The authorities did not condone homosexual sex but, although they would never have admitted it, through lack of manpower and resources were unable to stop it. The sharing of razor blades was another way the HIV virus was spread. Blunt blades were the cause of many shaving cuts. While the virus dies quickly when exposed to the air, a cut from a blade which had infected blood on it could lead to a new infection. Prisoners also tattooed each other using these blades, again increasing the risk. The wives of released prisoners came into a high-risk category when their husbands returned home to an active sexual relationship. As family members of prisoners the women also came within PFZ's focus group. They were often in a risk spiral for without a means of income 75 per cent of ex-prisoners re-offended within six months and could be in and out of prison on a regular basis. Left in poverty, the women themselves were often caught in crime and were imprisoned. Without other means of support many turned to prostitution.

When Carl returned from Namibia, Dolores Long advised us that she would visit PFZ to review our progress. Where I felt I was not making the required progress against my six months' objectives was in improving the accountancy systems. Robam kept the accounts for all areas of the organisation. Watching how he worked suggested to me that he did not really enjoy book-keeping for he seemed less than meticulous about keeping records up to date on a daily basis, yet at the same time he would not let the department heads such as Mellbin and Idah keep their own account books. They resented that, saying they never knew the financial situation of their departments. I suggested that as the organisation's accountant his responsibility should be to ensure that the department managers were keeping true and accurate account books rather than do the work himself. Robam's argument was that they did not know how to keep accounts but it seemed to me he didn't want to give them access to their account books because with the current reduced state of the bank balance he was transferring funds between different projects to meet expenses as they arose. As an interim measure Robam agreed to me teaching basic book-keeping to Mellbin and Idah. Worried that I was not keeping to my placement directives I spoke to George and Maurice and agreed that it would be best if I continued my present tack of trying to gain Robam's trust. If that failed to work, George would intervene and Dolores accepted the situation, pleased progress was being made overall.

I realised some of the problems with which Robam struggled when I attended a meeting of the PFZ Care Group at Kitwe with Francis and Robam. Prison Fellowship's Christian ministry in the prisons around the country was conducted by groups of volunteers from different churches known as care groups. The regulation and administration of the care groups came under the control of Francis, the organisation's chaplain. I accepted an invitation to meet the members of the Ndola care group though as my placement duties lay with the secular part of PFZ's organisation it was not necessary that I attend their weekly meetings even though they seemed to think I should. Missionary work was not part of my placement nor did I think it would be beneficial to my overall work if I was associated too closely with one group. It was in the same spirit of wanting to meet people but not to get too involved that I accepted Francis's invitation to accompany Robam and him to Kitwe. We were greeted warmly when we arrived at the Baptist Church Hall where the meeting was held but I was aware of tensions between Mr Kalifungwa, the leader of the group, and Francis about organisational matters while Robam was subjected to various veiled and some not-so-veiled remarks made about the failure of the national office to give financial aid to the local care groups. Money or what the group saw as the lack of their fair share of it was foremost in their minds for at one point during the evening I was questioned as to how much funding I had brought to PFZ. My response that VSOs brought skills not cash donations was not well received. I got a definite feeling that I was not believed. It was obvious that the care group members thought that the PFZ was financially well established and that nothing Robam said was going to persuade them otherwise. Patently, there was a widely accepted though erroneous view that PFZ had considerable funds. Perhaps even Francis believed the myth because he certainly did nothing to try and discount it and when on our way back to Ndola we stopped in Kitwe at The Pie Shop for takeaway food he ate well at PFZ's expense. My limited order had nothing to do with cash shortages. Zambian chefs enthusiastically add peri-peri sauce to their pie fillings and I don't like having my mouth feel as if it is on fire. I took the opportunity while we were eating to ask about why the care group members had kept harping on about an AGM. 'Annual' General Meeting was hardly the correct term. The last one had been held six years before. When I said that I was beginning to understand why the care groups knew little about the state of the organisation's finances, the reaction was defensive. I was told that it was the board of governors which called an AGM, not the national office, but as most of the care group members would have been scared to make any criticism of the board they took out their anger on the national office staff instead.

Pies might have been a welcome change from our usual diets but when it came to birthdays the volunteers splashed out. We didn't have a large choice of restaurants, Danny's or a Chinese off Broadway or Michaelangelo's, an Italian which opened only on Friday nights. This was still a luxury compared with the celebrations of most Zambians which were restricted to being invited to the front of the church during the Sunday service nearest the appropriate date, when the congregation sang 'Happy Birthday to You.' The enthusiasm with which both young and old rose and went to the front of the church was wonderful to see but then it was an achievement to have survived another year in the uncongenial circumstances many lived in. There was none of this for Brian, who had a birthday in February. Kevin organised a meal at Danny's Restaurant. In early January Dave Clinton and Carl had shared birthday celebrations when Dave and some of the other Lusaka volunteers had visited Ndola. I had ordered a cake for that occasion from Paterson's bakery. Brian and Kevin were both noted for their colourful language so I wasn't surprised when Kevin, anxious to get a cake for Brian, asked me where I bought the fucking cake. With Irish priests, Italian volunteers, Tony, Anna, Carl and I as well as Brian and Kevin, it was a very mixed but happy group who tucked into the Indian food at Danny's. Chatter and laughter around the table kept the noise level high so when Kevin went off to fetch the cake, I felt safe in whispering to Carl, 'Do you think it will say 'Have a happy fucking birthday'?' Unfortunately for me, the conversation had stopped as Kevin brought in the cake and my 'whisper' carried along the whole table. Embarrassing for me but everyone else thought it a great joke including Kevin who laughed loudest. A few weeks later when I had a birthday the cake was iced 'Happy F**king Birthday, Anne.' Carl told me later that when he, Brian and Kevin had gone to order the cake at Paterson's bakery none of them had had the courage to say to Miss Paterson what they wanted written on it. They wrote the words down on a piece of paper and handed it to her. I think the asterisks were the Paterson's idea.

With the Children at Zawi

Street sellers in Ndola

We are the champions (Street Children's Sports Day)

Mutinta and Bonnie are wed

Micro-Credit Class with Mark and Francis

Pounding maize at the PFZ Restaurant

I love my Christmas Box

Working with Robam

With Carl, at the Royal Golden Jubilee Celebrations 2002

My 61st Birthday Cake

The Eastern Cataract, Victoria Falls

White Rhino at the Mosi-oa-Tunya National Park

Dawn Patrol at S Luangwa Valley

A stately stroll at Letchwe

A traditional village scene

A home in the Chipulukusu Township, Ndola

Chapter 17

Zambia 1 – Nigeria 1

Much of our work was humdrum and could be rather depressing at times so any break from the norm was welcome. When the news spread that there was to be an international football match in the African Cup of Nations competition at the mining town of Chingola, about one hundred and thirty kilometres west of Ndola, many of the volunteers were keen to go. As the National Stadium in Lusaka was being repaired the fixture had had to be relocated to the ground of Chingola Rangers, a bit like holding a Scotland/England match at Inverness Caley's ground. E-mail messages passed back and forth between us and the final arrangements were that those wishing to go should gather in Kitwe (about halfway between Ndola and Chingola) at Helen Gosnell's home on the Friday evening.

Our party included a newcomer to the area, Vicky Rowan, an Irish dentist on a one-year placement. In her late twenties, her five-foot-four frame exuded energy. Dark hair set off a rosy-cheeked round face which seemed to be always wreathed in smiles while her professional skills were welcome not only when a crowned tooth came loose but also in sticking together the parts of my toilet which broke with monotonous regularity. 'Be at Zawi at 17.15 if you want a lift' had been Tony's instructions and we were. Even Kevin was on time. Tony drove carefully for Kitwe Road had one of Ndola's worst surfaces. There was little tarmac, just bumps and potholes. Kevin, Vicky and Carl got bounced around in the back seat while I held on tightly in the front. Some locals, shovelling earth into the worst craters, wanted a payment of K1,000 to let us past. 'Pay you on the way back,' Tony quipped and they laughingly stood back and let us through. Once out of Ndola, the road was in better condition which was just as well for lightning forked across a pitch-black sky. Torrential rain filled and hid holes in the road. Tony did his best but when a wheel found a pothole an eruption of muddy water splashed over bonnet and windscreen obscuring his already limited vision for the sky was so dark and heavy with rain-filled clouds that it was almost impossible to distinguish between the end of the day and the start of the night. On reaching Kitwe we had difficulty finding the bungalow which served as the offices of the CETZAM with whom Helen worked and where she had her rooms. It was a new address since I had last visited her. The bungalow, with a covered patio at the rear, was set back from the road in a large fenced-in garden. It had obviously been designed as a family house and Helen lived in two rooms to the back. The journey might have been difficult but we were at least dry when we arrived. Justin, Vicky Mulgatroyd and Mubiana, Vicky's boyfriend from Mongu in the west of the country, had travelled from Lusaka by bus and were drenched and soaked through when they showed up. Mike, coming from Kalulushi had arrived before the weather had deteriorated as had Sarah, another VSO youth programme student, who lived in Kabwe.

The rain did not stop the evening's fun. It pounded on the patio roof and added a further drumming to the music which blared from Helen's ghetto blaster as she cooked chicken and sausages on the braii. Her boyfriend, Dave, helped Sarah and I make salads. When we were joined by some of Helen's work colleagues, the rain was forgotten, as we toasted Helen's birthday in beer, and danced to the music. By the time we left to go to Cinderella's, a local nightspot, the rain had cleared. Watching the antics of the some of the dancers gave much more entertainment than actually being on the dance-floor. There was a cabaret act called 'The Dancing Dwarves', three diminutive men whose sense of rhythm had them foot-tapping and twirling at a fantastic rate while their audience clapped and cheered. All good fun but by the time we got back to Helen's I was so tired that I had no problems sleeping on the floor.

We were all up and ready when the minibus booked to take us

to Chingola arrived at 09.20. It was only about 65 kilometres to the ground and the match was not due to start until 14.00 hours but we still had to get tickets. Justin had tried to buy these in Lusaka before he left but they still had to be printed. They would be on sale outside the ground at 10.00. The road to Chingola, muddy after the previous night's storm, was busy. It seemed that nearly everyone in the Copperbelt was going to the game. Lots of mini-buses packed with optimistic Zambian supporters were accompanied by large Mercedes and 4x4s which hooted noisily but often without effect when trying to pass broken-down old bangers trundling along at a pace in keeping with their age. The sun beat down unmercifully on the heads of men and women who stood packed like sardines on the backs of lorries singing happily as they went along. As we got nearer Chingola, the mud had become sun-baked and every vehicle raised a cloud of red dust as it passed. The crowds of people walking along the side of the road were covered in it but no one appeared bothered although, unusual for Zambians, some were running. Whole families progressed in crocodile file at the rate of the slowest member. One family were pushing granddad in a wheelbarrow making sure that he and they made it to the stadium. The air was thick with excitement and hope of a home win as the crowd, young and old, headed in one direction, towards the ground of Chingola Rangers.

As we got nearer the arena, the crowds got thicker. The minibus had to slow down as the driver, horn tooting continually, wove his way through the throng. We did manage to get close to the ground but tickets still were not on sale nor did it look as if they would be available soon so the bus took us into the town centre where we could get food.

Back at the ground, tickets were on sale at last. There were long queues at each of the four windows of the ticket-booth. One member of our group stood in each of them. When Tony made it to the front of one queue, the ticket money was quickly passed to him. If it had seemed crowded earlier, now it was a boisterous, colourful mass of heaving, sweating people. Some knew what they were doing, others did not. Children wove their way in and out between adults getting in everyone's way. Mothers screamed at them to come back. Harassed police tried ineffectively to restore some kind of order. Street vendors set up stalls selling food, drink, and almost everything else you could think of including red frilly panties, but there were no items in the Zambian colours such as green, red and orange scarves and T-shirts on sale. Young boys with trays of hard-boiled eggs, which must be one of the original takeaway foods, moved up and down and in and out of the lines of people waiting for the gates to open. Pies, shaped a bit like Forfar bridies but very highly spiced, were a favourite. Drinks of every kind were available, water, orange juice, Coca-Cola, maize beer and even brandy. Two little boys, possibly no older than eight, were offering half-bottles for sale.

Having got our hard earned tickets and while still in line to get into the ground, a very officious policeman arrived to tell Tony and Mike that our party had to leave the queue. It took a little while before we realised that he thought we should be in a queue for the stand and even more time before he accepted that we did not have stand tickets. In his experience all whites sat in the stand. He then wanted to move our group to the head of the queue and was most puzzled when this offer was rejected. Others listened to this dialogue with interest but in silence until the policeman was safely out of sight. Then they made their feelings known. Those standing behind us thought we were mad not to have taken the offer. Those ahead of us let us know how they would have felt if we had moved. We were piggy-in-the-middle of what became a heated discussion which kept them and us occupied as we moved slowly nearer to the entrance gate. There seemed to be at least twice as many people hovering around us as had tickets but then there were many unofficial ways of getting in. The police would catch one ticket-less enthusiast as he climbed over the broken-glass topped wall and while they were busy administering their form of summary justice another twenty were up and over that same wall. Those inside the stadium were passing tickets back over the wall to those waiting outside so that they could be reused.

As we got nearer the turnstile, we were herded into single file between the stadium wall and an iron railing. Feeling something moving at my feet, I looked down and there were two wee boys creeping along between us and the wall. As I moved forward they moved forward. There was less chance of a police truncheon finding them if they were beside a group which included musungos. They got in. While I was showing my ticket, which was returned to me unmarked confirming my suspicion that tickets were being used more than once, the boys slipped through between my feet and were immediately lost in the crowd.

Inside reminded me of how I once experienced a rugby international at Murrayfield Stadium in Edinburgh when I was a youngster long before it was all seated.

We had to climb to the top of an earth bank to get to the tiered terracing. That was already full to crushing point. Women seeking to keep clothes clean had laid their chigenges along the rows but the spectators were pushed in so tightly that only the tiniest scraps of the multicoloured materials showed through. Everyone was pressed shoulder to shoulder with children held tightly on parents' laps. The aisles were packed to capacity with people sitting on the steps leaving no room for anyone getting up or down. Occasionally someone saw a friend and tried to squeeze across to join him by stepping over and on others who mostly accepted the disturbance with good humoured groans. They chattered, shouted to each other and sang, so happy to be there supporting their team. We were far too late to find a space on the terracing and had to content ourselves with a place where we could stand at the top of the banking. Helen, Vicky and I, the smallest members of our group, had to try and find peepholes through the crowd in front of us to see the pitch. The sun beat down and I was glad I had remembered to bring a hat only mine was pink not green, red and orange like some had hand-knitted ones which many of the crowd wore. The whole scene was like a Giles cartoon with people popping up everywhere. There were spectators clinging to the floodlighting towers, on the roofs of the two rather rickety stands which stood on either side of the pitch and some even sat on top of the broken-glass topped walls. I checked for supporters on top of the crossbars of the goals for they seemed to be everywhere else. The ground, home to a Copperbelt mining team, was about the size of a Scottish Second Division ground with a capacity of maybe three to four thousand. The pitch was surrounded by a running track. The playing area was fenced in with sharp razor wire, much nastier than barbed wire, discouraging anyone from trying to cross it. It was certainly needed that March day for whatever was the official capacity of the ground, it was well exceeded. It looked as if there were at least twice the number of spectators there should have been, almost all of them supporting Zambia.

The police band, very smart in French-navy uniforms, entertained the crowd until the teams and officials came out preceded by the FIFA flag carried proudly by youngsters in navy shorts and sparkling white T-shirts. Since the Nigerian team also play in green, the Zambian team were wearing their alternative colours, yellow and black. It was a good game. Both teams played with great enthusiasm and when a foul was committed there was no petty rolling around in agony by the offended but an eagerness to get up and get on with the game. Trainers with their magic sponges were not a feature for there were only two stoppages for injury in the whole match. Zambia tried very hard but their finishing failed to reward their effort. When players got the ball near the goalmouth they never quite managed to find the net. Then about thirty-five minutes into the game Nigeria broke away and scored. An almighty groan rose from the crowd. I thought the Zambian team might collapse after that but no, just before half-time, they equalised. The place went mad. A woman, who was standing behind me, celebrated her joy by thumping her fists repeatedly into my back. The crowd shouted and screamed their delight. The women began luluing, the high pitched yodelling that they love to do when excited. All in all, it was deafening and exhilarating.

Unfortunately that was the end of the scoring with a draw not good enough for Zambia to progress in the competition but good enough for Nigeria. Just before the end, the crowd got upset when the Zimbabwean referee ordered the Zambian coach from his dugout. Plastic bottles were thrown onto the pitch. The referee sent the players to the dressing-rooms but after an appeal to the crowd for order the game was played to a finish.

Our stance at the top of the terracing had one great advantage. Able to move quickly we were at the head of the disappointed, saddened and now much quieter crowd as everyone pushed towards the exits of the stadium. Our driver must have left before the end of the match for our minibus was waiting for us. If the standard of driving had impressed me on the way to Chingola it certainly did not on the return journey. It might have been his frustration at his country being eliminated from the cup which upset him, but he had to be threatened with no money at the end of the journey if he did not slow down and drive more carefully. He did.

Chapter 18

Christmas comes late in Zambia

The following Monday, in the time-honoured way in which sport is discussed in almost every workplace on Monday mornings, Maurice and Mellbin quizzed Carl about the international match while we stood in the office garden waiting for the doors to be unlocked. There was disappointment that Zambia was not progressing in the cup but pleasure in learning that the team had played well. Later at the management meeting I heard that the long-awaited consignment from The Samaritan Purse's Angle Tree Project in the USA had arrived. This shipment had been delayed at South African customs because of some slight discrepancies in the importation documents. It eventually reached Ndola weeks later than expected but was now securely stored in a warehouse in town. The cartons contained shoe-boxes wrapped in Christmas paper which had been filled by well-wishers in America with toys and many other goodies for disadvantaged Zambian children. Because many of these children came within PFZ's focus group, PFZ had in past years been responsible for distribution of the cartons. Expectation and excitement about when these eagerly anticipated gifts would arrive had been growing among the local children. The distribution ceremony was scheduled to take place on Saturday and I was asked if I would attend as official photographer, my only qualification being that I was the one person who had a camera.

This ceremony was to take place in the old cinema building on Broadway where I had attended the funeral of Bishop Chikwamba in November. Local churches had submitted lists of the number of children in their areas. Regina Kangwa, George's PA, had spent ages ensuring that the appropriate number of vouchers, each of which entitled one child to collect one box, had been sent to every participating church together with the time at which that church was to bring its children to the cinema. On the previous day every able-bodied man in Prison Fellowship had been involved in transporting the cartons, each packed with about seventeen/eighteen shoe-boxes, from the warehouse to the cinema, where they were stacked in six different piles, three for boys and three for girls, and into three age groups, two to four, five to eight and nine to fourteen years. Guards stayed in the cinema overnight in case anyone tried to break in.

Just as I was getting ready to leave in the evening Regina stopped me, asking what age and sex of child I wanted a box for and what would Carl want. My immediate reaction was to say I did not want a box as they were meant for the children but when I saw her face glowing with pleasure because she was able to make this offer I quickly bit the words back. It had taken a long time to gain the trust of the PFZ staff and a rebuff could have upset all my weeks of careful effort. Their culture was one where everything was seen as communal and by including Carl and me in the distribution we were being accepted as part of their community. Thinking quickly, the children at Zawi came to mind, and I said, 'A girl aged five to eight for me and a boy the same age for Carl.' Later as we ate our supper together I told Carl what had happened. He agreed that to have refused the boxes could have damaged the rapport we were building with our PFZ colleagues. The long-term benefit to PFZ from our placements depended on keeping that trust so while we both felt it was morally wrong to accept gifts meant for disadvantaged children, we were in a Catch-22 situation. We agreed that when the boxes arrived we would divide the contents between our little friends at Zawi, who maybe were not the disadvantaged children the gifts were intended for but who still did not have a lot.

To give some sense of ceremony to the presentation, a local dignitary had been invited to come and hand over some of the first boxes. As this was to happen at 08.00 hours I left Zawi just after 07.30 and strolled along Independence Avenue in the pleasant warm morning air. It was less than a kilometre to the cinema and on the way there I paused to admire the luxuriant bright-red foliage on a three-metre high poinsettia tree. While this poinsettia was gigantic in comparison to the pot plants sold in the UK in December, its flaming colour and Christmas associations seemed appropriate on this March day, when Christmas gifts were to be given to Zambian children. While pausing I became aware of a humming noise. It seemed little more than a buzz in the air but as I continued walking towards the cinema it got louder and louder. I walked faster. The babble became a clamour and by the time I reached the end of Independence Way and turned left into Maima Soko Road the clamour had risen to uproar. Once past some trees and an empty Lusaka coach, I saw why. The square in front of the cinema was swarming with children all pushing and thrusting, trying to get into the cinema. The crowds on the first day of a Harrods' sale were nothing compared with this. It was not the happy, laughing crowd of the football match. This was a mob made all the worse because it was children, all with just one thought in mind, getting through the cinema door and getting their hands on a Christmas box. Some of the older girls had little ones strapped on to their backs. All that meant was that there were four hands pushing instead of two. The children shouted and screamed at each other as the bigger, stronger ones thrust smaller youngsters out of the way. I looked in amazement wondering what had happened to all the carefully made arrange-ments for groups to come at different times. Adults were conspicuous by their absence. Just a few brave women hovered at the far end of the car park, desperately trying to keep their little groups beside them. The goggle-eyed faces of these children showed the same fear as that displayed on the ones in the mob – panic that all the boxes would have gone before they got one.

I had to try and get through that crowd if I was to be in my place in the cinema when the presentations started. When I stopped at the edge a policewoman detached herself from a little group of her colleagues and came towards me. Her companions remained under trees at the edge of the square taking shelter from the strengthening heat of the sun. They watched the melee but made no attempt to control it. I reversed my backpack which contained my camera so that it hung in front of me and clutching it to my chest like a breast-plate plunged into the crowd after the policewoman. Whether out of respect for her uniform or fear of the truncheon she held aloft or both, some children gave way to us but others, frenzied with just the one thought of getting through the door, held their ground. Buffeted and bruised we reached the cinema door, locked fast against the horde. My knocking on it was too much like the children's banging and was far too faint to be heard over the noise outside. The policewoman was far more effective. She used her truncheon and struck the door three times. When a voice muffled by the door asked who was there, she growled 'Your mama missionary,' confirming that she had known who I was without asking. A slight crack appeared, so little that all I could see was a thin slice of a brown face and one white eye. 'Wait,' we were told. After a few minutes and some scuffling behind the door, it opened just enough for me to squeeze quickly through. Once inside I recognised Newton Zulu, one of PFZ's health volunteers. His six foot gangly frame was assisted by four other young, strong men who put all their combined strength into holding the door in place while avid youngsters eager to make an opportunity out of its partial opening tried force it open. Charles Kachali, another health volunteer, slowly manoeuvred the heavy metal batten into its mountings to secure the door. When at last it clunked into position, we breathed a sigh of relief for if the mob had got their way we would have been trampled. It was only then that I realised my legs were trembling.

Inside was cool, dark and quiet after the pandemonium outside. The door-keepers asked why I hadn't gone to the back of the cinema where there was another entrance. I guessed everyone thought some-one else had told me to do that. When I made my way through to the shabby seating area of the cinema there were lights and a gentle murmur of conversation. Every seat in every row was filled with at least one child but often two were sharing. Most were dressed in their Sunday best, maybe well-worn but clean and pressed. Many were in western-style shirts, T-shirts and dresses which might originally have been bought at a store run by DAPP, a Danish organisation which bought clothes unsold in charity shops in the west and sold them very cheaply to people in developing countries. The clothes were sold or handed on many times through countless washings and dryings in the hot sun until they fell apart. These children were happy to wait patiently knowing that they had achieved what everyone outside wanted, a seat which ensured he or she would get a Christmas-paper-wrapped box. I took photographs of the stacks of boxes and some of the children before climbing up into the balcony and finding a window from which I could snap the heaving mass of children in the square outside. Time went by and our guest of honour still did not appear. Frequent inspections from the upstairs window showed that the crowd was continuing to grow. Some of the children had been there since first light, nearly three hours before. The temperature was rising as the sun climbed higher in the sky. No child was going to lose his/her hard-earned place to go and sit in what little shade there was at the edge of the car-park. Few had water to drink. There was a serious danger that one or more of these children would take heatstroke or die from dehydration but still they waited.

The temperature began to rise inside. The children sitting in the cinema seats had quietened, becoming sleepy in the heat. My blouse, spotlessly laundered by Harriet and immaculate when I left home, had become a sweat-soaked limp rag and my blue cotton skirt stuck to my legs every time I moved. I slipped out through the fire exit to the small yard behind the cinema hoping to cool off a little in the open air. Surrounded by high buildings and fenced in with two-metre high metal railings topped with the ubiquitous razor-wire, the ten-by-five metre yard was every bit as hot as inside. Four young men detailed as guards were stationed beside the pad-locked gate. They crouched against a high wall seeking what little protection it gave from the blazing sun. Tempted by the shade I joined them. Some of the cardboard cartons in which the shoe boxes had been packed had been flattened and laid like a carpet over the broken cement surface of the yard. They spoke about the boxes and how people in the United States had packed and sent them. Three of them moaned the fact that there were not more boxes, saying that rich Americans should be more generous. The fourth spoke of his dream of a day when Africans would not be dependent on handouts. One day, he said, Africans would not only get their rightful share of the world's material resources, they would get more. Today's wealthy nations would become poorer and would learn to suffer as Africa had suffered. He spoke of how the elite wealthy nations who form only twenty per cent of the world's population use eighty per cent of the world's resources to fuel their comfortable lifestyles knowing I belonged to one of these wealthy nations whose people unthinkingly use much more than their fair share of the world's riches.

Any embarrassment I felt diminished somewhat a moment later as I watched our distinguished visitor's shining-white, chauffeur-driven Mercedes buck its way along the dusty, rubbish strewn, potholed lane behind the cinema. Guards rushed to unlock the padlocks and unravel the yards of chain which secured the gate. George came forward to welcome our honoured guest, who alighted from his air-conditioned car and sashayed his way over the cardboard-paving to make an exuberant entrance through what had originally been the fire-door. Obviously pleased at having been asked to undertake this engagement he waved cheerily to the children, stopped to speak to the platform party and then inspected the stacks of boxes before taking his seat on the rostrum. We all stood to sing the National Anthem, *Stand and sing of Zambia, proud and free, Land of work and joy in unity.* We sang a hymn, said a prayer and received a homily on being thankful for gifts received. All of this probably took no more than thirty minutes but I was all too aware of the children still standing outside in the searing heat.

A gaily coloured box was taken from the stack for boys aged

two to four and handed to our guest. A tiny lad in a pale blue T-shirt in the front row was invited to come forward to receive it. I stood with camera poised ready to catch the moment but the little fellow, frightened by all the attention focused on him, became shy. No amount of persuasion could encourage him to come forward. Aware of a chance to be the star of the show, a girl sitting near him jumped into the breach. She bobbed a slight curtsey and smiled charmingly up at our guest who leaned forward to shake her hand before handing over the shoe box. As I clicked away with the camera, she ran her hand over her pink organza skirt just to ensure it was all in place then smiled straight into the lens. Everyone clapped and cheered and she smiled at the crowd, definitely a star in the making. The other children scrambled into line to receive a gift, and the box-giving got really underway. Mutinta tried to persuade our young star to exchange her shoe box for one prepared for a girl. Poor kid, she obviously thought that in getting the first box, she had received a very special one and that we were trying to cheat her by taking it back from her so in the end she left clutching the original box. I hoped that she was not too disappointed when she opened it.

After the first few presentations George and other PFZ staff also began handing out boxes and the presentations started to speed up. After a child had received a box, he/she left through the fire-door. I snapped the presentations for about half an hour before going out into the yard to see what was happening there. Some of the children looked almost traumatised as they staggered out, others clutched the boxes to their chests as if scared to lose this precious gift. Many just sat down in the first free space and looked to see what their box contained. I watched one little girl, maybe four or five, her hair tied in tight curls and wearing a pale green dress, take a small doll from her box and lifting it to her lips kiss it. One youngster had already started to colour in a page of a book. Another was flicking through a book. Boys were already swapping games. Watching the children's joy was wonderful but then I heard screaming and turned to see what had happened. An adult, presumably a parent, had arrived and taken a box from a child and marched off, followed by the child who was crying piteously. When I looked at Mutinta for guidance she shook her head. That was to be by no means the only child who having got a box, left without it. The following day I watched street vendors selling items which obviously had come from the boxes. But if you don't have money for food, what use are toys? Sometimes the contents would be sold to raise money not for food but for drink when the child would get no benefit at all from the box. That child might even be abused by a drunken parent.

Gradually the cinema emptied and then filled up again from those waiting in the car park and yet the car park numbers did not appear to reduce. Children still arrived though in much fewer numbers than before. One or two enterprising lads tried to go round more than once but when recognised were speedily evicted. There was heartbreak for those who had lost their vouchers, perhaps even had had them stolen. The box-giving went on all morning and into the early afternoon. Having used the two rolls of film I had been given, I headed home. Over the next few weeks, as I passed the woven cane-mats laid out on the pavements which served as stalls for the street vendors, I saw goods for sale which I was sure had come from the shoe boxes. I kept looking, praying that I would not see the little doll which had been so tenderly lifted from a box and kissed. Thankfully, I never did.

At Monday morning's devotion, the PFZ staff were congratulating each other. They thought the shoe box presentation had gone well. Despite my worries about the children standing in the sun, there had been only one report of a child taking ill. It was suggested, however, that if PFZ were still responsible for the presentation another year, it would be planned differently, with many small presentations in the townships where the children lived rather than one major event in town. Carl and I were told that the boxes allotted to us had been left at Mark's house on Independence Way, not far from Zawi. Carl promised to pick these up on his way home in the evening. He planned to pack them in his backpack so that the Zawi children would not see him with them. Harriet always waited until I arrived home before she left for her own home. I had just said cheerio to her and poured myself some water when a troubled Carl arrived with an empty backpack. What had been waiting for him at Mark's home were two cartons of boxes, not two boxes as we had expected. Our idea of splitting the contents between the children at Zawi was now impracticable and if the boxes were delivered to either of our houses the children would see and identify them. Not only would the Zawi children want their share of the contents we would be pestered by children coming from all around looking for toys or books. That was not what the people who donated the boxes had intended. We decided to offer the boxes to Brian and Kevin for the street children. They, the most disadvantaged of all children in Ndola, had not been included in the box distribution because without homes they were not listed in any area. Arrangements were made for Brian to collect the cartons in the Friends of Africa vehicle the following day and take them straight to the house he and Kevin shared with Father Don. They did not think it practical to give a box to a child who had nowhere to keep it so the four of us had an evening of fun opening each of the boxes in the two cartons and emptying out the contents. Brian could not resist having a cuddle at a soft, pink, teddy bear while Kevin and Carl tried a puzzle before crowning me with a hair-band decorated with a large purple and pink flower. We all tried to find out if we still retained some of our childhood skills with a yo-yo. Most boxes had toothpaste and toothbrushes but also lots of sweets. We stacked the dental items together along with the soap and face-cloths. They would be used in the night shelter. Brian planned to give each boy a glass jar with his own toothbrush and toothpaste. Toys and games would also go to the night shelter. They would be used either for communal fun for the boys or to ensure that there was a birthday present for a child on the appropriate day. Books, writing material, crayons and felt pens were saved for use at the

Open Community School which was attended by some of the street children and other disadvantaged children. We were still left with some very girly items such as hair slides and ribbons. These were carefully packed back in boxes to be taken to the children's hospice in Lusaka by the first one of us to travel to the city. After making sure by personally testing some of the toffee that it was still edible, we split our large sweet mountain into three, one lot for the night shelter and one for the school while the last would go with the dolls, ribbons and hair slides to the children's hospice.

Chapter 19

'AIDS may kill me in months or even years but hunger will kill me and my family tomorrow'

Distribution of the Christmas boxes left a feeling of euphoria in the office which deflated like a burst balloon when George, unhappy that the PFZ board had failed to confirm him in the position of executive director, gave notice of his intention to resign at the end of June. The atmosphere became strained. Although there were three months before George's resignation took effect, and the receipt of donations meant that the bank balance was healthier than it had been since Christmas, there was a feeling of insecurity and irresolution in the office. No one, other than Francis Mpzeni, who saw himself as the obvious candidate to be the new executive director, was sure what was going to happen and how it would affect their jobs. Even the very favourable six-month review that VSO had given Carl and me over the initial success of our placements at Prison Fellowship failed to raise spirits. Maurice, who was usually the powerhouse of new ideas, was busy with his own affairs. He and his fiancée, Martha, a nurse at Ndola General Hospital, were making arrangements to get married but the date had been altered at least three times. Getting their two families to agree the financial settlement that contained the bride price, the amount the bridegroom paid the bride's family, had been difficult. Maurice explained that in Zambia a man does not get recognition as an adult until he is married so although he was a university graduate with employment and a home he had no say in these negotiations and had to await patiently the outcome. Where traditionally in Europe the bride brought money to her husband, in Zambia the bride price was money or property given by the bridegroom to the bride's family so that he could establish his rights over the woman. When at last the family compact was complete it was disappointing to learn that the Saturday chosen for the wedding was one when neither Carl nor I would be able to attend the celebrations. We were scheduled to attend a VSO training seminar in Lusaka that weekend on HIV/AIDS.

Again I travelled on the early morning coach but this time I knew what to expect. Or I thought I did until the bus engine failed to start and all the passengers had to decant and move to a second bus. Anticipating a scramble for seats on the replacement bus I moved quickly but every passenger went exactly to the same seat in the second bus as they had occupied in the first. My newspaper was again passed round among my fellow travellers and my hair touched by a curious child in the row of seats behind. With subject of the seminar very much in mind I looked at my fellow travellers and wondered who among them was HIV positive. The likelihood was quite a few.

There were no accurate statistics of infection rates in Zambia in 2001. The stigma attached to being diagnosed as being HIV positive was so severe that those who were tested and found to be HIV positive kept that fact secret as long as possible. All this made it impossible to accurately calculate the infection rate. The World Health Organisation estimated that at least one in every six adults was HIV positive. There was a considerably higher rate of infection in urban as opposed to rural areas where the ratio might be one in every four. In a population of around eleven million, around one hundred thousand died each year from AIDS. Life expectancy had fallen below forty. As volunteers working in Zambia we were affected by the scale of the epidemic. The people and organisations we were working with in our placements had to struggle with the effects of its impact while on a personal level there was a danger of transmission when in contact with infected blood or in any sexual encounter. At the start of the seminar we were reminded once more of the personal risk and were prompted to help ourselves from the supply of condoms which was kept in a fridge in the VSO office kitchen. There was even a supply of discreet plain brown bags in which the condoms could be carried.

Dolores Long led the seminar. She gave us an overview of the National Strategic Framework which had been prepared by the National HIVAIDS/STD/TB Council (NAC), an organisation set up the previous year to advise the government on how to address the HIV/AIDS epidemic. This set out aims and objectives which included how to educate all Zambians, but particularly those in the most vulnerable categories, such as prostitutes and long-distance truckdrivers, on HIV/AIDS. It covered its plans on how to disseminate information about the disease, how it was transmitted, the protection which could be used against contracting it, and what help was available to people who were HIV positive and to their families. It also suggested ways of dealing with the stigma which a known sufferer could be subjected to. A woman who might have caught the disease from her husband could be thrown out of the family home and left destitute. An employee could be sacked. The VSOs at the meeting considered how the work each of us was doing in our placements and in VSO's Raise Awareness of AIDS in Southern Africa (RAISA) campaign complemented these plans.

Zambia's first known case of AIDS was reported in 1984. From that date the infection rate continued to rise as HIV spread throughout all levels of Zambian society. While most epidemics affect the poorest members of society worst, AIDS in Zambia and in other sub-Saharan African countries had spread throughout the total community. Its impact had affected all areas of the economy, weakening and stifling national development. Every sector of Zambia's economy was being impaired by the AIDS epidemic. Employers had to cope with the disruption of absenteeism through illness. Businesses had to meet the costs of medical care, funerals, recruitment and training of replacement staff. There was a lack of skilled personnel who could pass on their skills to the next generation. Quality suffered. Production costs soared. Most Zambians were involved in agriculture at some level, even if it was just growing food for personal consumption. As illness struck they were less likely to be fit to plant seeds or look after their crops. All of this aggravated an already desperate food situation. People already malnourished were now in danger of starving. AIDS had created a vicious downward spiral of social dislocation and economic deprivation.

That said, certain sections of the community were more vulnerable than others. Women were particularly at risk. The Zambian constitution states that all people are equal regardless of colour or sex but traditions such as the bride price meant most women were held to be subservient to their husbands. Most were culturally and economically dependent on their husbands so were unable to refuse conjugal relations or insist on protected sex. There was a great risk that a wife who refused her husband would be subjected to abuse. Many were aware of the risks to themselves when a husband returned to them after having sex with another woman but were helpless to safeguard themselves. There was also 'dry sex,' a practice enjoyed by men who encouraged women to insert a concoction of certain herbs into the vagina to dry it up. But dry sex could lead to tearing of the wall of the vagina, allowing the HIV virus to be absorbed into the blood stream more easily. Sexual cleansing was still prevalent when a male relative of the deceased had sex with the widow in the belief that this dispersed evil.

Babies could be infected by mother-to-child transmission. Without access to preventative drugs, around one-third of HIV-positive mothers gave birth to infected babies. It was estimated that approximately thirty thousand infants contracted the virus each year, either at birth or while breast feeding.

There was also a high level of sexual abuse of children. The high death toll from AIDS had led to many vulnerable orphans. There were more than half a million orphans in Zambia in 2001 and the number was rising daily. Many of them were looked after by a family member, and often treated as a poor relation that had to be grateful for a home. Others were left to survive on the streets as best they could. Men increasingly targeted younger sexual partners in the belief that they were HIV-negative. There was the myth of the 'virgin cure', that sex with a virgin could cure AIDS. There was little support for any child who tried to seek help from the authorities. It was unlikely that any official would act against an abuser.

Zambians become sexually active at a fairly young age. Often girls are encouraged to have sex with older boys or men in return for money or a gift. As a result there was a higher infection rate among girls in the age group 15–19 than among boys in the same age group. The girls were about six times more likely to be HIV positive than the boys. There were thousands of female sex-workers in Zambia. A survey suggested that around twenty per cent of women and twenty-nine per cent of men had taken part in paid-for sex. Many women became prostitutes to earn money to feed their families. There was a saying that 'AIDS may kill me in months or even years but hunger will kill me and my family tomorrow.' From the limited data available it was calculated that about two-thirds of prostitutes were HIV positive. Many of them worked in areas where long-distance truck drivers had overnight stops encouraging infection to travel along the main transport routes. Prostitutes also worked among seasonal labourers or migrant workers who spent much time away from their wives and who often took the infection back home when on a family visit.

The AIDS epidemic was having a disastrous effect on families, healthcare, education, and the economy and food production. The majority of people who suffered from AIDS were in their productive years. Often they were the breadwinners for their families. When they fell ill other family members had to try and earn money. This could mean that the children were kept from school, either because there were insufficient funds to pay for them to go or because they had to tend animals or crops or try to earn money in whatever way they could. They might also have to nurse and care for the sick. If there were any funds available the money would be spent on medicine and, later, on funeral expenses.

While many of these children would never complete their primary education even fewer of those aged between fourteen and eighteen were getting a secondary education. Teachers were dying at such a rate that teacher-training colleges were not turning out sufficient new graduates to fill the vacancies. Ruth Brewer spoke of the difficulties at the teacher-training college where she worked. They were struggling to fill the vacancies created by AIDS-related deaths

The Zambian health system, which had been underfunded for years, had almost completely collapsed under the strain of dealing with AIDS patients. Carers were struggling to cope with what little resources they had at a time when their own numbers were being depleted by illness and deaths from AIDS.

These were just some of the problems which the government of Zambia had to confront when dealing with this epidemic. As VSOs we were working with some of the most marginalised people, those who had few resources left. Many of us felt overwhelmed by the immensity of the problems this country was facing. In discussing the HIV/AIDS situation and the various actions different people were taking to help vulnerable people cope in these situations, we shared ideas and talked over some of the methods which had been successfully used in helping some of its victims. Dave Clinton and Emily Kippax spoke of the help being given to street orphans in Lusaka and how Zambian Open Community Schools were providing education for them; Carl talked about the education programmes PFZ volunteers were undertaking in the prisons; Justin Highstead was part of the team at the magazine *Trendsetters* who were using their pages to educate their adolescent readers on prevention and on dealing with stigma. Others were working in businesses where they were training new employees in skills which had been lost by deaths among the workforce. All of us were using every opportunity to talk openly about the disease, how it is transmitted and what precautions could be taken. Most of us were experiencing the same difficulties when doing this, the cultural resistance to talking about anything to do with sex, the determination of many of the churches that condoms should not be promoted, the conviction that people who fell victim to AIDS were being punished for sins, the strengths of the myths such as the 'virgin cure', and the tenacity of many who wanted to sweep everything to do with the epidemic under the carpet in the hope it would go away. Perhaps one of the most useful effects of the weekend was that each realised that we were not alone in experiencing difficulties. While there were differences in the kind of situations we each had to cope with, all of us were experiencing drawbacks in our placements as a direct result of the HIV/AIDS epidemic.

The atmosphere of depression conjured up by talking about this desperate situation through Friday afternoon and most of Saturday was put behind us when most of the volunteers spent Saturday evening relaxing in The Brown Frog. A shopping trip to Manda Hill had enabled me to replenish my own dwindling supply of toiletries as well as buy items for friends in Ndola. I had enjoyed being in Lusaka for the weekend, meeting up with the other volunteers, but was glad to be returning north on Sunday.

The Monday morning management meeting was a struggle of a different kind. George informed us that for this week only the meeting would be held at the Executive Lodge, a guesthouse in the North Rise area of Ndola. George advised Maurice, Francis, Robam, Mark and me that the Prison Fellowship Board wished the appointment of his successor as Executive Director to be made from the existing staff and had asked that the management committee propose a suitable candidate to the board. Francis sat back his chair confident that George was going to propose his name. He was completely dumfounded when George said that we had to choose between Francis and Maurice. Francis, cheeks bulging in annoyance, spluttered that the Prison Fellowship rules stated that the Director had to be a priest or pastor therefore Maurice was not eligible for the post. George, however, had done his homework and notified us that the rules said either a priest or pastor or someone holding a university degree, which covered Maurice, could hold the position.

Francis, unwilling to accept George's information, left the meeting to go home and check his copy of the rule-book. Maurice would only say that he needed time to consider his position before deciding whether his name could be presented as a nominee for the position. George closed the meeting with a reminder to all of us that our discussion was highly confidential.

It is one of the mysteries of management how the unofficial communication system in any organisation gets its information but that system in PFZ was just as active as any I had experienced in the UK. Even although George had taken exceptional care to prevent the discussions of our meeting being known, yet perhaps even because of his actions, rumours were circulating round the office. At supper that evening Carl reported some of these stories to me and it was surprising how accurate some of them were. It appeared one of the health volunteers had seen Francis near his home when he should have been at the meeting and with his demeanour indicating his dissatisfaction at events the staff had come to their own conclusions on what had been discussed and the possible outcomes. With no immediate developments, the rumours gradually died down but the general atmosphere of uncertainty and worry over the future prevailed. A change of director meant for many of the staff a doubt about their continuing employment at PFZ. Redundancy is a difficult situation in any country but in one where approximately eighty per cent of the population were not in paid employment it was disastrous. Mutinta, who was related to George through marriage (George's wife was her aunt), was worried about how the change of director would affect her. Kanyanta Sambie, who was being trained to take over the micro-credit unit when Mark returned to Canada in June, was still on probation. Mellbin was Maurice's cousin. That meant they belonged to the same tribe and obviously nepotism and tribal allegiances played a large part in the hiring and firing of staff. I knew that if the board appointed Francis I would have great difficulty in completing my placement. It was unlikely he would want me at PFZ.

It was ironic that just at a time when I was preparing mentally for a possible return home, one of my grumbles with PFZ was resolved. Once its bank balance had recovered a little a chair and a small sofa were purchased for both my home and Carl's. When the local joiner who made them said they were ready for collection none of the PFZ vehicles was available to transport them to Zawi. Torunn came to our rescue using her vehicle, a single cab Toyota Hilux. The two chairs along with Carl were locked under the canopy while I sat in the front passenger seat on top of a cushion, clutching tightly on to the other three to stop them falling on top of the hand-brake. My little home looked completely different now it had a comfortable seat. Torunn tried it out for comfort while I made tea. Maurice brought the sofa tied to the top of the PFZ Hilux a few days later, just in time for the arrival from the UK of my sister, Marjorie, and her daughter, Ruth.

I had arranged to take some of my annual leave while they were in Zambia and made enquiries about hiring a car. The quoted costs left me flabbergasted. The cheapest was US$100 a day. With a little help from George that figure was reduced to a more reasonable US$60 a day including full insurance for a small Suburu twin-cab truck. How comprehensive the insurance was, was open to doubt. I just prayed I did not have to depend on it. Mike Bird gave me details of a small game lodge/farm, Lechwe Lodge, about eighty kilometres south of Lusaka where he had stayed at Christmas and had enjoyed it. I booked for us to stay two nights after their arrival, giving them time to acclimatise.

Finding them somewhere to stay while in Ndola proved difficult and eventually Brian and Kevin lent me two foam mattresses. I pushed my bed into the corner of my bedroom and fixed my travelling mosquito net over it. The mattresses were placed on the floor under the larger net I normally used. There was not going to be a lot of space but I was sure we would manage. Marjorie and Ruth brought sleeping bags and towels with them.

Chapter 20

Visitors from home

Carl, who was meeting a friend off the same flight, shared the driving to Lusaka. After big hugs all round, we drove south in the Suburu to the outskirts of Kafue Town where a sign for Kafue fisheries and Lechwe Lodge directed us to turn west past the Nitrogen Chemicals factory and along a gravel road for over six kilometres. At the end of the rainy season, this was in much need of repair and we bounced around like corks in water. Lechwe Lodge was everything Mike had said. There was one main thatched-roof building which served as dining room with a small lounge off, which could be used for meetings/conferences. Guests were accommodated in thatched roof rondavels in the grounds. A lovely red poinsettia about two metres high grew beside the one we were led to. Marjorie and Ruth were delighted with their first experience of Africa, the heat, sounds and smells of a different continent, the blazing sun in a sapphire blue sky which gave a luminous quality to brick red earth. I was just pleased to have the luxury of a bathroom with running water and a working shower. It was in the bathroom that Marjorie had her first real African experience. She thought a large flat spider was a design on a bath tile until it moved. She was startled later when she opened her bag and found a tree-frog hiding there.

Lechwe covers an area or about 13 square kilometres of brachystegia and acacia woodlands and the game there includes giraffe, zebra, hartebeest and all the most common antelope of the region. It has none of the large predators other than crocodiles and there are plenty of them in the river. The best time to see game is early in the morning or at dusk so it was a bonus on an afternoon drive when we saw a family of giraffe. We also saw many species of birds: white egrets, green bee-eaters, wonderful blue kingfishers, yellow weaver birds, who plait reeds together to make complicated nests like small beehives hanging from trees, as well as lots of butterflies in yellows and oranges.

In the evening a log fire was lit in the grounds, the blaze warming in the cooler evening air. The bruising night-heat had disappeared along with the hot-wet season. April had brought the start of the warm, dry months. The scent of the wood smoke was relaxing as we sat beside the fire enjoying a sun-downer before dinner. The tinkling chorus set up by the cicadas and tree-frogs almost drowned the last calls of the birds as they settled for the night. When the warm colours of the sunset reflected on the water's surface, a lechwe, the breed of antelope which gave the lodge its name, came for a drink at the lily pond.

Leaving there for Ndola we made a quick stop at the VSO offices in Lusaka where Kate Greenaway asked what plans I had for my guests. When I mentioned among other things a planned visit by a group of us to the Chimfunshi Wildlife Orphanage west of Chingola, just south of the border with the DR Congo, she advised against it. The British High Commission in Lusaka had warned people had been attacked while using the road between Chingola and Solwezi, the one we would have to use. The orphanage situated on the banks of the Kafue River is a safe haven for orphaned chimpanzees, refugees from war-torn DR Congo where it was suspected that their parents had been the victims of poachers, who supplied an illegal export trade. She recommended that we thought very carefully before going.

I went back to work the following day, leaving Marjorie and Ruth to do some gentle exploring of Ndola. Later they visited PFZ where Marjorie, who did silk screening as a hobby, was particularly intrigued with the tie and dye work being done in the tailoring department. Pieces of plain white cotton material were folded in specific ways then one corner of the folded material was dipped first in a tub of hot wax heating on a charcoal brazier, then into a bubbling vat of coloured dye. When the material was opened up, the areas where the wax had held were white and the remainder coloured. It was then stretched out on the grass to dry. Mutinta was particularly happy to meet Marjorie and Ruth. When she knew of their visit she had asked if they would buy a wedding ring for her in the UK and bring it over with them. It was almost impossible to buy a gold ring in Ndola at that time. Over the previous weeks letters and catalogues had been posted back and forth between Zambia and Edinburgh and an appropriate ring had been bought for her.

One of the highlights of Marjorie and Ruth's stay in Ndola was their visit to the township of Chipulukusu where PFZ ran its micro-credit project. Kanyanta Sambie offered to take them and Carl's friend on a tour round part of the township. Sambie said they could carry cameras but he advised that they carry them in bags and ask before taking any pictures. Carl, Francis Chibembe, another of the micro staff, and I tagged along. We set off early, before the temperature rose, and climbed up Vitanda Street's gentle hill where we passed the Copperbelt Brewery, home to Rhino and Mosi, the local beers. Once into the residential Lowenthal Road the road began to slope downhill again past well-kept bungalows which sat back off the street in gardens with high fences often topped with razor wire or walls finished with pieces of broken glass. Leaving the main town behind we followed the road for Lubumbashi in the DCR, a single track of poorly surfaced road, for around a kilometre before turning off onto a narrow earth path, beaten hard by the many feet which trod over it daily. There had been no rain for a few weeks but the grass on either side of the path was shoulder high. Sometimes we had to stand to the side to let pass those going in the other direction but it was mostly they who stood back in surprise to watch the quite unusual sight of musungos walking to Chipulukusu. We squeezed past men struggling with ancient bicycles which were so grossly overloaded with bags of charcoal that the men had problems keeping them upright. Many of them had illegally crossed the Congolese border but as the people of Ndola needed the charcoal the authorities turned a blind eye and so the charcoal sellers pushed their ancient bicycles back and forth over an unmarked border.

Crossing the railway track meant listening carefully for the sound of a train as this was the line which went north-west to Lubumbashi in the DR Congo. One branch then goes further north in the DR Congo while another heads west to Angola's Atlantic seaport, Benguela, a journey of more than two thousand kilometres. The local residents had none of my concerns. Some wandered along the middle of the track while a cart being pulled by a bullock had its wheels balanced on the rails.

From the train track it was a short distance to the first houses in the township. We wandered through small streets of houses built mostly from mud bricks. The more prosperous ones had roofs made from corrugated iron sheeting held down with large stones. Most of the others had thatch made from reeds taken from the nearby river. A few had cardboard which had either been replaced after the rains or was badly misshapen having been soaked and dried so often during the wet season. Occasionally we passed a small ruin. Houses which did not have roofs strong enough to keep the rain from the mud bricks disintegrated and collapsed, sometimes around the family sheltering there.

We passed a number of wells of the type where water is raised by pumping a handle. Three women drawing water offered me an almost Biblical scene. When her container was filled, one woman swung it up onto her head as if it weighed little more than a feather and strolled off without even a hand raised to steady it. Sometimes a water source was just an open pipe where the water trickled away to be sucked up by the dry earth. At one such well where the ground was not absorbing the water quite so quickly naked youngsters were having a great time splashing around in the mud.

As we wandered down little lanes between the houses, Sambie and Francis Chibembe stopped from time to time to introduce us to people they knew or to speak to some of PFZ's micro credit clients. Some of these ran cottage industries, weaving baskets from dried reeds, making rag rugs, beating out pails and containers from sheets of metal, but many, probably too many, were shopkeepers, people who had built stalls from pieces of wood roughly nailed together. Sometimes these kiosks were covered with faded advertisements for such as Omo soap-powder, Coca-Cola or Lifebuoy soap. Their stock was meagre, some eggs, a few bread rolls, a tin of shoe-polish, soap, wax candles and maybe a few cheap, caramel-type sweets. All stalls had some little plastic bags tied to strings hanging from the roof. The white coloured ones contained mealie meal and the blue ones soap-powder. The shopkeeper made his profit by buying a twenty-five kilo bag of mealie meal and splitting it into amounts his customers could afford to buy. Similarly the packets of soap-powder had been broken down into affordable units. The profit margins were low, almost too low, and competition fierce so many of the micro-credit clients were struggling to repay their loans.

At one home where we stopped, the lady of the house invited us to enter. Knowing that in keeping with local etiquette such an invitation would include some refreshments, at the very least the offer of a drink of water, accepting what was offered would mean depriving her family of what little they had. Sambie gave me a reassuring nod. Going from the brilliant sunshine outside to the dark interior meant our eyes took some time to adjust but gradually I saw that the house was split into two rooms. The living area was crowded with furniture. We sat on chairs which had been positioned backs to the walls to form a square round a small wicker table. Hand embroidered, turquoise-blue chairbacks edged with cream crochet protected them. A Biblical picture of Jesus teaching children was pinned on the wall behind where I was sitting. The open doorway to the sleeping quarters was curtained with a piece of chigenge material. Our hostess, handing round a plastic plate with pieces of watermelon, was obviously very pleased that we had accepted her hospitality but her children, perhaps checking that there would be some melon left for them, peeped round the door to see what was happening then ran off giggling.

The sun was now high in the sky. As we passed an open area of sparse grass where a few tethered cows strained to find grazing we hurried because the stench from the hut that served as an abattoir was absolutely foul. It was here that I had helped choose a cow for the prisoners' Christmas dinner. A few hens scratched around and two goats meandered into our path with their goatherd desperately trying to round them up.

At a church, four concrete walls with a corrugated iron roof, Peter, the pastor, who was a member of the Ndola care group invited us in. The furnishings were one table, a few low benches and nothing else, not even a picture on the walls, but it was pleasantly cool inside. Some children who had been playing nearby were curious and followed us. Peter told us some of the local children came there for lessons but whether these were scholastic or Biblical was not clear. He encouraged them to sing for us. Without further prompting they formed themselves into a semicircle in front of us. With eyes shining bright they raised their dusty faces towards us and sang. They ranged in age from around four to about ten or eleven and were dressed in a ragged assortment of multicoloured grubby T-shirts and shorts. Only minutes before they had been playing and scrambling around on the hard-packed earth in front of the church. Now they lifted up their voices in song all the more beautiful because it flowed so effortlessly. Having thanked them and handed out some sweets purchased at one of the local stalls, we were ready to move on. Time was passing and we had to walk all the way back, preferably before the African sun reached its midday zenith. Zambians tried to stay in shade during the worst heat of the day and we were aiming to follow their example. It was a tired group who made it back to Ndola where we took Sambie for an nshima lunch at the PFZ restaurant.

Marjorie and Ruth spent much of their time in Ndola strolling around its dusty streets, discovering for themselves the places I had mentioned in letters including Kaunda Avenue, the site of the memorial to Northern Rhodesians who died in the two World Wars. They were able to tell me about places I had not visited. My chances to explore were restricted to weekends and then I had shopping and other jobs to do and also many public buildings were closed at weekends. We spent a morning in the small Copperbelt Museum on Buteko Avenue which illustrated something of the geology of the region and of how and when the mining industry had been started. Africans had used copper to make tools as early as the Stone Age but it was not until the start of the twentieth century that commercial mining began. In 1902 an Australian mining engineer, Tom Davey, came across ancient copper workings at an area known to the Africans as Kabwe. Because he broke pieces of rock from the *kopje* (small hill) he called the area Broken Hill but after Independence in 1964 the name reverted back to Kabwe. Excited by his discovery he encouraged another prospector, William Collier, to look for ancient mine workings in Ndola and Luanshya. In response to a request from an elderly local man to shoot some meat, Collier took a shot at a roan antelope bull which, when it died, fell on an area of dark grey shale in which there were very fine seams of green malachite, a source of copper. These two incidents were the start of the development of the mining industry. The region became known as the Copperbelt. Collier called the area Roan Antelope after the animal he had shot as was the mine he set up on that site.

Ruth, who has a degree from the Edinburgh College of Art, visited a small art gallery in the town. This had been built in an open piece of ground behind the park near a stepped area which could have been used as an outdoor theatre but which, sadly, like so much of Ndola, had been left unattended and at the mercy of the weather. At the gallery she met some fellow artists including one who was making papier mache sculptures. Some of his work, statues of people that represented sections of the community, had recently cheered up the roundabout at the intersection of Broadway with the main road from the south. However, there had been complaints from some of the evangelical churches because one was of a woman in traditional costume of grass skirt and not much else. It had been removed and repainted so that her breasts were discretely covered.

It seemed ironic that among a populace where women kept their legs covered but openly and naturally breast-fed babies, it was the uncovered breasts which caused offence.

Marjorie had said on arriving that she wanted to experience life in Zambia as I was living it so for our journey to Livingstone to see the Victoria Falls I arranged for us to travel by bus. The journey was long and tiring, even with an overnight stop in Lusaka and if I thought the lovely location at the Zambezi Waterfront had made Marjorie forget the discomfort of the journey, I was mistaken. When I was beginning to relax with a Rhino beer, she announced that she did not care how we travelled back to Lusaka or what it cost but she was not going back on the bus. She was not prepared to suffer again the discomfort of the coach journey. Arrangements were made for us to fly back to Lusaka.

Viewing the Victoria Falls from the Zambian side was the first priority on our list of things to do, so we ordered a taxi to take us there. Ernest, our driver, turned out to be very helpful. Most Zambian taxi-drivers will tell you their names and ask yours. To them it is polite, but it is also a way of ensuring that if you take a taxi you will name the driver you want. Entrance to the Falls national park cost US$3 each. The parking area was beside the curio market, where hundreds of carved animals, some large, some small, stood side by side in displays laid out to catch the attention of the tourists. Tribal masks hung beside copper plaques and strings of wooden beads. Ernest came to our rescue when the craftsmen surrounded us. If one of us looked even mildly interested in something such as a carved elephant or a copper bracelet, they were pressing it into our hands, not realising that the pressure they were putting on us to buy was frightening us off. Ernest, seeing Marjorie walk away from one stall, bargained on her behalf for a carved chief's stick, a wooden pole just over a metre in length which had a carved head at one end and tapered off at the other, a copy of one traditionally carried by a paramount chief.

Ernest led the way to the best viewpoints where what I saw was a completely different panorama from the one I had seen in December. Then there was much less water in the river and rock showed through between the different sections. In April, after one of the heaviest rainy seasons in recent years, it was one sheet of water along the total escarpment, much of it hidden by the spray from 750 million litres of water cascading over it every minute. We stood looking into the mist while marvelling at the spectacle and listening to the roar of water striking water in the ravine over one hundred metres below. Beautiful rainbows glistened through the spray. The escarpment is divided by islands in the river into seven different waterfalls. Going east from Zambia to west in Zimbabwe these are the Eastern Cataract, Armchair Falls, Rainbow Falls, Horseshoe Falls, Main Falls, Cataract Falls and Devil's Cataract although with the extra high water level in the Zambezi it was impossible to identify these different areas.

The spray which rose high in the air was raining down on us causing Ruth to take care of her camera for the spray could get into the lens. We were soaked to the skin but that did not matter. The hot sun would soon dry our clothes. We moved from one viewpoint to the next, stepping carefully through the rain forest, itself a direct result of the conditions created by the Falls, for the paths were wet and slippery. The barriers at the viewpoints were often just a fence made from a few pieces of wood. Sometimes there was a very steep drop into the water, just feet away from the viewpoint. We followed the path down watery uneven steps towards the Knife-edge Bridge which crossed the chasm to the next set of viewpoints. The bridge, aptly named, was a narrow metal span of about twenty metres which looked as if it had been made from a Meccano set. The spray there was so heavy that we could hardly see the other end of the bridge and the end nearest us had yellow and black 'warning' tape stretched between the rails of the bridge and a branch of a tree. A stream of water ran across the bridge creating its own little waterfall where it fell off the end. We chose instead to walk back round the south side of the promontory so that we could look at the view to the road/rail bridge which crossed the river and the foaming white water rapids, known as the Boiling Point, flowing fast below it.

The forest too was different from how it had looked at Christmas for colourful flowers bloomed in the undergrowth. Small yellow heads peeped up through the grass as did tall plants with little white flowers. On the side away from the Falls a few trees supported vivid pink creepers while some clumps resembling bluebells in pinks and blues peeped through the grass. Bright colourful butterflies fluttered by, settling here and there on a grass stem. Ernest continued his self-appointed role as our guide and told us how in geographical terms the Falls are relatively new. They were formed around one million years ago. Originally the escarpment was much further downstream from the present one. The fast flowing water had over hundreds of thousands of years eroded the edge of the waterfall and gradually gouged out channels through the basalt rock. As one escarpment was formed the water would gradually wear down the rock until it found a fault line behind the rock and then that wall would weaken and collapse. Gradually over thousands of years the escarpment line had retreated upstream by over ninety metres. The Devil's Cataract on the Zimbabwean side, the most westerly waterfall, showed evidence of the continuing sequence – how the power of fast flowing water hollows out a series of deep gorges through rock.

When I made a comment about 'The Smoke that Thunders' Ernest said that the correct translation is 'The Smoke that Rises'. Apparently, David Livingstone not only misspelt the name '*Musi-o-Tunya*' given to the Falls by the Kololo chief, Sebituane, as '*Mosi-oa-Tunya*' but also translated it incorrectly. The earlier name, '*Shungu na Mutitima*,' was used by the Tonga people who originally inhabited the land where the town of Livingstone now stands until they were driven out by the invading Kololos. They also had another saying of the Falls which translated something like 'A foolish man would think he could make a fire from it.'

The spectacle was so overwhelming that it was difficult to drag ourselves away from it. Ernest suggested that we walk upstream a little and view the turbulence in the river above the escarpment as the water rushes towards the edge. The little weir the volunteers and I had crossed at Christmas when we walked over this part of the river to the pool on the lip of the Falls was hardly visible under the present flow of water. When looking at the speed of the flow I found it difficult to take on board that we had actually crossed over there. Our clothes dried off in the sun as we watched the cloud of spray which would be seen miles away.

The following morning we hitched a lift to the Zimbabwean town of Victoria Falls. At that time holders of British passports did not need a visa to enter Zimbabwe. We had a super view as we sat perched high on the back of a safari vehicle trundling down the road to the border. Once again we became damp from the spray from the Falls as we crossed the rail/road bridge which spans the Zambezi and is the border between Zambia and Zimbabwe.

In need of some local currency I changed a few pounds at a bank in Victoria Falls into Zimbabwean dollars at a rate of eighty dollars to the pound (today in 2008 the rate is in millions and rising daily) before we made our way to the Safari Lodge some distance out in the bush. The lodge, built from wood and thatch so that it blended into the landscape, was set high at the top of an embankment and the restaurant had views which looked down over a watering-hole. We sat at a table near the window and watched buffalo, bushbuck and impala come for a drink as we enjoyed a buffet breakfast. Extra entertainment came from an ongoing contest between the waiters who were setting up tables for lunch and a monkey which grabbed the beautifully folded napkins, unfolded them and threw them on the floor.

On our way back to Victoria Falls town by hotel minicoach, we passed an elephant using its trunk to uproot a small tree at the side of the road. The driver stopped so that we could photograph it but refused to open the bus doors for someone who wanted to get out for a better photographic shot. We moved around inside the bus all eagerly pointing our Pentaxes and Canons trying for the best angle as the elephant inconsiderately moved around. Suddenly we were thrown all over the floor as the driver revved his engine and took off as if he was Michael Schumacher in Formula 1. There were moans, grumbles and splutters of annoyance at the alarming take-off but as I climbed back to my seat I saw through the rear window that there was a second elephant, rather large and very annoyed with trunk and ears flapping, chasing us up the road. We had all been so engrossed in our photography we hadn't heard it trumpeting or the thump of its feet as it got nearer. The driver had and he knew to take immediate action for that elephant was moving fast. This was no cartoon jumbo. This was a raging two-ton animal, a mass of muscle which would do dreadful damage if it caught up with us. We hung on to anything which seemed solid and safe as the driver forced the accelerator down to the floorboards and the coach swung round corners in the road on two wheels to an accompaniment of squeals and shrieks from terrified passengers. Then whether the elephant thought it had chased us off its patch, the hill was too steep for it or it just got fed up, it suddenly slowed then stopped in its tracks, gave one last, very loud bellow, turned round and meandered off. The driver must have scored in the tips he received when he reached the centre of Vic Falls but the poor man was still shaking from his efforts and from the fear of what might have happened but also from knowing that he had to drive back that same road.

Having decided that because the spray was so heavy we would not go to view the Falls from the Zimbabwean side, we walked back through the customs post and over the bridge where we stopped to watch the bungee jumping. I could not believe that anyone would pay for the privilege of throwing themselves off the bridge yet there was a queue waiting to do so. They were talking noisily and excitedly among themselves which must have been a sign of nervous tension. Once back into Zambia, we picked up a taxi, though not Ernest, at the customs post to take us back to The Waterfront. Unlike the

Zimbabwean side of the river where there was lots of liveliness, street-sellers, souvenir shops, cafes, places offering elephant rides and white-water rafting, on this side of the river the terrain was almost completely undeveloped, much as nature had formed it. There were just a few boys trying to sell copper bracelets to tourists and the curio market inside the park area. There was not even a booth selling cold drinks.

Over the next few days we took a safari trip in the Mosi-oa-Tunya National Park, enjoyed a sunset cruise when we watched some of the same animals we had seen in the park come to the water's edge for their evening drink, visited the museum in Livingstone and searched for souvenirs. Relaxing by the small swimming pool at The Waterfront, we were eating lunch at a table nearby when Ruth noticed something move under one of the sun beds. She mentioned to one of the waiters that it looked like a snake. At first he disbelieved her but then he too saw it. A green mamba, about a metre long, was intertwined through the wooden slats of the sun bed just feet away from where we had been sitting. The waiter called for back-up. The head waiter arrived as did almost every member of staff. They gathered around, looking, but no one was keen on getting too near the snake. The instructions to deal with it were passed down the pecking order. Eventually the boy who was responsible for looking after the pool was instructed to take the long-handled net used for removing debris from the pool and use it to catch the snake. Everyone else took a few steps back as the pool-boy moved tentatively forward. As he swung the net over the sun bed, the snake, perhaps disturbed by the noise, unwound itself from the wooden frame and slipped through the fence at the rear and into long grass. It was some time before anyone used the sun beds again and then the cushions were lifted first and frames carefully checked.

Time was running out for Marjorie and Ruth. Ernest drove us through Livingstone and out to the airport and the return journey to Lusaka. We passed the armed police checkpoint accepting it as just a normal hitch during the journey. The airport building was small, just one large hall with a few sectioned off areas and we had to pay an airport tax of US $5 each but once that had been completed there were few other formalities. The plane was a small eighteen-seater belonging to Zambian Airways. Our fellow passengers appeared to be mostly business men and women to whom the flight was just part of their day. As the plane soared into the sky we looked out the windows for one last view of the Zambezi, wide and blue until it reached the prominent white stretch of foam which marked the Falls.

Marjorie and Ruth had one final night in the comfort of Lusaka's four-star Taj Pamodzi Hotel before leaving on the Thursday evening flight for London. Sue Clay drove us to the airport. Dave accompanied by Emily drove Carl, who was travelling on the same flight. He was going home to attend his sister's wedding. We waited while Marjorie, Ruth and Carl paid the airport tax, US $20 for an international flight, and when that flight was called watched as they lifted their luggage onto the security scanners. At Lusaka airport, all luggage, both that about to be checked-in and the hand baggage which will be carried on to the plane, had to be screened before the passenger reached the check-in desk. What we did not realise was that once they had done this they had to go directly to the departure lounge and could not spend time saying good-byes to relatives and friends. I suddenly felt so lost. They had gone and I hadn't even said goodbye or given them a kiss and a cuddle. It would be nearly eighteen months before I was home and saw them again.

Sue, Emily, Dave and I wandered slowly back to the car park for the return journey into town. To cheer me up, we went out for a meal then on to a casino. I had never been in one before. We agreed an amount we were each prepared to lose and with beginners' luck I managed to not only keep my original stake but have enough to pay for the drinks. The following morning I was back on the coach heading for Ndola. This time my little house did not seem quite so welcoming as it had when I returned after the Christmas break. It seemed empty. The mattresses which Marjorie and Ruth had been using were still there reminding me that while I was on my own again they would be home in Edinburgh.

Chapter 21

Lunch, Supper, Dinner

During Marjorie and Ruth's visit I realised that it had been handy to have a spare mattress. Vicky Rowan, the Irish dentist, whose placement was in Francisdale some way out of Ndola could join in the weekend fun if she stayed overnight with me. We visited an Indian shop on Chisokene Street, an area little frequented by the European community where household goods were cheaper than at Shoprite. During the week when it was not needed as a mattress, it made a reasonable headboard. At the weekends we pulled it out, laid it on the living room floor, tied my spare mosquito net to a rope above it, and Vicky had a bed in town.

Along with all the other VSOs, in June I received an invitation to lunch at the residence of the British High Commissioner in Lusaka, an annual event to celebrate the Queen's official birthday. As it was to be held on a Thursday, Carl, who had returned from the UK, and I had to ask George for permission to go and I was unsure of the reaction we would get but consent was willingly given. It appeared that everyone at PFZ felt honoured because we had received the invitation. On the evening before the big event Mike Bird arrived from Kalulushi. He, Carl, Jolene, Carl's sister who was visiting him, and I set off for Lusaka on one of the first morning buses. Not wanting to arrive at the reception travel stained I packed my 'good' pale yellow dress and a pair of strappy sandals in my backpack and changed at the VSO office after I arrived in Lusaka.

Having bargained with a taxi to take us to the Residency on Independence Avenue, we were welcomed by the High Commissioner, Mr Thomas Young, tall and slim, dressed in a light-grey lounge suit, and by his wife, equally tall and slim and very elegant in a floral-printed silk dress. They greeted us, made a few pleasant remarks, before turning to greet their next set of guests while we moved on to meet the Deputy High Commissioner, a buxom lady perhaps in her late forties, dressed more business-like in navy and white, accompanied by her husband.

The well-watered long green lawns were so relaxing on the eyes after living with the Zambian burnt-red countryside. The lawns were surrounded by beds of multicoloured flowers and shrubs. A privet hedge protected a rose garden where the profusion of brilliant blooms perfumed the air. Music also came from the rose garden. A small, rotund conductor stood on a raised platform and beat time with his baton as the musicians in a brass band played well-known melodies. Waiters appeared with trays laden with glasses of wine and soft drinks. Spirits were served at a table where the white tablecloth could hardly be seen under so many different varieties of drinks. People wandered around glass in hand. The green lawns made an ideal backdrop for the multicoloured clothes of the guests, ladies in bright dresses of reds, blues, pinks, yellows and whites, a few Indian ladies in beautiful saris of soft flimsy materials which floated out behind them when they walked, men in jazzy psychedelic Zambian shirts and an ex-pat Scot wearing a kilt of red tartan. The king of Barotseland, seated on a throne-like chair under a canopy, was surrounded by his bodyguard, six warriors sans weapons, who sported lion skins and red mop-caps. The canopy made it difficult to see his traditional dress. It was his bodyguard which attracted attention. The sheen on the rippling black muscles of their powerful physiques was certain to set many a feminine heart a-flutter, including mine. Equally certain was that only the foolhardy would dare tangle with them. White pergola-type marquees had been erected on the lawns in front of the house. In their shade, chefs fully kitted out in their kitchen whites and high hats, presided over tables laden with platters of smoked salmon, poached fresh salmon, roast beef, large hams and many different accompanying salads. There were straw-berries and cream and a wonderful selection of British cheeses and biscuits, food that spoke of home to us volunteers.

Lunch over, the High Commissioner and the President's representative gave their official speeches and at their close Mr Young toasted 'Zambia,' and the President's representative, a member of his government, proposed a toast to Her Majesty and we all wished her well. We stood to attention for *God Save the Queen* and the Zambian national anthem, *Stand and sing of Zambia, proud and free*. The socialising went on for some time as a piper from the British Airways Pipe Band played traditional Scots airs.

I took the opportunity to talk to Zambians from the business and professional fields and to representatives from the various embassies and high commissions which were based in Lusaka. As funding for some of PFZ's projects came from certain of these embassies and new funding might come from these or from others, these were important connections. I wandered around taking the opportunity of making contacts, speaking to as many people as possible. By the end of the afternoon, I had made some new acquaintances including the chairman of the Zambian Caledonian Society, the wearer of the kilt.

A few days later I was a guest at another official function, Bonaventure (Bonnie) Zimba and Mutinta's engagement supper held in the garden of George's house. It was an engagement party unlike any other I had ever attended. Chairs were set out church style with a centre aisle. The young couple walked down this until they stood in front of a table, decorated with a pretty cloth and a vase of artificial flowers. George stood behind the table holding a large family-style Bible. The engagement ring was placed on a page of the open Bible and prayers were said for the young couple. The ring was lifted by Bonnie and slipped onto Mutinta's finger to a background of cheering and luluing from the assembled relatives and friends. A bunch of flowers was placed in his hand and as he gave these to Mutinta he placed a very chaste kiss on her cheek. Mutinta looked radiant. At one point she had believed that this evening would never happen. The two families had had difficulty agreeing a bride price. Mutinta, in her late twenties, was much older than the average Zambian bride. Bonnie's family had taken that into account and offered a reduced bride price while Mutinta's family maintained that as she was in employment and had a home the price should be inflated, not reduced. When it looked as if a settlement would never be agreed Mutinta had been told to forget Bonnie and find another husband. 'For years they've been telling me to get married,' she sobbed one Monday morning. 'Now I want to get married they won't let me.' A little more negotiation had brought the agreement longed for by Mutinta and Bonnie. Now the way was clear for their wedding in September and the ring Marjorie had carried from the UK would be needed after all.

At work there was much to catch up on. No indication had been given as to who the board would appoint to replace George. One afternoon while Robam was bringing the account-books up to date and I was preparing some training material, Chama came into the Accountancy Department to tell us that George had a visitor. George wanted all staff currently in the office to meet the Rev. Brian Greenaway who had arrived from the UK. Chama was still bringing in extra folding chairs as along with the rest of the staff Robam and I filed into George's small room. It was a tight squeeze. Our visitor was not in the least what I expected. Brian was a large, powerfully built man perhaps in his late fifties. Dressed in a denim jacket and jeans he had pulled his fading red hair back in a ponytail that was partially covered by a large brimmed hat slung on the back of his neck and held by a toggled cord. He looked relaxed and comfortable with his ageing hippie look.

When George invited Brian to tell us something about himself he started by saying 'I was a Hell's Angel. Anne will explain.' Not only was I the sole British person there, I was the only one old enough to remember the Hell's Angels. But how to describe a Hell's Angel? All I could think of was someone nasty and of fights between rival gangs of motor-cyclists in London and along the south coast of the UK in the 60s and early 70s. I stuttered out some such nonsense before Brian explained that to be a Hell's Angel meant you were a member of a motor-cycle gang who dressed in denim or black leather, decorated with chains and Nazi-style paraphernalia, and who went through initiation rites which often involved getting into fights with other gangs along with other anti-social behaviour. A normal weekend for such a gang was to ride at speed in convoy from London to Brighton on the south coast and instigate a fight with a rival gang. He had been in trouble with the police on several occasions but on one such weekend he was involved in a fight when someone was killed. He spoke sorrowfully when he said that he still did not know if he had been the one who held the knife which had caused the death. There had been many involved in the fight and most had been armed with knives or other weapons. Along with others, Brian was arrested and charged with man-slaughter, not murder, but he said that his own conscience told him that a murder charge might have been more deserved. Found guilty, he had been sentenced to fifteen years and had served ten when released. While in Dartmoor prison, he realised the futility of his lifestyle and after many discussions with a prison chaplain converted to Christianity. Not, he said, one of these recanting scroungers who appear to change to get assistance. He had taken the opportunities available to him to study theology and was now an ordained Anglican priest. Before release from prison, he had decided that, in atonement for his past sins, his life's work would be with the homeless, those who sought shelter from the weather under bridges and in doorways and who often lived in no more than cardboard boxes.

Listening to him talking there was none of the 'See how good I've become,' just a practical assertion that the homeless needed help and it was his job to provide it. He said he was not a very good Christian but he tried and that he was fed up with all those 'perfect Christians' who will not admit they are less than perfect. I did not know what my Zambian colleagues made of that comment but then they were amazed that there were homeless people in a country as rich as Britain. Many of the questions put to him were about how such a situation could happen because the British welfare state seemed like utopia to poverty-stricken Zambians. They could not appreciate that some people slip through the social security safety net and live in conditions which have many similarities to those endured by Zambian street-children. Brian said that to help those people, and certainly before any evangelising could be undertaken, the conditions in which they lived had to be experienced. He had regularly spent days and nights living amongst them, taking them food and blankets and living the same miserable existence as they did.

I had a wee smile when he asked if he had been speaking too long; given such a captive audience a Zambian pastor would have gone on for hours. Brian went on to explain that he had come to Zambia to visit a prisoner in the Condemned Section at Mukabeko Prison in Kabwe, who having obtained Brian's name through some mysterious remote connection had written to him on several occasions. Having met up with his correspondent, Brian decided to ask Prison Fellowship Zambia to give this particular prisoner ongoing spiritual help. Francis, quick to point out that he too had been a prisoner and who also had become a Christian while in prison, agreed to attend to Brian's request. From the general conversation about prison-life, Robam's contribution suggested he knew more about prison life than would have been acquired simply from visiting prisoners. If he was an ex-prisoner, he had not said so perhaps because a prison record would not be an asset to someone with the title 'accountant.'

The message Brian delivered was not what the Zambians expected. He asked why was PFZ doing this or not doing that, and, what was the use of us 'sitting on our arses' when the Lord's work had to be done? When asked how he was enjoying living in Zambia, Brian spoke about the friendliness of the people and how he was enjoying the warmth of the sun. But to the horror and disbelief of the Zambians present he said he was fed up eating nshima. It reminded him too much of the porridge served up during his prison days. My suggestion that he might like to come home with me when I would cook us a British-style meal was immediately accepted with a smile. When we left at around 16.00 hours I was sure there were sighs of relief. Francis said he would bring the PFZ Venture to Zawi to collect Brian at around 20.00 hours and drive him back to the guesthouse where he, Brian, was staying.

Brian and I walked back to Zawi, visiting the park en route. I explained what PFZ were attempting to do at the park and Brian met some of the ex-prisoners currently working there. Few of them spoke English but Gift Njombe acted as interpreter. Gift had looked after Mark's garden at the house on Independence Way. As this had always been well kept Gift had been given charge of the manual gardening work at the park. Mutinta had taken over the managerial side. Brian spoke about his life and work and asked how I came to be at PFZ. Back at Zawi, I cooked our supper and remembering his background and PFZ's stance on alcohol, I first offered Coca-Cola or orange juice but then added there was also some cold beer in the fridge. He laughed as he accepted a beer saying he had considered buying a bottle of wine but thought that I might be offended. Supper was chicken pieces in a white sauce with potatoes and cauliflower followed by apple crumble and custard. Brian spoke of his early home life. His father had left his pregnant mother when he was four and his sister even younger. That made his mother bitter and she started drinking and hitting the children. When he was eight, she remarried and his stepfather was a bully. By ten he was in a Dr Barnardo's home and in his own words 'completely unmanageable.' At fifteen he had been loose on the streets, getting money wherever he could, carrying a knife and using drugs, a ready recruit for Hells' Angels. He was excellent company and our conversation ranged over many different topics, including PFZ. Considering how short a time Brian was with the staff of PFZ it was surprising how quickly he had summed up their characters. We agreed that while George and Maurice were men with a strong commitment to helping others he thought Francis lacked love and compassion. Perhaps being in prison had taught Brian to sum people up quickly. We finished the meal but sat on at the table enjoying the beer and the chat so when Francis arrived much earlier than expected our beer bottles were very evident. His eyes kept straying to them. As Brian picked up his jacket in preparation for leaving, he thanked me for the meal, then, winking, said, 'It was a good whisky.' Francis was confused. Perhaps he thought Brian was a hypocrite for Brian, the repentant sinner, was not acting as Francis thought he should. He was drinking alcohol but then so was I. No doubt some comment would be made about that in the next few days. I stood at the door and watched them leave, two men who had so much in common, who worshipped the same God but who carried out His teachings so differently. Brian preached love and forgiveness while Francis threatened hell and damnation. The following evening in the company of Tony, Anna, Brian and Kevin, I told the story of my visitor and got a ticking-off. I should not have entertained an ex-Hell's Angel, even if a reformed one, on my own. Nothing would convince them that at no time had I felt threatened in any way. Brian had been more Heaven's Angel than Hell's Angel.

Chapter 22

Total Eclipse plus a Sports Day

The number of VSOs on the Copperbelt swelled to five with the arrival of Dan Cashdan.

In his mid-twenties, his bouncy nature brought to mind Tigger, Winnie the Pooh's friend. Based in Kitwe he was using his IT expertise to help the Copperbelt Health Education Programme (CHEP) improve their systems. Along with Dan, Vicky Rowan, Carl and his sister Jolene, I spent June 21 Lusaka with Dave and Emily and other staff members from Zambian Open Community Schools (ZOCS) at one of their schools. ZOCS schools provided education for children from disadvantaged backgrounds, street-children or those whose families could not afford school fees. There was much confusion about whether the day of the total eclipse of the sun was an official holiday for all but what was certain was that all schoolchildren had a holiday on that day. ZOCS had told their children that if they went to their schools there would be food for them.

Travelling in a ZOCS minibus, we drove through a township on the edge of the city where there was squalor on a level I had not seen before. Even the main road through the township was rutted and in a dreadful state of repair. The place stank of burning rubbish. Fires smouldering in the ditches gave off clouds of dirty-grey smoke which draped itself over the houses like a dingy shroud. These seemed to be in a much more dilapidated state than any I had previously seen. Many of them looked as if they would collapse if someone leaned against a wall. The impression was one of despondency and despair. When we reached the school, it was surrounded by a two-metre high wall topped with broken glass. Heavy gates were set in one wall. Inside, the ground was sun-baked red earth with the centre dominated by a flagpost set in a concrete reminiscent of a very simply built market cross. A few cream-coloured low buildings, classrooms and offices, had been erected near the walls and formed a square round the flagpost.

There were already one or two members of staff and a number of children present and gradually their number increased until there were around fifty youngsters. Dave explained a little about what a solar eclipse was, how the moon would pass directly between the sun and the earth so that its shadow would fall between the sun and the earth completely blocking out the sun. Dave and one of the teachers explained that this would happen shortly after 11.00 hours and that the children were not to be frightened as the sky darkened. The eclipse would last for just over three minutes when gradually the sun would reappear. All of us emphasised that they must not look at the sun with unprotected eyes. We did not have nearly a sufficient number of spectacles, cardboard frames with the special dark plastic lenses, to give each child a pair but there were enough for us to share them with the children. These spectacles were the fashion item of the month in Lusaka. Everyone wanted a pair. One young street-child, a girl, had crawled around under the market traders' stalls collecting grains of maize from among the dirt. When she had a bagful she sold it to a trader. She kept on doing that until she had raised enough to buy a pair of eclipse spectacles. They were more important to her than the food which normally she would have bought with any money she earned.

There was bustle and stir and a flutter of agitation as we watched the moon take the first small bite out of the sun. We used sheets of paper with pin-holes bored in them, and even the space between fingers and thumbs to project onto a building wall an image of what was happening in the sky. The air was filled with excitement because what we were experiencing was new to all of us. There was apprehension among the children who were still unsure of what was happening. Even among the adults there was a sense of expectation for what we were watching was unfamiliar and remarkable. The youngsters laughed and giggled with excitement and nerves as they squabbled over the spectacles, skipping back and forward between groups as they tried to find out what each was doing. I found I had a tail, three young girls, possibly about twelve years old. I asked their names, Rachel, Bethhya and Tabitha. All three were about the same height but Rachel wore a pink dress while the other two had red T-shirts and dark skirts. They chattered together in Nyanja, their local language, before one of them would ask me a question in English. When they tried to teach me a few words of Nyanja, '*Bwanji*' – 'Hello' and '*Muli bwanji?*' – 'How are you?' my attempts at the 'bw' sound brought gales of laughter. We shared a set of eclipse spectacles and there was even more laughter when I put those on with my own glasses on top. But this was the only way I could view this fantastic natural phenomenon which minute by minute was unfolding before our eyes.

As the shadow of the moon obscured more and more of the sun, daylight began to diminish. The blue of the sky gradually darkened, azure into ultramarine, indigo to midnight. Lower, towards the horizon, in every direction, the colour lightened again, first a deep turquoise, then shades of sea-green, citron, pale yellow, peach, apricot until the horizon was a line of shining gold, a luminous glow which lit it in every direction. It was as if there was an all round sunset. There was much flurried activity among the birds. Clamorous screeching flocks of them flew hither and thither then as the sky grew very dark they found somewhere to settle and their hustle and bustle suddenly ceased. Even the children were silent. Knowing what was happening did not stop the sensation that this was almost a supernatural experience. The air was still warm but I felt cold and shivery. Everything became so still that as the last tiny part of the sun disappeared, you could have heard a pin drop. Darkness was complete. There was only the moon encircled with a halo, a corona of silver light in an otherwise pitch-dark sky. It was then that the children began to sing, a soft, sorrowful African lament. They moved as one and formed a circle round the centre flagpost.

Hands on the waist of the one in front they undulated to the rhythm of their song, feet beating out the tempo, as they swayed three steps forward, two back. It so suited the ghostly ambience of the event, the wonder of what we were experiencing. Watching the eclipse was emotional; the singing made it seem ethereal.

The three and a half minutes of the total eclipse felt like eternity. One part of me wanted the darkness and the children's singing to go on for much longer. Another part wanted the sun to reappear with all its warmth and light. Gradually it did. First just a hint of gold gleaming through the moon's halo, then little by little its brilliance began to lighten the sky. Colour and warmth returned. The birds began to sing again. The ring of children broke up. They became an excited chattering mass, talking about what they had seen, squabbling once more over the spectacles so that they could have a last look at what was happening.

With the sun once more scorching us with its midday heat, and when the boys became more interested in a game with a football made from supermarket bags carefully tied into a ball, the youngsters were fed with soft bread rolls and bananas. Not wanting to deplete the supplies meant for the children, Dave borrowed the ZOCS vehicle and drove our volunteer group back into Lusaka, to the Brown Frog where we, almost as excited as the children, enjoyed swapping stories of our experience of the eclipse. Perhaps the best story came from the lady who owned the Brown Frog. She had been seated in her garden, watching the eclipse through the special lenses when just before total darkness fell, an owl, seeking a perch, had landed on her head. She had the scratches to prove it.

For the pupils of ZOCS' seventeen schools, all of which were based in or around Lusaka, the following day, Friday, was Sports Day. Each school had four teams, a volleyball team, a netball team and two football teams, one of boys and one of girls, all wearing different coloured football shirts. Dave, a lifelong Manchester City FC fan, had written to City, explaining the work he was doing with disadvantaged Zambian children and how they lacked equipment.

The response to the request in the Man City fan magazine that second-hand football kits be handed in at the club for onward transportation to Zambia had been overwhelming. While many sent in single football jerseys or a single kit, junior football teams responded with complete team sets. Many of the shirts were in Manchester City's pale-blue, and for months after youngsters sporting Manchester City colours could be seen walking around Lusaka, but strips of every colour, stripe and pattern had been donated. There were shirts in Newcastle's black and white colours, Southampton's red and white stripes, Glasgow Celtic's green and white bands and from almost every senior football club in the UK with a few European ones as well, together with those from school and junior club teams. Manchester City FC received so many that the logistics of getting all the equipment to Zambia posed a problem. When British Airways was asked for help, the airline responded by not only transporting the equipment donated by the club and the football jerseys to Zambia, it flew Dave back to Manchester to be presented with the gifts at a Manchester City match. Dave and the other ZOCS staff had put an enormous amount of work into making Sports Day a memorable occasion for all the ZOCS youngsters. When I was in Lusaka for the High Commissioner's lunch, he mentioned to me that all was going according to plan except that the local company which had promised to provide trophies for the winning teams had withdrawn its offer. When Dave disclosed just how small an amount of money was required to buy the cups and medals but that the ZOCS financial resources would not stretch to covering it, I volunteered to provide the money for the trophies. As a result I would be at the Sports Day in the role of an honoured guest who at the end of the day would present the trophies to the winning teams. To do justice to the occasion I had once again brought the 'good' dress with me.

Vicky and Jolene and I watched some of the early matches. We wandered around the playing fields of burnt-brown grass, watching as volleyball teams batted balls back and forth and the netball goal-shooters and goal-attackers worked their way into the shooting circles and took aim. The girls' football matches were every bit as hard fought as the boys' with supporters yelling their encouragement from the touchlines. Emily's tall, slender figure moved around sorting minor problems and doing much of the backroom work needed to ensure the smooth running of such an event. As the day wore on, the heat got stronger. The youngsters did not seem to mind. Spectators became covered in dust which rose in clouds as competitors dashed around the burnt-dry grass. The surfaces of the football pitches had little or no grass when play started but after many bare feet had pounded back and forth kicking a ball from one end to the other, these surfaces had been reduced to dust.

Late in the morning, Vicky borrowed Dave's car and she, Jolene and I set off for Manda Hill Shopping Centre to collect sandwiches from Subway for our group. En route, Vicky planned to call at the Irish Embassy which was in the same area of the city. She had dropped her passport in the Zambezi when on a visit to Livingstone. Although it had been rescued it was water-damaged and she wanted it replaced. Dave did warn us that the car was low in fuel and asked that we fill up at the petrol station near Manda Hill. The warning light came on almost immediately as we drove off. Our route took us south to north across the outskirts of Lusaka and although we were provided with detailed instructions on which roads to take we lost our way ending up in a rather threadbare township. With the midday sun high overhead there were no shadows to suggest a bearing. Aware that our fuel was now getting dangerously low, I began to think about who would go to seek out a jerrycan of black market fuel for we would never find a petrol-station in a township, and who would stay with the car? If we all went and left the car parked, it was more than likely that we would return to find it stripped of all moveable parts. We were not exactly in a dangerous situation but it was becoming risky and it would be better if we could get quickly back to a main road. As we hesitatingly turned a corner in the potholed road, we saw at the side of the road two road surveyors taking measurements with a theodolite. Before they could move on Vicky stopped and asked for directions. Once we knew where we were going it did not take us long to reach the Great East Road and find the petrol station. Then the problem was, was it a petrol engine or a diesel one? No one had thought to ask. We thought it was petrol but asked the young pump-attendant for advice. He lifted back the cover on the opening for the tank, sniffed and announced 'petrol'. His look suggested that women like us should not be allowed out in a car.

With a full tank our next stop was Subway at Manda Hill. Having collected the sandwiches I was looking forward to getting back to the sports field and getting tucked in. But first we had to go to the Irish Embassy. Vicky parked outside the Embassy gates and left Jolene and me in the car, saying she would not be long. When we were still there after fifteen minutes, we began to joke about what the Irish mean by 'not long.' Time went on and the guard from the gate came to check on why we were still there. More time passed and the guard came back. He was bothered. To leave us sitting there was obviously contradictory to his instructions. Eventually he persuaded us to wait in the Embassy reception. Reluctantly, assuming that Vicky had to reappear soon, we got out the car. As I went to shut the car door I noticed that the seat-belt was about to get caught in it and lent down to push the belt inside. Unfortunately I also pushed my thumb inside and it got caught as I slammed the door. For about two seconds I didn't feel a thing. Then the pain hit. It felt like a comic strip picture when the bashed thumb is shown about three times its normal size and radiating pain and heat. Jolene and the guard looked as sick as I felt. I wanted to hold it tightly to try and relieve the pressure but of course that did not help. The guard was still shepherding us into reception when Vicky reappeared. One look at our faces told her something had happened. Ever the trained medic, she rushed me to a cloakroom where she held my thumb under cold running water, before trying to check what damage had been done. I vaguely remember saying 'I'm going to faint'. When I came round I was lying on the floor looking up at rows of shelves lined with files and three anxious faces, Vicky, the ambassador and the embassy doctor. Part of my placement was to network with any organisation useful to PFZ and in fainting I had now met the Irish ambassador but I would have preferred to have been on my feet when the introductions were made. Certainly, he would not forget who I was. Satisfied that I wasn't seriously hurt, the two men left me to Vicky's ministrations, some pain-killers and a bandage. She apologised for the delay. She had been speaking to the embassy staff about the use of a vehicle which would let her extend the scope of her dental work.

We had no problem finding our way back to the sports ground. The others got tucked hungrily into their Subway batons but mine no longer felt so appetising. I was more interested in when I could next take painkillers. We watched the last of the knock-out matches and cheered on the finalists and when at last the final whistle blew I hurriedly changed into my dress so that I at least looked the part of a celebrity invited to present the prizes. Carl and Jolene left before the presentations but Vicky stayed partly to ensure I was physically well and partly to enjoy the festive mood of the occasion. The excited youngsters, as high as kites, were chattering like monkeys, many of them still colourfully dressed in their team colours, as they squeezed into a small pavilion at the sports ground. A table decorated with a frieze of black and white paper footballs had been set on a dais at one end of the hall. On it sat the cups, gleaming as if they were silver, and cardboard boxes filled with prizes, parcels covered in bright coloured paper. I joined the platform party. First to be called forward was the captain of the winning boys' football team. Dave handed me a trophy which I, in turn, presented to the team captain. In the time-honoured way, he kissed the trophy before holding it up so the cheering crowd could see it. Ignoring the pain in my thumb I shook his hand, then as they came forward to receive their medals, shook hands with every member of his team. By the time I had presented eleven trophies, shaken hands with and given medals to four football teams, two netball teams and two volley-ball teams, and the man-of-the-match from each final, I couldn't feel the throb in my thumb, my whole hand was numb. But then not only had Vicky given me as many pain-killers as was permissible but also I felt part of the fantastic spirit of elation that filled that small pavilion. The coloured paper was soon ripped from the prizes, mainly football shirts, balls or items such as goal-keepers' gloves, which had been part of the Manchester consignment. Those were held high so that all could see. Everyone is exultant when they win a hard-fought competition but these deprived children had never experienced anything like this. They cheered themselves and each other until they were hoarse. Those who had not won wanted to at least touch a trophy but protective arms ensured these remained in the possession of the champions. When food arrived, the mood quietened slightly and Dave suggested that he, Emily, Vicky and I take the opportunity to slip silently away. I was pleased to have a chance to get back to Dave's house and rest for Saturday was going to be a busy day. Maurice and I had to be at Lusaka Airport to meet and greet a team of twelve people from the UK based Tearfund, a Christian relief and development agency, when they arrived from London via Amsterdam and Nairobi before travelling with them by coach to Ndola. All members of the team had some medical training. They would be working in the prisons alongside the PFZ staff and volunteers for the next six weeks.

Chapter 23

Medical Assistance

When George had asked me to take responsibility for the programme of this Tearfund team and also a second team which was to come a few weeks later it had appeared a simple request until I discovered that there were no records of what had happened in previous years. Finding out meant asking questions and that required time and thought, for my Zambian colleagues answered only the questions I asked seldom venturing any further information. They didn't mean to be unhelpful or rude, it was just their way. Gradually things fell into place. Arrangements were made for an extension to the lease on the house Mark had occupied. His placement complete he had returned to Canada. While it was going to be a tight squeeze the house would accommodate twelve people once extra mattresses, pillows and household equipment was added to what was already there. Maurice organised a coach to transport the team from Lusaka to Ndola and obtained the special clearance required from the prison authorities to allow them to work in the prisons. A request that the team spend at least one week in a rural area had been covered by arranging a trip to the prison in Solwezi, a small town approximately three hundred kilometres to the west of Ndola. Francis had been asked to make contact with the care group there and arrange accommodation for a group of twenty, the team, the PFZ staff and local volunteers who would be travelling with them, including two local doctors and two nurses, one of whom was Maurice's wife, Martha.

The team, eleven women and one man, all medical students, needed time to adjust to both heat and altitude. During those first few days Maurice, Carl and some of PFZ's health volunteers briefed them on conditions in the prisons, the most common health problems suffered by the prisoners, the HIV/AIDS situation and the projects currently being undertaken by PFZ. Introductory visits to Kansenshe and Ndola Remand Prisons were included.

George had only a few days left before his resignation became final and was busy tidying up his work and trying to leave everything ready for his still to be appointed successor. He suggested that I suspend my standard Thursday afternoon training sessions during the duration of the team's visit but I was still involved in other projects, including preparing and writing fund-raising proposals. Often budgets which had accompanied many of these had been very poorly constructed and as a result the funds provided by donors were often inadequate for the purpose for which they were needed. Now I paid close attention to all budgets accompanying fund-raising proposals

When George requested that I join him for a few minutes and I entered his room, Francis was already there, sitting on a chair across the desk from George. Francis normally tried to sit at the side of the desk, giving the impression that he was on the 'management' side of it. I wondered why he had changed his position. His leg was swinging backwards and forwards, usually an indication that he was annoyed. When George invited me to sit, I pulled a chair forward from under the window but remained standing. That gave me the advantage of height, at five foot two something I seldom had. A gut feeling told me that this was a time when height might be an asset.

George began by saying that Francis had just told him I hadn't prepared the budget for the Tearfund's visit and was just keeping notes on scraps of paper. Francis was using a tactic he often employed, attack as a form of defence, which suggested that he was in trouble over something. Transferring the attack onto someone else was not going to work for Francis this time, for the relative budget was complete with one exception, the cost of accommodation in Solwezi, the information he was supposed to provide. The budget was lying in a file on my desk and was up to date. I had even begun to enter the actual costs and work out variations. Asking to be excused for a few moments I collected the relevant file.

I opened the file and laid it on George's desk. Speaking very deliberately I informed George that he would find the budget, complete with all the information I had been given with one exception. Perhaps Pastor Mpzeni could tell us why despite being asked on many occasions to provide details of the accommodation in Solwezi, I was still awaiting that information. George would remember the pastor had been instructed to look into this and provide the relative information. When George asked Francis to confirm that this was correct, Francis began to splutter that weeks ago he had given me details of a guesthouse and the cost. I didn't let him finish before I cut in to remind him that he had been informed immediately that the guesthouse chosen was far too expensive and would have used almost the total budget supplied by the Tearfund to meet their team's expenses. He had known he had to find alternative accommodation. When asked by George if that also was correct he took a quick glance at me and reluctantly agreed it was. When told by George to get in touch with the Solwezi care group at once and find out what other accommodation was available, he almost slunk out of the room. Allowing myself to relax I apologised to George for what looked like my loss of temper but I had a suspicion that it had not been unexpected for he had had a sight of the budget when it was almost complete.

When I returned to the accountancy department, Mellbin, Mutinta, Regina, Chama and Knox had joined Sambie and Robam. All had been discussing what could possibly be going on and became silent as soon as I walked through the door. Caught talking about what could have happened and of how I had suddenly turned into an outraged musungo, they were obviously waiting apprehensively to see if they too would be the recipients of a second angry outburst. It was only then that I remembered that in Zambian society it was very bad manners to lose one's temper. No one there was going to risk encouraging me to make that social faux pas twice. Only I hadn't lost my temper, just become very angry and determined not to be bullied as I had been during my first weeks in Ndola., when, still unsure whether I had committed a cultural error by writing about my concerns over the house, I had not defended myself against Francis' tirade. Once those gathered in the accountancy room realised that I was quite calm and not about to blow my top at them, there was awed admiration that I had not only defended myself against Francis's attack, I had counter-attacked. Sambie remarked that he had read in newspapers that Mrs Thatcher, the British Prime Minister, had been called the Iron Woman. Maybe that title was appropriate for me.

A walk back to my home at Zawi gave me time to cool off completely. After a lunch of rubbery cheese sandwiches I locked my door and had started to walk back to work when I remembered my promise to collect details and contact numbers of the VSOs working in and around Solwezi in the hope that one of them might be able to suggest a suitable guesthouse in that town. Not wanting to be late, I turned quickly and re-entered my house, lifted the list which was lying on the desk/dressing table in my bedroom and turned to leave. As I stood on the small rug at my bedside, it slid on the polished floor and I lost my balance. I put my left hand down to break my fall. As I hit the concrete floor, I knew immediately I had hurt my wrist. Carefully nursing my left wrist in my thumb-bandaged right hand, I slowly clambered up until I could sit on the edge of the bed. I stayed there for some time feeling sick but gradually got sufficient strength back to telephone the office for help. When there was no reply, I waited then tried again. As by that time it was well after 14.00 hours, I guessed that the office telephone line was once more out of order. Unless I walked to the house on Independence I couldn't contact Carl. Feeling groggy the two-hundred metre walk did not seem a viable option. I couldn't contact Anna for she and Tony would be at school but Brian and Kevin had mobile phones. Kevin answered my call and assured me help was on its way.

He had put in some groundwork before he arrived. He had spoken to one of the Irish priests who recommended that he take me to Dr Fernandez, a Portuguese doctor who had a surgery on Independence Avenue. The reception/waiting area was empty when we entered but a nurse in a white uniform arrived almost immediately. Once she had taken some particulars, I was shown into the surgery. The doctor, an olive-skinned man possibly in his late fifties, put the cigarette he was smoking in an ashtray before taking a very cursory look at my very swollen wrist and stating that an X-ray would be necessary. For that I would have to go to another clinic. His chauffeur was instructed to take us there in a rather ancient Mercedes. This second clinic turned out to be poky, badly lit rooms at the top of a short dark stair, the door to which was squeezed between two shops on Buteko Avenue. Again, there were no other patients and I was attended to immediately. The equipment looked ancient but the radiologist was enthusiastic and efficient and in due course Kevin was presented with an envelope containing X-rays to take back to Dr Fernandez who studied the plates for some time. His eyes were screwed up more against the smoke from the cigarette which hung from the corner of his mouth than concentration on the plates but he eventually announced that I had not broken any bones, just sprained my wrist rather badly. The cigarette was laid in an ashtray just long enough to let him bandage my wrist. Once supported by an elastic bandage and a sling, the severe pain reduced to a tolerable ache. I was given a prescription for pain-killers and anti-inflammatory pills. Aware that because I am asthmatic my GP at home would not allow me anti-inflammatory medicines in case they activated an attack. I queried the wisdom of taking these. I was told to stop worrying. Just pay the bill, less than ten pounds, and go home. As we made toward the door, it burst open and George rushed in wanting to know how I was. When I did not reappear after lunch, he was worried I was still upset from the morning controversy and had driven to Zawi where some of the children were able to tell him I had had a fall and had gone to the doctor. Their information gathering would have done credit to any intelligence agency. Just how they had come by all that information

I did not know other than they had seen Kevin arrive, then both of us drive off, and that I was holding my arm. Still not quite reassured that I had suffered nothing worse than a sprained wrist and a few bruises on my rear, George followed us to Zawi where Kevin made tea before leaving to go back to work. George was able to tell me that he had been in touch with a church contact in Solwezi who thought that the Catholic Church had a guest-house which could accommodate the Tearfund team and also those of the PFZ staff who were travelling with them. When on the following day I returned to work with my arm in a sling, I heard from various members of staff that according to Francis, my sore arm was a punishment from God because I had lost my temper with him, one of His pastors.

Life was difficult. With a strapped-up left wrist and a bandaged thumb on my right hand something as simple as washing my face was awkward. The filled water-containers were heavy. Holding a facecloth between the fingers of my right hand I tried dipping it in the water and rubbing that over my face and body which did get rid of some of the perspiration, but I did not feel clean. Vicky, alerted by Kevin to my problems, arrived on Friday night in her own newly acquired vehicle, a small single cab truck. I was pleased to see her for many reasons but most of all because I wanted her advice regarding the anti-inflammatory pills. I still had not taken any. Without access to medical books, she thought that in not taking them it could take longer for the swelling in my wrist to reduce, but nothing worse.

The next few days would have been very difficult if I had not had the support of the volunteer group. Carl cooked meals, Mike, over from Kalulushi for the weekend, filled every water container he could find, Anna shopped for me and Vicky continued her lady's maid act of helping me wash my hair. Gradually the pain in my thumb lessened and I began to be able to use my right hand more. I still had to keep the thumb covered and I was definitely going to lose the nail but having even the partial use of one hand made life much easier.

Over the following two weeks Robam was only too pleased to be my driver. He and I had been working better together since my outburst in the office. Mike, at the end of his placement but before returning to the UK was computerising the PFZ accounts using equipment recently acquired through Tools with a Mission. Robam helped me buy and deliver the lunch supplies to whichever Copperbelt prison the medical team and Tearfund team were working in. They would spend two to three days in one prison, ministering medically and spiritually to the inmates. After hymn singing and prayers any prisoner wishing medical attention could request to be seen by a doctor. Few prisoners did not have a problem of some sort. The poor prison diet aggravated their already reduced immune systems making them very susceptible to illnesses but as eleven of the Tearfund members were young women there was an extra attraction for men who might not have spoken to a woman for months, perhaps even years, in wishing to see a doctor. Many of the medical problems were fairly minor but there were usually one or two serious bouts of malaria and often there would be men suffering from TB, a skin disease or a tummy complaint with occasionally someone very seriously ill. Those who had a sexually transmitted disease (STD) were desperately looking for relief from their condition. Tables were set up in the prison compound and prisoners would queue at one of these. A doctor would quickly assess a prisoner's condition before directing him to wait beside a specific table where he would be treated. A prisoner called forward to the table which dealt with those suspected of having an STD would stand in front of it, drop his pants and present his penis for inspection. Treatment was usually administered in private but watching the agony on the faces of those who had recently received a painful relief-giving injection showed just how uncomfortable were the consequences of catching an STD.

One of the prisons the medical teams worked in was a prison acting as a farm, a rehabilitation unit south-east of Ndola, sited near the border with DR Congo. Prisoners in farm prisons were usually those nearing the end of their sentences or whose crimes had been very minor. Land around the prison was cultivated by the inmates and because of this the prisoners not only enjoyed a better diet but were subject to a lower level of security than at prisons such as Kansenshi or Ndola Remand. As usual Robam and I had collected the buns, fillings, fruit and soft drinks for the lunches and set off in the Venture. We watched carefully for a signpost tacked to a tree indicating the road to the prison but Robam became seriously worried when he thought we had passed it and had unknowingly crossed into the DR Congo pedicle. Had he been on his own it was unlikely there would have been a problem. Having me with him caused a serious dilemma. While he didn't need a visa to enter the DR Congo, I did. He thought that if we had crossed over the border and were caught by officials there was a high risk that we would be arrested as illegal immigrants or even spies. Then just as he was beginning to panic and suggest that we turn back at the next possible turning-point, we found the long-awaited sign pointing us in the direction of the prison. Because we were travelling so slowly on a badly rutted road, we had not covered as great a distance as we thought we had. With huge sighs of relief all round we delivered the lunch supplies before rattling and rolling our way back to Ndola and our lunch-break.

The trip to Solwezi went ahead during the fourth week of the team's stay. Solwezi is over three hundred kilometres distant from Ndola so the plan was to leave Ndola at first light, shortly after 06.00 hours, when the morning was still cool. Those travelling included the twelve members of the Tearfund team, Maurice and Martha, Francis, Carl, two doctors, a nursing colleague of Martha's, and me. The doctors worked and lived in Kitwe. The coach would stop there en route to collect them. The rest of us met at the house on Independence Avenue where the team were staying and when the coach arrived we helped the bus boy load the medical equipment and our luggage and climbed aboard.

We might have been ready to set off for Solwezi but the driver was not. He had to speak to his boss so instead of heading north-west he drove south down Blantyre Avenue and into Makolu where he stopped near the site of Ndola's famous Slave-Tree. It is a very old *mupupa* (afzelia quanzensis) tree which unfortunately had two parasitic creepers entwined around it, almost strangling and obscuring it. In the early 1950s it had been declared a National Monument. More than a century before it was where slave-traders met slave-raiders to talk business. The records of the Ndola Boma included a statement made in 1939 by an old Arab called Mwalabyu in which he admitted that in his youth he had been part of a gang who used a stockade under the tree as a base from which to make raids to capture slaves. Mwalabyu claimed to have met David Livingstone. Livingstone is still highly respected in Zambia today for the strong fight he made against the slave trade. Chuma, one of Livingstone's devoted companions, was a slave until freed by him. By 1870, the slave trade had been stopped in Europe but it still flourished in Zanzibar, Turkey, Persia and Arabia. Europeans still bought coffee, cocoa, sugar and cotton grown by slave labour. The search for slaves to man the plantations which grew these commodities pushed further and further into the African interior. The slave-raiders, armed with guns and gunpowder provided by the slave-traders, travelled great distances to round up their merchandise, men, women and children. Once purchased by the slave-traders these poor unfortunate people, yoked and chained together, were forced to walk to one of a number of slave-markets on the Indian Ocean coast, a distance of over two thousand kilometres.

Our driver was more concerned about contacting his boss than in allowing us time to look at and photograph the Slave-tree but eventually he got back behind the steering wheel of the bus and headed towards Kitwe passing colourful advertising hoardings recommending Sunlight Soap, Coca-Cola and the latest 4x4 model from Toyota. The two doctors worked at Kitwe's Central Hospital, but even though we were late in arriving there we still had to wait for nearly an hour before they arrived. Their reason for the delay was that because there had been an emergency at the hospital they had been late in finishing their shift, after which they had had to return to their quarters to shower and change but in true Zambian custom had seen no necessity to hurry.

It was nearly 09.00 hours by the time we left Kitwe and the cool morning air had been warmed by the sun's rays but the temperature in the bus was still comfortable. Later, with no air-conditioning, it became very hot. There was little change in the scenery in the next stretch of road with little settlements further and further apart. There was only one small town, Chambishi, not much more than a large village, between Kitwe and Chingola. On the western outskirts of Chingola the huge open-cast Ngacha mine had left a ghastly grey scar but Zambians would not be unhappy about that if its presence meant an improvement in the local economy. After Chingola the road lay about thirty kilometres south of the border with the DR Congo and ran parallel to it. With little diversity in the countryside and as the temperature in the bus rose, many of us dozed, tired after the early start.

I must have been in a deeper sleep than a doze for when disturbed by an interruption in the motion of the bus, I had to struggle to waken and then was horrified to see a man, armed and dressed in combat clothes, climb aboard the bus. For a few seconds I sat rooted to my seat as he ordered us out of the bus but it was only then that I realised he was a member of the Zambian armed forces. We had reached the crossing over the Lunga River but the bridge had been destroyed. I never heard exactly what happened to the original bridge but presumably years of water pounding against it during countless wet seasons had weakened it until it had collapsed. It had been replaced with a temporary wooden structure. Because of unsureness about the weight the replacement was capable of bearing, loads were being lightened before a vehicle crossed. We waited while the driver drove over carefully and then with the bus safely across we walked over to join it.

Solwezi had only one tarred road, the main road passing through it en route for Mwinlunga or to Lubumbashi in the DR

Congo, and the town had been built linear fashion along it. Because of its strategic position it had several fuel stations and our first action on arriving was to refuel the bus. That completed, we headed for the Catholic Guest House, a small complex sited in a road which ran parallel to the main road, where we were welcomed by the nuns who ran it. Our accommodation was a number of rooms of different sizes with mattresses on the floor. Getting everyone organised into their rooms took time but eventually the eleven Tearfund girls and I were lodged in two larger rooms some distance from the others. PFZ had been told that the guesthouse could accommodate our party easily. 'Easily' was optimistic but we would manage for three nights and the location of the guest-house was convenient for the prison, less than a ten-minute walk away.

Once everyone was settled, Maurice, Francis and I were driven to the prison to introduce ourselves to the officer-in-charge and to meet members of the Solwezi PFZ care group. We could have walked there in the same time as it took to drive for the road was the usual rutted hard-packed red earth and it seemed selfish to ask the driver to make this journey after the hours he had spent at the wheel getting us to Solwezi, but it seemed that our standing would be diminished if we arrived on foot. The officer-in-charge welcomed us as did three members of the local care group who had been holding a prayer meeting for the two hundred or so inmates. When we left arrangements had been made so that the clinic could begin early the following morning. Unfortunately while we were up at the crack of dawn and ready to go, the prison authorities were not. Someone had mislaid the keys to the gate. No one could get in or out. We hung around while a search was made. After some considerable time and when the keys had still not been found the officer-in-charge gave the order for the bolt to be sawn through much to the amusement of the prisoners. Carl's facetious suggestion that we tunnel in was not appreciated.

Eventually to an accompaniment of derisory calls from the prisoners and the embarrassment of the guards the gates were at last opened and our equipment was carried in. While the Tearfund group carried out their well-practised routine of getting organised, one of the guards showed me round. He unlocked the door from the compound yard into the area where the prisoners stayed. Smaller than other prisons I had been in, it was equally bleak and lacking in facilities, just a few mud-brick blocks which served as communal cells and an open-to-the-air washing area of shoulder-high walls, but the atmosphere seemed more relaxed and friendly. I didn't know if that was because it was smaller and the prisoners were all together rather than separated by wire fences into different groups or because the prisoners had felt free to shout their jocular comments about the keys without apparent fear of reprisals.

After a hard day's work the team went back to the guesthouse to try and get rid of the sweat and dust. While the Roman Catholic Church did not insist on the anti-alcohol stance required by other denominations, the temperance rule at the guesthouse suited PFZ's stance on alcohol so supper of chicken and rice was washed down with Coca-Cola. President Chiluba had decreed that Zambia was 'A Christian Country' but while a very high percentage of Zambians attended church each week, there was little toleration among the various denominations regarding the differing tenets held. And there were many different denominations. The United Church of Zambia covered only certain of the Protestant churches such as the Methodists and Presbyterians. There were also Anglicans, Roman Catholics, Lutherans, Dutch Reform, Jehovah's Witnesses, Seven Day Adventists and a great number of evangelical churches linked to those in America's southern states which went under such names as The Bread of Life, The Apostolic Pentecostal Assemblies and the Assemblies of God. Each sect felt sure that its interpretation of the Bible was the correct and only one. A pastor attached to PFZ in Ndola who belonged to one of the evangelical churches had said in my hearing that he did not think that Roman Catholics could be Christian because they drank alcohol. The underlying distrust was so great that I had been warned that when I received the bill for accommodation and meals in Solwezi from the nuns I should check it carefully to ensure that they were not charging for too many meals and drinks. In an attempt to ensure that there was no dubiety regarding the number of drinks charged everyone in our party was told that if they ordered any drinks other than the ones served with a meal they had to be paid for by the person ordering them. Maurice backed me on this, aware that some of our party might be only too happy to say 'put it on the bill.'

At the end of the second day, Carl and I met some of the VSOs who worked in and around Solwezi. Our e-mailed instructions were to meet them at the town's one restaurant. Having arrived first, we ordered beers before realising that the two Zambian doctors from the PFZ team were already there enjoying a meal. As the place was empty except for us, and aware that we had ordered the 'censured' alcohol, we felt there was little we could do but ask if we could join the doctors. As Carl sat down and swung his legs under the table there was a clink of glass. It appeared that the doctors, quicker than Carl and I, had hidden their forbidden drink below the table. What was helpful was that when the doctors heard that all VSOs were registered with the Corpmed Clinic in Lusaka, they advised I went there as soon as possible to get my still swollen wrist X-rayed. After four weeks and with little improvement it was unlikely it was only sprained.

Chapter 24

'When the sun rises in Africa...'

It was dark on Sunday night by the time Carl and I eventually made it back to Zawi at the end of the Solwezi trip. Even in the pathetic light given off by the security lights positioned above each front door, it was obvious that something had happened at Carl's house. The dilapidated old car which usually sat outside his bedroom window had been pulled back some metres onto the road which ran round the compound. The car's original paintwork had been scratched and dented but had still looked white when we left. Now it was now black. As we walked nearer, we saw that the front of his house including the roof and rone pipes had been scorched and many of the glass window panes were cracked or broken. Mike, who had been staying there while computerising the PFZ accounts, explained what had happened. The gardeners in the park had been curious when they saw smoke and flames coming from Zawi and seeing that the fire was spreading from the car to Carl's house they had climbed the wall and pulled the burning car back from the house. Thankfully there had been no injuries more serious than various hands blistered when they pulled at the car's bumper. Tweza was being blamed. He and Chilomba loved playing in the car. They had driven many imaginary miles together turning the steering-wheel this way and that and moving the gearstick back and forward. On Friday he had been seen with matches. Over the next few days it was a very sober Tweza who wandered around Zawi, so different from his usual mischievous and cheery self. Carl was of the opinion Tweza's father had used a heavy hand when dealing with his son's misdemeanour.

While Maurice, Carl and I all made it to the office on Monday morning Francis had decided that he needed a day off. I could understand why for I was exhausted after the journey but I wanted to tidy up the Tearfund accounts. The monies spent were within the budget but I still had to pay out the away-from-home allowances of K100,000 (less than £20) to each of the PFZ staff who had been on the trip. I had argued against making these payments saying they were not required as the staff had all their expenses paid over the weekend but was told that it was normal Zambian custom. Francis' payment was put in an envelope and locked away with the remainder of the cash so that he could collect it when next he was in the office. Carl and I had agreed earlier that we felt it inappropriate for us to take the money so he arranged to pay his allowance into one of the health department projects while I credited the park's accounts with mine.

Maurice, appreciating that I was very tired after the Solwezi trip, suggested that I take Tuesday off and have a rest. The pain in my wrist was making sleep difficult so when I was wakened from a sound sleep by a loud banging on my front-door very early in the morning I was not in the most amiable of moods. Unlocking the glass door I could see Francis through the mosquito netting-covered window in the outside wooden door. Opening the door only slightly, I wasn't given time to ask what he wanted before he barked at me that he wanted his money. At first I couldn't think what money then I realised it was the payment of K100,000. When I did at last realise why he had come I saw red. The last thing I needed was my neighbours thinking I kept large sums of cash in the house. And he had wakened me from a much needed sleep. This time there was no play-acting. I left him in no doubt that his money was in the office and that I did not appreciate being wakened by his banging on my door. Neighbours, attracted by the noise, were gathering to find out what the row was about. I knew that I was making a mistake for he would never forgive me for raising my voice to him. It was culturally incorrect for a woman to lose her temper with a man and certainly never with a pastor. At the time, I just didn't care. Giving me a look of unconcealed animosity, he pushed through the crowd and stomped off. Francis and I had never been friends and now it was extremely unlikely we ever would be.

The park was desperately underfunded and my donation of K100,000 enabled us purchase some much needed items such as poison for the snakes which lurked in the anthill. One of the staff had already suffered a snakebite. He refused to go to hospital demanding instead to be taken to a tribal healer who used something known as 'a black stone' on the bite. The treatment must have been effective for the gardener was back at work the following day. The purchased poison having been thrown into the anthill did not kill all the snakes but those that survived were killed by slashing when they tried to escape the fumes inside. Since the park was situated very near my home, I encouraged the gardeners in their policy of extermination. Also I was expecting a visit from my nephew, Kenneth Tully, a college-educated gardener. He had arranged to take his annual leave entitlement in a oner so that he could work with Gift and the park staff, sharing with them some of his skills, including propagating plants and record keeping while he would learn something about African horticulture from them. He was arriving on Saturday, July 28, but I travelled to Lusaka the previous day giving me time to visit the clinic in Cairo Road. An X-ray confirmed that my wrist was broken in two places and it was set in plaster. Kenneth and I had the weekend in Lusaka before travelling to Ndola with the second Tearfund team who were due to fly into Lusaka on the Monday. He knew exactly how he wanted to spend his weekend. We visited the botanic gardens at Munda Wanga at Chilanga on the outskirts of Lusaka.

'*Munda Wanga*' means 'My Garden.' We wandered round the well laid-out paths, walked over manicured lawns, crossed ornamental bridges over a stream, looked at colourful flower beds, some filled with canna lilies, tall iris-like plants in red, orange and yellow, stood under a rose covered pergola, examined trees of all shapes and sizes and looked at a new rock garden which had just been planted. Kenneth, notebook in hand, recorded all that interested him. The gardens were originally developed by Ralph Sander on five acres of land which he leased from the Government in 1952. His work with the Game Department encouraged him to use part of the garden as a sanctuary for orphaned animals from the wild and a zoological park developed from that. By 1964 when Zambia became independent Munda Wanga had grown to forty acres, had a staff of nine, and with a collection of over fifty thousand varieties of trees, shrubs and plants had become possibly the most comprehensive collection of plants in Africa. When Sander died in 1978, the ownership of Munda Wanga passed to the Government but with the economic struggle of the next few years and without Sander's enthusiasm the gardens and the zoo were both left to deteriorate. After a varied history Munda Wanga was privatised in 1998 and with the help of local sponsors and interested volunteers had been restored to much of its former glory. Even here I was able to network on behalf of PFZ for the botanical manager at Munda Wanga was Douglas Gibbs, a VSO, and an arrangement was made for some of the PFZ park staff to visit Munda Wanga.

The next few days were spent introducing the new arrivals to the PFZ staff and showing them around Ndola. The new team were mostly students but unlike the first team, had no particular skills. The Tearfund's objectives in sending teams to Third World countries such as Zambia included them learning something of the problems of the people and giving practical help while sharing Christian worship. The PFZ management had decided that this team would work in the park. Gift and Kenneth got on well together and began to make plans about what could be achieved in the short time that Kenneth and the team were in Ndola. With no access to machinery manual labour was required but with the help of twenty prisoners a large area in the park was cleared, dug over and made ready so that the park staff could plant grass when the rains returned in October/ November. Gates made from opened-up oil drums had been erected to make the park secure and the words 'Prison Fellowship Zambia' were painted in blue on the lime-washed wall near them. The area round the small memorial to men from Ndola who had died in two world wars, a broken pillar set in a small walled garden, was tidied up, paths to it were edged and the flower beds beside them planted with roses, salvias and marigolds. Preparations were started on a car park and foundations dug for an *insaka*.

Kenneth, captain of the Tillicoultry Company of the Boys' Brigade in Scotland, had arranged to meet some of the local Ndola company. Each Friday night their efforts were heard at Zawi. If enthusiasm could have created great music, their efforts would have sounded wonderful. Led by a drum-major swinging a home-made baton, the band played trumpets, bugles and even a euphonium. They banged on drums and clashed cymbals with great gusto and panache. Considering that there was a large part of the left-hand cymbal missing and the tension adjusters on the drums had given up with age, they created a commendable sound. Kenneth was made welcome especially when he produced two footballs brought from the UK. He visited the community project the boys were working on, digging a well in one of the local townships, but was horrified when he saw the boys, aged between eight and twelve, digging at the bottom of a hole over six metres deep with no protection. When asked about shoring, the adults appeared surprised and said it was not needed and anyway there was no wood available.

Kenneth's last week in Zambia was a proper holiday. Everyone who visits Zambia tries to see the Victoria Falls and on this my third visit they looked different again. With less water in the river than in April there was not quite so much spray and this time I saw them from the Zimbabwean side as well as the Zambian. From there Livingstone Island lost its ghostly image. We were able to see the trees and vegetation on this small isle which measures less than two hundred and fifty metres long and no more than one hundred metres at its widest point and which sits on the very edge of the cataract. It was from here that David Livingstone in November 1855 first saw the Falls while attempting to find a route from the centre of Africa to the Indian Ocean. Although the sight of the cataract must have made him realise that the Zambezi was not navigable, putting paid to his dream of establishing a trade route which as well as promoting Christianity would provide Africans with a means of selling items such as palm oil and ivory thus discouraging them from selling fellow Africans into slavery, he was still stunned by the beauty of the area. He is credited with the phrase 'scenes so lovely must have been gazed upon by angels in their flight' although it is thought the words were actually penned by his publisher, John Murray.

Time was limited so flying to Mfuwe International Airport was the quickest way to get to the South Luangwa National Park, an area of over 9,000 square kilometres where the game density is on a par with parks such as the Kruger or Serengeti, the great advantage for visitors being that there are fewer of them. It was a fantastic opportunity to visit a true wilderness accompanied by well qualified guides.

A green 4WD with raised seats at the rear was waiting to take us on the nine kilometre journey to the Kafunta River Lodge. We were greeted at the Lodge by Anke Cowan, who along with her husband Ron, own and manage it. The main insaka had been built round a wild mango tree. It separated the dining area from the bar-cum-lounge, both of which were open to and looked out (at slightly different angles) across the flood-plain of the Luangwa River. Small palm trees planted in ceramic pots and the sweet scented smoke and bursts of sparks which rose from a recently lit log fire, set in an oval of irregularly shaped stones lent a friendly atmosphere. Groups of typically African wooden chairs, with backs of five rounded spars set in a fan design, were set round low tables. A tea tray laid on one of the tables made me feel right at home. The evening game-drive would set off in an hour and that dinner would be served on its return. The morning game-drive started at six o'clock and we would get a wake-up call at five which would give us time to have a light breakfast before setting out. Anka reminded us that we were in an open area where animals roamed. This was their habitat and these animals were wild. We were not to go strolling around. We were not even allowed to walk between our chalet and the main insaka without a guard as the area was patrolled by armed guards at all times. A bell rung in the chalet would grab their attention.

Our wood and thatch chalet, one of eight set apart among in riverine forest, was built on stilts, approximately one metre from the ground. Our guide hopped up the six wooden steps leading to the door, threw it open and proudly showed us round our home for the next three days. Before leaving he pointed out the bell we were to use when calling for a guide. Left to ourselves, we sank into the large, squashy cushions in chairs set on a veranda which over-looked the flood plain where antelope grazed in the company of baboons but there was little time to enjoy the luxury. Our first game-drive in the South Luangwa National Park was due to begin.

Ron Cowan was waiting beside a 4WD. He introduced himself and Jacob, our guide for the evening, as well as our fellow game viewers Philip and Amanda, a young South African couple. Nearby another vehicle was being loaded with a second set of guests. Jacob was going to take us into the park via the Nkwali Pontoon, an entrance used only by vehicles from the lodges. He sat in the front beside our driver, Nelson, and we started off passing by the electrically charged fence built to stop elephants raiding the vegetable garden belonging to the lodge.

It was only about one and a half kilometres over scrub land to the pontoon. A slipway had been dug out from the sandy river bank. Pink hippo mouths showed above the water and crocodiles waited to enjoy an evening meal of anyone thrown into the river but Nelson had done this many times before. A wire rope was strung across the river. When three men on the pontoon caught the wire in 'G' shaped notches carved into the head of wooden clubs and pulled, the pontoon slid slowly over the water.

The gradient on the north bank slipway was not so steep but

Nelson had to use the four-wheel drive traction to take the vehicle through soft sand. While we crossed an area of open grassland, driving through grazing herds of impala and puku, Jacob gave us some background information on the Luangwa valley. Lying south of and over six hundred metres below the Muchinga Escarpment it is a rift valley similar to but thought to be older than the Great Rift Valley which runs south through eastern Africa. Its ancient rock strata belongs to the karoo period and was laid down somewhere between one hundred and seventy-five and three hundred million years ago. Portuguese settlers of the sixteenth century left reminders here of their occupation as did Stone Age man. The Luangwa River, a tributary of the Zambezi, is over six hundred and sixty kilometres long. Over thousands of years it has on many occasions altered its course through the valley leaving mineral-rich earth on the valley floor which gives nutrients for its diversified vegetation which in turn supports the herbivores. It was some of these herbivores, a group of four zebras, which halted Jacob's talk. These were Burchell's zebra, the plains zebra. They are common to many countries from southern Ethiopia to the north of South Africa.

Over the next hour and a half we drove over gravel roads which took us through floodplain grasslands and riverine forest, stopping often to look at giraffe, a herd of buffalo, elephant, baboon, bush-tailed mongoose, civit, genet, porcupine, kudu and waterbuck as well as many different species of birds, including herons, egrets, storks, bee-eaters and orioles. Over four hundred species of birds have been recorded in the Luangwa valley. A large giraffe stood in the middle of the track we were driving on, and for around five minutes kept completely still. From its height advantage it looked down on us as if to say 'Move away.' This was a wonderful photographic moment and our cameras were clicking madly. Eventually it got fed up waiting on us making the first move. In a most graceful and majestic manner it turned slowly round and sauntered up the centre of the track. Watching a family of elephant including a very young calf cross the road in front of us was a magical moment and Jacob was as excited as we were when he pointed out a honey badger, a small black mammal with a grey-white back and a face like a dog's. Although widespread throughout the country, they are seldom seen.

As dusk began to fall, Nelson parked the 4WD on a hillock overlooking the river. We listened to the birdsong though the hippos with their chorus of grunts did their best to drown it out. Their heads with huge yawning mouths popped up from below the water while ripples would show where one had submerged. Beautiful bright green bee-eaters flew out from nests burrowed in the sandy cliff beside the river. We climbed out of our seats and stretched our legs while Nelson and Jacob prepared sun-downers and nibbles. There is something magical about enjoying a gin and tonic while listening to the music of the jungle, a medley of birdsong and animal calls, smelling the scent of the bush and watching the colours of an African sunset reflect in the surface of the river.

We savoured the moment, until the last streak of orange/pink light had faded. All aboard once more, we set off with a brilliant spotlight attached to the top of the windscreen and headlights full on. The spotlight picked out groups of zebra and families of giraffe as well as a herd of recumbent buffalo but we had still not seen any of the big cat family. Jacob directed Nelson to try various sites where lions were known to roam but with no success. Then just as we had almost given up seeing any, we drove over a hillock into the sand of a dried up river bed. There in the headlights, almost completely camouflaged because their coats were the shade of the sand, were three sleepy lionesses, curled up like domestic cats. They were unfazed by our presence, hardly bothering to even open an eye. Jacob reckoned that they had recently made a kill and were sleeping off their feed. It was growing late but now we had seen lion, and we headed out of the park by the main gate and to dinner. No one would be late in turning in with an early start the following morning.

Sunrise was still some way off when we rang for the guide to escort us to the main insaka but by the time we had breakfasted, loaded up and been driven to the Mfuwe Bridge entrance to the park the first streaks of red were showing through the trees. Dawn breaks quickly in Africa. We had hardly driven any distance when Jacob pointed to a slight depression in the land where a family of elephant including two calves were using their trunks to pull down branches of trees so that they could reach the tender shoots at the top. A herd of buffalo was on the move. At first only a few were visible as they streamed out from an area of woodland but the herd was stretched out and there must have been between two to three hundred rapidly moving animals. Heading for a *dambo*, a pool of water, they crossed the road a short distance from us. We headed east along the area known as the elephant loop. White egrets, pink and lilac orioles, emerald green bee-eaters, bright blue kingfishers displayed their glorious colours and an eagle soared above. Near the river we could hear the hippos' chorus, all definitely bass singers. On the sandy soil at the river's edge, the crocodiles, some as long as three/four metres, were basking in the early morning sun. Two hippos were cropping grass near some bushes. Out of the river we could appreciate how huge they truly are. Jacob could tell that these were naughty boys who had been driven out of the herd for trying to mate with the 'wrong' female. Certain animals have strict rules about which males can mate with the females. The herds of impala which we passed were bachelors. At some time in the future one of them would fight the stag for the right to service his harem. A group of lionesses with cubs were more than a little unhappy when we stopped nearby to take photos. Jacob hissed out urgent instructions for us to sit down when one showed signs of getting ready to spring. And we did.

Heading towards the Lion Plain, we came across giraffe nibbling at the treetops. Eight different subspecies of giraffe have been identified and one known as Thornicroft's giraffe inhabits the Luangwa valley. Their colouring is slightly different from other giraffe found in southern Africa, darker patches on the body, lighter patches on the neck and white legs below the knee. There is a local superstition that the skin of someone who eats giraffe meat will become covered in patches similar to the giraffe and because of this they have never been hunted or poached. In the 70s when the economic situation in Zambia was very poor, animals were poached for food. Later in the 80s commercial poachers came looking for rhino horn. This was particularly sought after in China and the Middle East to make dagger handles. Zambia's black rhino population was thought to be completely wiped out but there have been unsubstantiated sightings so it is possible that a few animals still exist in the wild. Poaching for ivory was also rife but the elephant population fared better than that of the black rhino. While their numbers were reduced they have recovered. The government now realise that Zambian wildlife is an asset when encouraging tourists to visit their country and it takes a very strong stance against poaching.

During the evening drive a pride of six or seven lionesses walked round and past the vehicle and I felt we had got a little too near for comfort. We were assured that they saw only one item, not a vehicle with six humans on board but it was unnerving to watch so many walk past while we sat completely unprotected. When we drove through trees after dark our guides kept playing the spotlight on the branches, ensuring that we did not drive under a leopard waiting to pounce. Some spotted-hyenas looked just as evil as I had always imagined them. The highlight of the evening was the sighting an aardvark. It was a fleeting glimpse as it scurried under bushes but its long snout and huge ears were unmistakeable. It eats termites and has powerful legs designed to dig up their nests.

On our second morning we collected an armed guard, Mr Bottle, and set off on a walking safari. Jacob drove the 4WD over the pontoon and some way into the woodlands where we left it tucked in under some bushes where it should not attract the attention of baboons or monkeys. We walked in single file, Mr Bottle at the front, followed by Jacob, then we four tourists in a line at the back. If possible we were to step in the same places as Jacob and Mr Bottle, giving less chance of standing on a snake. If threatened by an animal, we were under no circumstances to run as the animal would run faster than us. To hammer home his point, Jacob mentioned that only recently a qualified guide from one of the other lodges had been killed when he had tried to outrun an elephant. The flood-plain terrain over which we were walking at that time was the sun-baked silt left by the river's floods during the rainy season and resembled a frozen ploughed field.

A little apprehensive at first, I soon began to relax and enjoy the experience. Being on the ground near a giraffe makes you realise just how tall it is. There was so much to learn about the ecology of the park. At between twelve and fourteen degrees south of the Equator, it gets plenty of heat and light and the typical annual rainfall of around one thousand millimetres is sufficient to encourage strong vegetational growth in the mineral-rich soil left by the river. The 'bush' takes a variety of forms. Riverine forest grows near the river and typically consists of ebony, sausage trees, many varieties of fig and mangosteen. Munga woodland is scrub where thorny trees and bushes such as acacia grow and mopane woodlands where the trees are known as 'butterfly trees' because of the shape of their leaves. These contain nutrients valuable to many grazing animals. Mopane trees can grow to a height of twenty-five metres and because of the high ceiling effect created by their branches are sometimes known as cathedral mopane. And there are the baobab trees, huge leafless monsters, described by Livingstone as 'a giant carrot planted upside down'. These jumbo-sized monsters are found at various places in the park and some could be well over one thousand years old. A tree cut down when the Kariba Dam was being built on the Zambezi was found to be around that age.

As the morning progressed the heat of the sun became intense. Mostly we were walking on rough uneven ground and that became tiring. Jacob was leading us in a circle back to where the vehicle had been parked when we saw a hippo in the distance. We were between it and the river, the most dangerous place to be. Hippos are almost blind but they have a fantastic sense of smell and they do not take kindly to anything they sense standing between them and their natural habitat, water. Watching it raise its nose and sniff, we were sure it knew of our presence. Telling us to be as quiet as possible Jacob guided Philip, Amanda, Kenneth and me to a high knoll round a large tree, while he and Mr Bottle remained in front of the tree, Mr Bottle in firing position with his rifle aimed at the animal. We stood silent and still, eyes glued to the approaching animal. It came slowly, looking towards where we were, aware that there was something unusual in its vicinity but still not panicked. For what appeared to be minutes but would in fact have been only seconds we all stood, frozen, hardly breathing before it turned and gathering speed took off down a gully which would lead to the water. Our adrenalin rush was over.

The vehicle had been untouched and once its covers had been removed we drove off to a quieter spot where we stopped for coffee before resuming our drive past Chichele Hill and Chichele Presidential Lodge, the president's private lodge during Kenneth Kaunda's time in office. When part of the parastatal 'National Hotels' it had been left to decay but had recently been sold. The new management had rebuilt much of it and it was soon to open it as a game lodge.

The highlight of the evening drive was when a leopard stalked past the vehicle. It was so close I could have put my hand out and stroked its magnificent coat. The animal's smooth movement was effortless as it glided past. About ten metres ahead of us, it stopped, raised its head and listened then took off at such an accelerated pace that it disappeared in seconds. From the same direction we heard the squeals of the bushbuck caught in the leopard's claws but by the time we reached the site of the kill the leopard was dragging the bloody carcass of the small antelope up into the branches of a tree where it would be safe from attacks by hyenas. Even the family of lionesses and quite large cubs seen later seemed tame in comparison. Somewhere I have read that 'When the sun rises in the African bush, the antelope has to be up and running for otherwise it will be caught and eaten. When the sun rises in the African bush the lion has to be up and running for if it does not make a kill it will starve. This shows that when the sun rises in the African bush everything has to be up and running.' Apparently it is not only when the sun rises that everything has to be up and running.

Chapter 25

'... And Sorrow and Sighing'

This time I knew what to expect when at the airport I said 'Cheerio' to Kenneth but although I was a little down on my return journey to Ndola there was good news waiting for me. Allan Keppeso had made some repairs to my house. He was hopeful that the roof would no longer leak and best of all water pipes had been led from the city's water-main supply to the house. The work hadn't been completed in a tidy manner for the pipe lay above ground waiting to trip up the unwary who walked behind the houses at Zawi but I not only had water coming from the taps, I had a supply of hot water. Eight months after it had been installed the hot water tank worked.

Even without the supervision of a director, PFZ was continuing to operate but gradually the cohesion between departments was loosening. There was certainly less interaction between the spiritual ministry and the vocational departments. Perhaps this stemmed from the different attitudes taken by Francis and Maurice and the cat-and-mouse play that was going on between them, each worried that the other was going to be appointed Executive Director. Funding had been an almost constant problem during the time I had been at PFZ but as the cash-flow problems became really acute there were more and more angry exchanges at management meetings With the departures of Mark and George the management committee consisted of Francis, Maurice, Robam and myself. Regular donations from churches in America dried up. These had been made by friends of George, contacts made when he studied in the USA. Francis would not accept that fund-raising was part of his job specification so donations from local churches were few and small. Donors such as foreign embassies were prepared to provide funding for specific programmes but expected the recipient organisation to be able to meet their day-to-day running expenses. Because Dr Mathani, the chairman of the PFZ board, was known locally to be a dollar-millionaire it was generally believed that PFZ was a well-sponsored organisation. Nothing could have been further from the truth yet even Francis had difficult in accepting this. The care-groups, volunteers who took the Christian mission into prisons around the country, were sure that funds which should have been given to them were being creamed off by the PFZ staff but Robam had to scrape the bottom of the barrel to pay the electricity bill, which meant insufficient funds to meet the telephone bill. We could use the computers but had no e-mail connection. The annual rental of the mailbox at the post office was not a large sum but there was not even enough to pay that so for over a week we had neither written or electronic mail. The only positive result of this was that Robam, who now needed my help in his endeavours to explain the financial situation to Francis and the care-group chairmen, was prepared to let me see at least some of the accounts. It appeared from even a cursory glance that PFZ existed only by robbing Peter to pay Paul.

While all of this was going on Maurice and I were both very involved in trying to interest certain international embassies in Lusaka in PFZ projects. I combined a visit to the Japanese embassy with my return visit to the Corpmed Clinic. After the embassy security guards had checked my identity and confirmed that I had previously made an appointment, I was escorted to a comfortable but impersonal interview room where I renewed my acquaintance with an attaché I had met at the British High Commission in June. He was interested in the PFZ proposal, funding for children's playground equipment for the park, but said that the embassy had had applications from over one hundred organisations and had funding for only five. PFZ would be advised of the outcome in due course. While our appeal made their short list the eventual outcome was 'No.'

The plaster was removed from my arm but the muscles in arm and hand had weakened considerably. I arranged to see the physiotherapist but it was obvious that I could not keep travelling the two hundred miles from Ndola to Lusaka two or three times a week for physio so it was suggested that I try the Ndola Central Hospital. The out-patient entrance to the hospital was in Nkana Road. Following signs I worked my way through queues of waiting people in corridors which had once been cream but were now a grubby milky-white until I found the physiotherapy department. The area designated 'waiting' had a bashed and scarred wooden bench but I sat there for little more than a few minutes before a lady in a white coat came forward. Telling my tale, I showed her the letter of explanation from the physiotherapist in Lusaka. She was confident that the hospital could help me, but was I aware that I would have to pay? A form was completed in triplicate and I was given two copies, one for myself and one for the Treasurer's Department at the hospital. I joined the queue of expectant mums and people on crutches I had passed on my way in. All were waiting to pay fees before getting treatment. Slowly we progressed towards a window where one solitary clerk took his time about working out what each patient had to pay. I was charged at non-resident rates, K70,000 for ten sessions, approximately £1.40 per session.

Back at the Physiotherapy Department, we agreed a time table of three one hourly visits per week before starting the first of the ten sessions. Mr Mwinga, my therapist, had worked with two VSOs in Malawi and knew Mr Manda, the physiotherapist at the clinic in Lusaka. The treatment of my injury did not require the use of complicated equipment which was just as well for the department didn't have any. Once my arm muscles had been heated in warm water my treatment involved moving weights, the type I remember from a grocer's shop in my childhood, across the table with the side of my hand, trying to turn a rotating bar set into a frame and scrunching up a towel with my fingers. At times I had to bite my lip to stop myself crying out for the exercises were painful but gradually as the sessions went on there was more movement and flexibility in my wrist.

One lunchtime towards the end of September as Carl and I were tucking into rubbery-cheese sandwiches, we had a visit from Harriet, our maid who had been on maternity leave. She brought baby Brian with her. He was four months old and a darling. When Carl started jumping him up in the air and catching him, his chuckles got louder and louder. Ruth, her sister, kept our houses clean and made a very good job of washing and ironing but she kept moving things around and both Carl and I had a feeling that she had been looking through our papers, something neither of us had ever suspected Harriet of doing. While Harriet was keen to return to work there still appeared to be a problem. We spoke together for ages before finding out what it was. She shamefacedly admitted that she and her husband were to separate. They had been married for just over a year and for most of that time she has been either pregnant or nursing the baby. She seemed terribly confused about what was to happen to her, saying that her husband, also called Brian, wanted her to return to her father. Her father had agreed but would take her back only when Brian had paid him compensation for returning 'damaged goods.' At that time her husband did not have money to make the compensation payment so she would have to stay with him until the payment was made. He expected a bonus at Christmas and would make the payment then. Worried about Harriet and aware that wife-beating was not unusual I asked what she meant by 'damaged goods' and did she get any of the 'damaged goods' money? Thankfully there had been no beating but because she had had a baby it was unlikely that another man would want to wed her so she was 'damaged.' None of the compensation money would go to her.

Harriet confided that she did not want to stay with her husband until Christmas because 'he was playing around with girls.' If he contacted AIDS he would most probably pass it on to her, an almost certain death sentence in Zambia. Nor did she want to return to her father's house. Harriet's dislike of her step-mother appeared to be fully reciprocated. Harriet thought that if she was earning she could rent one room in which she could stay with baby Brian. If there was a dispute about custody of the child, it was more than likely that a Zambian court would give custody to the father. However, at that time, Brian's father was not interested in having him. Unfortunately that could change when the baby became older but as long as Harriet was breast-feeding Brian he would stay with his mother. Sympathetic to her plight, Carl and I both agreed that she could bring baby Brian to Zawi with her when she returned to work at the beginning of November while giving her some money which would help her keep going until she received her first pay. The timing suited Carl and me. The first year of our placements ended in October and we were due some holiday entitlement.

After the departure of the second Tearfund team the Thursday training sessions re-started. Although my living-room was not large I found it the most convenient place to host these sessions. One Thursday after PFZ staff left I began making preparations for supper. That evening I was expecting Torunn, Anna, Tony, Brian and Kevin as well as Carl. When the phone rang I had no premonition of bad news. It was Carole, Mike's partner. Mike had returned to the UK for a break before taking up a new placement. We expected him back in the Copperbelt the following week. Carole was phoning to say that Mike would not be returning. Mike, just forty-one years old and the volunteer of all of us most conscious of the need to keep fit, had suffered a severe stroke and died. I gabbled some words of consolation, knew I was talking too much and probably making little sense but felt that I had to keep speaking to her. I promised that everyone in Zambia who had to be told would be, and that we would keep in touch. When I laid the phone back on its receiver, I sat down on the settee completely dazed trying to take in what I had heard. I had the unpleasant duty of breaking the news to the others.

I was still sitting when Carl knocked on the door. On his way home from work he had bought bread for supper. One look at my face told him something had happened. Younger and unused to death among his peer-group he was even more stunned than I was. We sat looking at each other, still trying to take in the news. Slowly the first effects of the shock began to wear off and I made mugs of tea. We decided to let our supper continue when we would break the news to the others. Carl, however, phoned Dan Cashdan to tell him. Mike had been planning to stay with Dan in Kitwe when he returned and had left much of his luggage at Dan's house. Carl, knowing that Dan was still grieving over a family bereavement which had happened before he came to Zambia, suggested that rather than be on his own that night he might like to join us in Ndola. As people arrived and the news broke everyone felt a great sadness.

Gradually as people got over the initial shock conversation began to flow although from time-to-time someone would slip quietly outside, needing to be with their own thoughts. The following morning, my PFZ colleagues, especially Robam and Sambie with whom Mike had worked for just over two weeks, were shocked. The average lifespan of a Zambian at that time was thirty-seven. The newspapers were full of obituaries of people much younger than Mike but his death at forty-one still surprised them. It was not the suddenness of it that upset them for Zambians were well-used to the amazing swiftness with which death could strike, it was the fact that it had happened to a volunteer when home in Britain. Mike had made so many friends among the people of the Copperbelt that a local radio station, Radio Ichengelo, broadcast a tribute to his memory. I still have a cassette recording of that broadcast.

Chapter 26

Wedding Bells

While I was attending the hospital for physiotherapy, Mutinta was making the final preparations for her wedding. I received a formal cream and gold wedding invitation from Col L.D.L. Phiri & Mrs C. Barbosa, her parents. There was a phone number to which I should reply and below that was a little note, 'Strictly by card. No children.'

I also received a less formal invitation from Mutinta to her Bridal Shower. I had heard enough to know that this held a greater significance for a Zambian bride than a hen party did for a British bride so was delighted when Robam said that he had permission to use the Venture to take his wife, Mary, and me to the house where the party was being held. Regina and Marjorie had also been asked but Regina was ill and Marjorie Fwolishi had confided in me that she would not be going to the Bridal Shower as it was expected that you took a gift and she had no money to buy one. As a volunteer she had no income other than the pittance she received from PFZ's Health Department for travelling expenses when she visited the female prisoners at Kansenshi. She often walked to the prison so that she could use her travel allowance to buy food for herself and Audrey, her two-year-old daughter. Mutinta had told her to come anyway but she did not feel that would be correct. It would have been unfortunate if she had missed the Bridal Shower for she had few opportunities to enjoy a day out. It took some persuasion before she agreed to taking one of the two casserole dishes I had purchased as my present.

The house in Lowenthal where the Bridal Shower was held had a lovely garden with long manicured green lawns which stretched up a slope from the road. A large woven mat had been laid on a flat area of grass. A semicircle of white plastic chairs were set out on one side of it and a tented pergola decorated with balloons and some potted plants had been erected on the other. Mary laid her gaily wrapped gift on the mat beside some other colourful parcels before finding a seat in the shade of a tree. She was pregnant and wore a loose fitting dress in a red and blue print with matching turban. Having carefully watched what she did, I laid my parcel near hers and took a seat beside her. Marjorie joined us. The tree branches did not cut out the full glare of the sun and I wished I had brought a hat. Mary too was obviously feeling the heat. I asked when her baby was due. The look on her face told me that I had committed a social gaffe. While I knew better than to discuss such a topic in mixed company it never occurred to me that it could not be talked about when there were only women present and the Bridal Shower was an all-female occasion. She whispered 'December.'

Taped music was being played and I hoped no pun was intended when I realised it was Scott Joplin's theme from the film *The Sting*. It was at least a change from religious tunes. There was no sign of Mutinta. A few of her guests were wearing western-style clothes but most were dressed in local-style rainbow-coloured costumes with matching turbans of unbelievable complexity. All carried chigenges which matched the multicoloured prints of their dresses and when one or two started to dance round the growing pile of presents they wrapped the chigenges round their gyrating hips, hips which swivelled at a fantastic rate. Marjorie, who was dressed in western-style clothes, wanted to join the dancers but would not do so until she had borrowed a chigenge. Then kicking off her shoes she swung her slender hips with the best of them. When I asked where Mutinta was, I was told 'In the house with the matrons.' This is the occasion when a bride is taught the duties of a wife, in particular how to please her husband. It was considered too embarrassing for the mothers of the bride and bridegroom to undertake this instruction, so two matrons, friends of the family, were invited to teach the bride about the birds and the bees and what to expect on her wedding night.

A ladies' choir danced and sang. Hot food was served at a buffet. Large dishes of chicken, beef, nshima, rice, coleslaw and rape (a green vegetable similar to spinach) were laid out on a table along with soft drinks and we helped ourselves, but Mutinta was still not among the company. We had more singing, some prayers, and eventually when two girls started beating out a rhythm on drums, a dancing procession began to make its way slowly from the house. Its members, with Mutinta covered by a chigenge tucked in behind one of the ladies, doing a formal three steps forward, two back stately processional dance, made their way into the circle and round the mass of presents. Mutinta was led round until she was in front of the pergola when they made a great ceremony of getting her seated while keeping her covered. Her legs were stretched out in front of her and her shoes removed before her arms were stretched out on top of her legs, palms down. When the cover was taken off her head, she kept looking down. Even when one of the ladies spoke to her there were no smiles. She remained in that pose, not moving as the two women who had arranged her sat on the ground one on each side of her. These were neutral supporters, presumably the matrons who had performed the teaching which had been undertaken in the house.

There was more singing, dancing and praying, a Bible reading from the Book of Ruth and even a homily which was thought appropriate on being obedient to and pleasing the husband. The guests began to ululate and gradually this built to a crescendo. This announced the arrival of the bridegroom-to-be. When the garden gates were opened Bonnie, carrying a bunch of red roses and accompanied by two friends, entered and made his way through the crowds of women until opposite the pergola. Alone, Bonnie moved forward until he was in front of Mutinta. For the first time since she had been brought in and seated in the pergola she appeared to waken. When she almost threw herself forward into his arms she got a quick hug from Bonnie before her supporters pulled her gently back into her seat. They asked her if she would accept this man. I did not hear her answer but it must have been 'Yes' for the ceremony continued as Bonnie was led away by his friends.

Now came the opening of the parcels and this was obviously the part of the celebrations many of the women had been waiting for. The mistress-of-ceremonies lifted a parcel from the mound of those laid on the mat, read the gift card and invited the donor to come forward and present her gift to the bride. A short poem or saying had been written on the gift card. This described the contents of the parcel and how it could be used and was read by the mistress-of-ceremonies as the donor danced her way towards the pergola and presented the parcel to Mutinta, only it was one of the supporters who received it and opened it. The guests screamed with laughter at some of the poems and the antics of the dancers. Most of the poems were in Bemba or Tonga. (Mutunta's mother came from the Tonga tribe originally from southern Zambia while her father belonged one of the tribes which traditionally came from the east, near the Malawian border. This had caused problems when they met and wanted to marry as the elders of her father's tribe disapproved of a match with someone from a different tribe.) I did not understand much of what was being said but what was obvious was that much of it was at best risqué, at worst downright bawdy, but women who found it embarrassing to speak about a forthcoming birth laughed and giggled over the actions of some of the dancers which were extremely sexually explicit. If the bride did not know what was expected of her on her wedding night before this she certainly should have after watching this.

This all took time and it looked as if it would take most of the evening before the last parcel had been handed over. Not knowing about the gift card poem or the dancing, my gift carried only the simple congratulations that I would have used in the UK. Thankfully Robam called to collect Mary and me before my parcel had been chosen. My attempts to dance Zambian style would have had the other women guests crying with laughter.

219

By the end of September the weather had become very sultry. Humidity was high. It was hot and muggy even throughout the night when temperatures never dropped below thirty degrees Celsius. It would at least another month before the rains started so it was no surprise when Mutinta and Bonnie's wedding day dawned hot and sticky. I did not expect the wedding ceremony to start at 11.00 sharp but felt I could not be late as good time-keeping regularly came into my management talks. George Chanda was the only person at the church when Carl and I arrived. Mutinta and Bonnie were members of The Bread of Life Church where George was the pastor, but that church did not have its own building. The Baptist Church had been rented and decorated for the occasion with vases of red and yellow roses. As midday approached the church became warmer and warmer. Other guests began arrive. The organist played hymn tunes on an electronic organ but no one paid much attention. A ripple of excitement passed through the church heralding the arrival of the bridegroom's party. The women guests excitedly began ululating when the music changed to traditional African with its definite beat as the three groomsmen, all over six feet tall, dressed in black suits, black shirts with pastel-shaded satin ties and wearing shades, sashayed down the aisle. Hands at shoulder level, they swayed first to one side, then to the other in their synchronised rumba-style progression through the church. Two page-boys, in gold satin waistcoats and black trousers, followed. They attempted to duplicate the groomsmen's actions. It was superb and brought back memories of the Bond film, *Dr No* when during a New Orleans funeral scene the mourners twirled to the beat of the jazz. But this was a wedding not a funeral and the women's ululating rose to a crescendo if the groomsmen entered; it became absolutely ear-splitting as they welcomed Bonnie. Also dressed in black, but in a straight-cut, long jacket, he wore a white shirt with a wing collar but no tie and sported a gold satin waistcoat. Waiting until he had sole occupancy of the aisle, he began his solo dance. Centre of attraction, object of all the women's ululating and called greetings, the moment was his and he enjoyed it to the full. His dance was unhurried, stately yet rhythmic.

The bride's procession was led by two young flower-girls in white organza dresses carrying baskets of flowers decorated with gold ribbons. They were followed by three bridesmaids in satin dresses and coats in a style made famous by Jackie Kennedy when she was America's First Lady, matching dress and coat in a semi-fitting style. One was in creamy peach, one in gold and one in olive green. The groomsmen's ties matched the colours of the brides-maids' outfits. Each bridesmaid had gold ribbons in her hair and carried a bouquet of artificial flowers in cream and gold. In a dance similar to that performed by the groomsmen, their display was also impeccably choreographed. A matron-of-honour, a slightly older lady in a cream suit with matching large-brimmed hat, accompanied by two small girls in green satin dresses with white lace trimmings, came next Their dance was simpler but their feet lightly tripped the fantastic as they swayed to the beat of the African music. As they reached the communion table and took their assigned places, the music, in the course of one beat, changed to *The Trumpet Voluntary* and Mutinta made her entrance. Her traditional bride's dress in white satin, had a sweetheart neckline, fitting waistline and full skirt with a train which swept the carpet as she walked. Her face, suitably solemn, could be seen through her short white veil and in gloved hands she carried a bouquet similar to those of her bridesmaids. Her father had his arm through hers suggesting that he was getting support from her rather than giving it.

The service began with the congregation singing *To God be the Glory*. The reading from the Bible came from the Old Testament (King James version, of course), Ruth 2, verses 16 and 17, 'For whither thou goest, I will go: and where thou lodgest, I will lodge: thy people shall be my people and thy God, my God. Where thou diest, will I die and there will I be buried, the Lord do so to me and more also if ought but death part thee and me'. What was not mentioned was that Ruth made this vow to Naomi, the mother of her late husband, not to Boaz, her intended second husband. In the sermon that followed the preacher used the reading to emphasis that women must be obedient to their husbands at all times. Carl was amused at my reaction to the preacher's words, but did agree that they were to our Western culture decidedly chauvinistic.

The words said by George in the actual marriage ceremony were very similar to those used at home in the UK. Maurice, Mellbin and his wife arrived during the service but it was not until George invited all pastors present to come forward and bless the newly married couple that I realised that Francis Mpzeni and his wife had also come in late. Six or seven pastors all crowded round the kneeling couple, each taking his turn at the mike to give his blessing. After the register was signed, the bride and groom left the church to the accompaniment of African music while bubbles were blown over them. Bubbles were a good idea for they are much easier to get rid of than confetti, but there again they were used because confetti is both expensive and difficult to get in Zambia. At Mutinta's request, Carl had brought some from the UK when he was home in May which we saved until we were outside the church. Again there was the beautiful choreographed dancing with the groomsmen and bridesmaids intermingling as they left the church. Apparently they practise together for months before the wedding with the end result seeming effortless.

There was no opportunity to take a photograph of only the bridal couple. When they posed for photographs it was the total bridal group, the bride and groom, bridesmaids, groomsmen, flower girls, page boys, matron-of-honour and one small boy in a red T-shirt, after which they climbed into waiting cars which had been decorated with lots of multicoloured balloons and which with horns sounding continuously drove off in convoy out onto Broadway.

Once back home, T-shirts and shorts were much more comfortable clothes to relax in on a hot September afternoon before dressing once more for the reception which according to the invitation began at 17.00 hours. The children at Zawi had been dismayed when I first wore shorts in the compound, refusing to speak to me for it was indiscreet for a woman to show her legs above the knees. Gradually they had got used to the idea and now they no longer even noticed. However, out of respect for Zambian custom, I never walked outside the Zawi compound wearing shorts.

When we arrived at the Chinese Restaurant for the reception there was very little happening. The bar was closed and ushers, eight friends of the bridal pair, were in the process of preparing the restaurant for the reception. That night it had been rented by Mutinta's family. When we arrived the ushers were sweeping the floor and setting out tables. A long table, the High Table, was covered with white muslin and gold paper and decorated with yellow roses and gold ribbons. Candlesticks made from soft drinks bottles covered in orange crepe-paper and tied with gold ribbons were set in front of each seat. Balloons and Christmas-tree lights were strung around the room, especially in the centre of the High Table where they illuminated the seats which would be occupied by the bridal couple. Plastic chairs, which had been rented for the night, were set out 'theatre' style facing the High Table, leaving a square open area in front of it, in the centre of which sat a table with the wedding cake.

The High Table was for Mutinta and Bonnie, their groomsmen, bridesmaids and matron-of-honour. Mutinta had told me that about one hundred guests and been invited but that it was difficult to know how many people to cater for. Apparently anyone who thought that they should have received an invitation could turn up and had to be fed along with the invited guests. Now I understood the wording 'Strictly by card. No children' on the invitation, as an attempt to restrict the number of uninvited guests.

As guests began to arrive we took our seats and gradually the room began to fill up. Robam, Mary, Melbin and his wife, Margaret, joined us. Dress at the wedding service had been a mixture of Zambian and western styles. Now most of the women wore traditional dress but the men wore suits. When the bridal party arrived there were

223

around thirty people in the uninvited section. Again the entrance was spectacular, with complicated choreographed dances presented against a background of taped music, drum beating and hand-clapping, topped with the excited ululating by the women guests. The groomsmen came first. They had changed their black shirts for open-necked satin ones in colours which matched the bridesmaids' outfits. The bridesmaids allowed them their moment of glory before stylishly sashaying in, after which the matron-of-honour led in the bride and groom. Mutinta had changed her dress. She had told me that two different relations had offered to lend her a wedding dress. It appeared she wanted to please both of them for the regal white satin of the morning had given way to a figure-hugging ivory which opened out just above her knees, a style often favoured by Shirley Bassey. The bridal party took their places, the bride and groom in the centre with the groomsmen on their right and the ladies on their left.

Once seated, those at the High Table were served with cans of soft drinks. In a low tone Mellbin told us that the bridal party had already eaten. The entertainment began when friends of Bonnie and Mutinta sang. Speeches were made by family members and friends before the buffet was served. There was a pecking order for this. First the family members, followed by the pastors, then the invited guests while those who had not been invited brought up the rear. Watching the respect given to the pastors made me realise once again just how much importance is given to them in Zambian society.

It was uncomfortably hot standing in the queue waiting to be served and I must have looked tired for one of the ushers asked if I would like him to bring food to me. Two very full plates of chicken, beef, rice and salad arrived for Carl and me. Remembering Zambian manners we left a little salad on the plates. Food over, the bride and groom cut their cake and five youngsters dressed in gold waistcoats gradually danced their way through the crowd towards it. Each was given a tier by the matron-of-honour and they, together with the chief bridesmaid and groomsman, danced their cakes away for cutting.

Before taking to the floor for the Zambian version of the Bridal Waltz, Mutinta and Bonnie sang a very beautiful and sentimental love duet. Mutinta, a tuneful soprano, often led the singing at PFZ's Monday morning devotion. They had the floor to themselves for some minutes before the guests were invited to meet and greet the new Mr and Mrs Bonaventure Zimba. In a line-up similar to the welcoming reception at a Scottish wedding, we stood in a line waiting our turn to wish the newly-weds well and to hand our presents to the matron-of-honour, who stood at Mutinta's side. Shortly after that Carl and I left with the offer of a lift home from Maurice. Dancing would continue for some time before the bride and groom left on their honeymoon, a few days in Livingstone.

Chapter 27

Slaves and Spices

The October temperatures had risen to their uncomfortable peak when having completed one year at PFZ, Carl and I were given two weeks' leave. Adventure as well as relief from the heat encouraged both of us to think about Zanzibar. Travelling together on the two-day train journey from Kapiri Mposhi to Dar es Salaam gave us company and a level of security. The gates onto the station platform were opened half an hour before the scheduled departure time and then there was one almighty scramble by the crowds as they fought for unreserved places in the third class. People who had managed to get seats leant out of windows and shouted to their friends and family to join them; others ran along the platform looking for empty carriages; hurrying mothers pulled children along behind them; elderly women were helped by younger members of their family who tried to cajole them into walking faster. Some clambered aboard a carriage only to be pushed off by those who had already claimed it. We made our more leisurely way to the front of the train where all we had to do was find our reserved seats in carriage D, compartment 4. Looking back I could see that in the struggle to get seats many had lost precious possessions. Here and there a chigenge lay abandoned, a battered case had broken open, its contents scattered across the platform and two brown-paper parcels sat near the door to the station. Worse still was the young child who had become separated from his family and who stood forlorn and tearful waiting for someone to return and collect him. Thankfully someone did.

An old-fashioned carriage with bench seats one on each side and two folding bunks above them became our home for the next two days. We watched the passing scenery, played cards and Scrabble, negotiated with customs officials who asked for unnecessary documentation, avoided the currency traders and cheered on a giraffe who tried to race the train. We met fellow passengers while stretching our legs at one of the many official and unofficial stops. At one of those we bought bananas which looked like small stubby green fingers and tasted delicious from a local woman and watched the chefs on the train going in the opposite direction at an official stop bargain for supplies of chicken so fresh that they were still alive.

In the area near the Great Ruaha River the land rises over 1,250 metres in 1,000 kilometres. When the train entered the first of the many tunnels through the hills, we sat in the dark until we emerged minutes later into the bright sunshine on the other side of a hill. It was the problems of the terrain that had delayed the building of this railway. When just months after Zambia had achieved independence, the then President Nyerere of Tanzania made a state visit to China in February 1965 at which Chou En-lai, the Chinese premier, indicated his country's sympathy for the newly independent African states.

Zambia's economic situation worsened when UN sanctions applied to Southern Rhodesia after UDI cut Zambia off from its traditional export routes through South Africa and Mozambique and there was unrest in other neighbouring countries. There had been a road to Dar es Salaam used and maintained by the military during two world wars but the demand placed on it after the Southern Rhodesian UDI was far above what the structure of the road could take and Zambia had to borrow £6.5 million from the World Bank to upgrade the road to a standard suitable for heavy-duty traffic. China agreed to build the badly needed railway in September 1967, providing an interest free loan of £167 million to Zambia and Tanzania which would enable these countries meet the cost of the railway. Work began in July 1969 and the laying of 1,860 kilometres of track was completed in 1975. In 2001 peace had been restored in many of Zambia's neighbouring countries and commercial traffic had resorted to traditional routes so without the remunerative goods traffic and despite the number of people using its service the TAZARA Railway was struggling economically.

Arriving in Dar was for us like being the rope in a tug of war.

Taxi drivers circled round us, all jabbering, pushing and pulling, and we had difficulty staying together. Carl's height did help control the situation a little and he managed to secure a reasonable deal for the journey to the Jambo Inn, Swahili for 'welcome,' clean and secure but not much more. Waking the following morning to the muezzin's call to prayer was our introduction to a city so different to Ndola, even to Lusaka. The smell of the sea and sand was in the air. People hurried about their business. Those dressed in formal European clothes rubbed shoulders with colourful Africans, women in burkas, men in burnooses or with long shirts hanging over their trousers with even the occasional red fez. Heavily loaded lorries thundered round narrow streets oblivious to the donkey-carts and cyclists. Glossy Mercedes manoeuvred round *dala-dalas*, the local minibuses, as they stopped to disgorge their multifarious passengers and freight in streets lined with high cream-coloured buildings. The ferries and hydrofoils left from a pier near St Joseph's Cathedral and the Old Boma, Dar's oldest surviving building, and Carl and I made our way there for the crossing to Zanzibar.

An hour and a half later the perfumed air, heavy with the scent of spices, especially cloves, welcomed us even before the hydrofoil docked. Osmali Arabs believe Zanzibar means 'Fair is the island' but an alternative derivation could be 'Negro Coast' from '*Zangh*' meaning 'negro' (the first inhabitants of the island) and '*bar*' meaning 'coast'. Whichever it is, the island of Zanzibar is an autonomously administered region so our first stop was immigration. Dhows, the traditional sailing ships, were at anchor in a separate harbour. Their high prows, painted in blues and greens, and raised rear decks flanked low midships, characteristics of Zanzibar's Arab heritage which conjured up images of smugglers and swashbuckling pirates but when booking rooms at an hotel we were greeted with 'Salaam, peace be with you,' to which we responded, 'And with you.'

Stone Town, the old capital and cultural core of Zanzibar, is a maze of small wynds, tunnels and lanes. Especially intriguing were the Zanzibar doors. Traditionally the door was the first part of a house to be erected. Burton, the nineteenth-century British explorer said of the doors that 'the higher the tenement, the bigger the gateway, the heavier the padlock and the huger the iron studs which nail the door of heavy timber, the greater the owner's dignity.' Wandering on through the narrow streets we saw many of these beautifully carved doors on our walk to the old slave market or what little was left of it. Most of it had been demolished. The young guide who took us to the slave chambers below the Anglican Missionary Hospital told us that about 75 slaves would be kept for two days without food or water in each of these rooms, none more than four feet high and not terribly large. The only air came from tiny slit windows. If the slaves survived they were considered strong enough to be auctioned. If they died their bodies were pushed into deep channels dug through the rooms where water would carry the bodies out to sea. Some of the shackles with which they were chained were still attached to the walls. When we were in the room where the women and children were held Carl asked:

'What would I get for Anne?'

'First, you will have to leave her here for two days without food and water to see if she survives,' was the response, not a suggestion I appreciated.

The Anglican cathedral, built in 1887, stands on what was the site of the actual market. In front of the altar is a circle on the floor which represents the stake at which the slaves were flogged in front of prospective buyers to show how the slave could endure pain and also to demonstrate his physical strength. The marble round this area is red, representing the blood shed. A small wooden crucifix hangs near the stained glass memorial window to David Livingstone. The wood from which the crucifix was carved came from the tree under which Livingstone died at Chitambo in Zambia. Near the seafront one of the buildings bears a plaque which reads 'This building was the British Consulate from 1841 to 1874. Here at different times lived Burton, Speke, Grant and Kirk. David Livingstone lived here and in this house his body rested on its long journey home.'

Round Ras Shangani point in Suicide Alley is a house which once belonged to Tippu Tip, a wealthy nineteenth century slaver, perhaps the most notorious of the slavers and certainly an enemy of Livingstone's who reported to London details of a massacre at Nyamgwe in DR Congo in which Tippu Tip was involved. Livingstone's report helped considerably in the bringing about the outlawing of slavery in this part of the world. Along with Carl and in the footsteps of nearly every tourist who had ever visited Stone Town, I climbed to a rooftop bar to enjoy a sun-downer while watching the Technicolour spectacle of the setting sun. The horizon, the black silhouette of the African mainland, a land long known as the dark continent, was tinged with gold as the huge vermilion sun slipped below it, washing both sky and sea in glorious colour before all faded into the tropical night. Long before the days of tourists many others had watched this fantastic sight. As they prepared for their expeditions into the unknown interior of this continent were explorers such as Livingstone and Stanley fired with excitement when they watched this nightly extravaganza? But what words can express the depths of depression that the men, women and children forced into slavery must have felt as they watched the outline of the only land they had ever known disappear into the darkness for ever?

There were many references to the slave trade as we toured the island, caves where slaves were kept even after the trade became illegal; a ruined palace where the mortar for the stones had been mixed with the blood of slaves in the belief that that would make the mortar stronger. On unsignposted roads we lost our way more than once and fell foul of the authorities when it was pointed out at a police check that the car we had hired was not insured. The policeman eventually gave up hope of getting a personal donation for Carl kept insisting that we would go to the police station and pay any fine due and a sudden malfunction of my hearing-aids prevented me hearing his expostulations. When in response to his 'You are not listening, Madame,' I replied 'I'm sorry, I'm deaf,' he gave up and waved us through. But there was also much needed relaxation in walking along miles of glorious white beaches where local fishermen were landing their catches, beach braiis, scuba-diving among coral islands with black and white zebra fish for company, watching red colobus monkeys swinging from tree to tree in the Jozani Forest in the south of the island and best of all, swimming with dolphins. As our boatman let his craft float towards them, we donned masks and flippers and, trying not to splash, slipped over the side of the boat in to the water. Even without my specs I could see the shape of the dolphin which swam along beside me. It was near enough to touch but that would have been impolite to this large gentle creature. Screwing up my eyes to try and see more clearly I could just make out its face. When it moved off another took its place. They interwove their way between us, effortlessly lifting themselves out of the water and re-entering so smoothly that there was scarcely a ripple. Then in a second, the whole school moved off at a speed no human swimmer could have matched. Getting back in the boat when my recently out-of-plaster wrist would not bear my weight was not so pleasant but with a pull from above and a shove from below I made it.

We had one last night in Stone Town before catching the hydro-foil to Dar and taking a taxi to the station. When it lacked buzz and crowds we knew that something was amiss. For some unexplained reason the time we expected the train to leave (there was no time stated on the tickets) was two hours after when it actually departed. When we were standing in the station at Dar the train with our reserved compartment was trundling its way south-west towards the Zambian border. A few seconds' disbelief then realisation hit that we either had to stay on in Dar for another three days or find an alternative way back. 'Come on,' I said. 'Let's see if we can fly back to Lusaka.'

We were subject to very strict security checks at Dar es Salaam airport when checking in for the flight back to Lusaka but then it was less than two months since the 9/11 terrorist attacks on New

York and Washington and prior to that Dar itself had suffered a bomb attack in 1998. In Zambia the attacks on New York and Washington had made only a few columns coverage in the newspapers. On September 9 I was unaware what had happened until I was home at Zawi after work when my sister, Marjorie, phoned from the UK. Arriving in Lusaka, Carl and I called at the VSO office to update Dolores that the PFZ board had appointed Rev. Lawrence Temfwe as executive director on an interim, part-time basis, before bussing it home to Ndola.

Chapter 28

Wheeling and Dealing

Back at work the holiday in Zanzibar was soon just a memory. Lawrence Temfwe had taken up the reins at PFZ and everyone was very busy. As budget preparation was still inadequate, I got clearance to construct a three-day course that would teach the staff on how to prepare budgets and also how to use these to monitor progress by comparing actual expenditure against budgeted. With Lawrence's backing, the senior staff had to attend. Robam allowed me some access to the PFZ account books and he had taken on board one or two suggestions of mine on very basic book keeping but frustratingly he would not allow me a complete overview when I might have been able to give more help. As usual the lack of funding was causing problems and Lawrence accepted that I prepare a course on fund-raising, one which all the staff would attend early in the New Year. As it was an area that I did not have a lot of experience in, I ordered books from the UK. Once they arrived I had plenty of swotting up to do before preparing a variety of teaching procedures such as discussions, practical exercises, puzzles and games.

Also at Lawrence's request, Carl and I were putting together a management report on all sections of the PFZ organisation for presentation to the Board when its members met in February which meant looking at the aims and objectives of PFZ and at all the component parts of the organisation and its management and staff. We spent hours asking staff questions, listening to the replies, always having to remember that Zambians seldom give information unless it is specifically asked for. Now, one year on, experience had taught us to expect this and we had some idea of how to overcome many of the hurdles it created. As the report was to be confidential, much of the work assessing the information given and the writing of the report was done at home. I often worked at home. It was much easier to do preparation for training when not continually interrupted as frequently happened when in the office. Many visitors to the office who had no business in the accountancy department still stopped by to say 'Hello,' which in Zambian terms usually meant at least a ten-minute conversation. At home there were diversions too. Harriet, working once more at Zawi, brought her baby, Brian, with her. Wrapped in a piece of chigenge material, he spent most of the day, either sleeping on the settee or tied onto Harriet's back while she washed and ironed clothes or polished floors. He didn't have toys but he laughed happily when the Zawi children called to see him banging pot and pan lids with wooden spoons.

Harriet's husband Brian had received a Christmas bonus from his employer, money which he could use to compensate her father for returning 'damaged goods'. However, if Harriet was pregnant her father would refuse to take her. She asked for time-off to enable her meet her husband at the hospital where she would get a pregnancy test. If it was positive, Brian would sign the papers which would allow her to have an abortion there and then. She said that if that was the case she probably would not feel well enough to return to work so would it be OK if she took the rest of the day off? I pleaded with her to take time to think about what an abortion would mean, but she wouldn't listen, saying, 'If he keeps sleeping with other girls, he will get AIDS. Then he will give it to me and if I get ill and die, who will look after baby Brian? He has money today to pay my father but if he does not hand it over soon, he will spend it. This is my one chance to be free of that risk.' Thankfully there was no pregnancy. Once the payment was made to her father, technically she was returned to his home. As she was not fond of her step-mother, the last place she wanted to be was in her father's home so she continued to stay with a friend.

Some of the VSO volunteers and their friends planned to spend the festive season together at a camp in the Kasanka National Park east of the DR Congo pedicle and near the village of Chitambo where David Livingstone died. Cooking would be done for us by the camp staff but we had to supply the ingredients. Vicky Rowan, Susanne Bradley, an Irish lass who had replaced Brian Higgins on the street children project when his one-year placement ended, and I spent ages working out menus, followed by large shopping lists. As the crow flies Kasanka is about one hundred and sixty kilometres from Ndola. By road, circumventing the DR Congo pedicle, it is twice that. There were many travellers on the roads and excitement levels in the country were high for a general election was scheduled for December 26. President Chiluba's attempts to have the constitution amended so that he could stand for a third term had been unsuccessful. The Movement for Multiparty Democracy (MMD,) the President's party, had put forward Levy Mwanawasa, a lawyer, as their candidate. Ten other political parties, including United National Independence Party (UNIP), the party of the ex-President Kenneth Kaunda, were contesting the election. Tension was building as polling-day approached. The electoral system was first past the post but electors had had to register earlier that year and many had found that difficult for registration centres had opened for restricted times only, particularly in parts of the country where the MMD were not popular. The MMD had also strengthened its chances of being re-elected by choosing a date when the university students were on holiday which had the effect of disenfranchising many students who were registered to vote in Lusaka but who on their Christmas break were staying with their families throughout the country and few could afford to travel back to Lusaka to vote. Unlike opposition parties the MMD had funds available to enhance their campaign. Truck loads of new bicycles were seen on the road north from Lusaka and the story was that these were awarded to party workers. As being given a bicycle was almost the equivalent of being given a car in the UK, many were prepared to be party workers. Advice to volunteers from the VSO office was to avoid getting into discussions about politics and to stay well clear of polling stations on election day. There was little confidence that the day would pass peacefully.

When we arrived at Kasanka two days before Christmas, we found that a polling station had been built at the entrance to the park though where we were staying at Wasa Lodge, the park's main camp, was about ten kilometres from there. Kasanka has been a national park since 1972 but in 1990 the management of it was passed to the Kasanka Trust which tried to revitalise an area previously ravaged by poachers searching out animals for food and elephants for ivory. By Christmas 2001 elephants had returned although still not in large numbers and while zebra and giraffe were rare there were hippo and many different species of antelope including the very rare sitatunga.

The guide-book suggested that the Kundalila Falls was one of the most beautiful in all of Zambia and it was there that we chose to spend Christmas Day. A gently running stream drops 80 metres over the edge of the Muchinga escarpment. The planned highlight of our visit was a swim in the crystal-clear pool below the falls. The path which zigzagged through trees down to the pool was steep and slippery and at times I had to grab a branch of a tree to stop me slithering down but the view from below the waterfall was worth the effort. The curtain of water was not wide but its uninterrupted cascade, burnished by the midday sun, sparkled as if a silver veil had been thrown over the cliff and through the narrow ravine. To get to the pool meant scrambling over boulders which had fallen from the rock face but the water was crystal clear, deep, very cold and very refreshing. Most of us splashed around, happy to be able to swim in water which was free of the risk of bilharzia, a disease caused by a parasitic worm common in most lakes and slow-moving water, while some of the more adventurous climbed up the rock face at the side of the waterfall. A forked bolt of lighting in a suddenly darkened sky followed by a tremendous roll of thunder which reverberated deafeningly through the narrow gorge brought our fun to an abrupt end. Scrambling into clothes, we lost no time in tackling the ascent up the almost vertical path before a tropical downpour made the gruelling climb even more hazardous.

Leaving Kasanka the following day, we passed the polling station with its long but orderly queue of those waiting to vote. The election passed relatively peacefully, what rioting there was being mainly confined to Lusaka. The actions of the MMD led to some criticism by international observers, but with only 29 per cent of the vote it was declared the winning party and although three of the opposition parties challenged this ruling in the High Court, Levy Mwanawasa was declared President of the Republic of Zambia.

In mid-January, when the staff at PFZ returned to work after their Christmas break there was one lovely piece of good news. Mary Mukubwa, Robam's wife, had given birth to a boy. I was pleased for them for their little girl had died while still very young.

I was immediately involved in the fund-raising course. Working on a very tight budget I negotiated with a local non-government school to rent a classroom for two weeks. (Zambian schoolchildren have their long break in January.) We looked at why we needed to fund-raise and why everyone in the organisation had a part to play, something not always accepted. Many continued in their delusion that PFZ was well funded, always a good excuse for not taking action. Even many of those who did accept that fund-raising was urgently required lacked the enthusiasm needed to be successful at it. The course material tried to encourage the 'God helps those who help themselves' rather than 'God will provide.' For when He didn't it appeared to be accepted that 'God didn't provide because we had sinned and didn't deserve it.'

I wanted to bring out to my colleagues that there were different kinds of fund-raising, not just the begging bowl, the request for donations, but in a cash-strapped organisation such as PFZ the seed money required to start fund-raising was often difficult to find so plans had to be those which were in keeping with the money available. Staff and volunteers had to appreciate that starting a project was not enough, perseverance was required. Between Christmas and New Year I had been lucky to get a seat on a flight back to the UK and make a short visit to my family. During my days home I collected many different ideas on fund-raising tactics used in the UK, from charity Christmas Cards to volunteer supermarket packers, talent money projects to charity shops, and sponsored walks. The item which caught the attention of my Zambian colleagues was a newspaper photograph of the 'Calendar Girls'. I hadn't been sure whether or not to include it but it was a wonderful image of the courage and ingenuity fund-raising requires and those at PFZ were flabbergasted to discover that British women needed to take such exceptional action.

While at home I managed to acquire some management training videos which I thought would be useful for everyone at PFZ. A VSO grant to the PFZ Health Department had allowed Maurice and Carl to reorganise their office space. A small area had been set aside for training and as the grant had included money for a TV and video these were now securely locked in a metal casing high on the wall. One of the videos showed the dining-room team at Gleneagles Hotel in Scotland at a staff debriefing, when the waiters and waitresses were complaining that the management had allowed too many diners to be booked into the restaurant at the same time. The management's objectives of a fully booked restaurant had been met, but staff's objectives of giving a professional service had not. The sumptuousness of the dining room left most of my Zambian colleagues astounded. There were open mouths, eyes on stalks and gasps of 'Have you been there, Ann-ne?' so it was only after they extracted a promise that they could look at the video again at the end of the session that we got back to the object of the exercise, a discussion on the importance of everyone's aims and objectives being met. All were prepared to accept that one of the common aims and objectives of hotel management and waiting staff was to give the best possible service to the guests. What some were not prepared to accept was that the waiting staff had the right to complain that their management could be in error. To Zambians the waiting staff were being disrespectful to their bosses. A lot of time and patience went into convincing my colleagues that unless constructive criticism was allowed the aims and objectives of neither the hotel management nor the waiting staff were not going to be met.

Having finished the fund-raising course and with video training well underway, the management report for the board became my main focus of attention. Both Carl and I wanted to make that as professional as possible. The board meeting was to be held on Saturday, February 23, and we had been asked to attend and give a presentation on the report. But the week before the board meeting was due to take place PFZ got caught up in a huge dilemma. At first most of us did not know what had happened; only that it was serious. During many heated discussions in the director's room between Lawrence, Robam, and Francis the windows were closed to ensure that the staff could not overhear what was said. When George made a return visit speculation was rife. Gradually it emerged that in February of the previous year, when Francis had made a visit to the care-group in Mansa in northern Zambia, a visit George and I had dropped out of, he had taken with him funds which had been donated for one particular ex-prisoner who stayed there and who was maintaining that not all the money had been handed over. It appeared that Francis had told the ex-prisoner that he was short of money for the return journey to Ndola so he had retained K400,000. Robam was adamant Francis had not told him about this. When the ex-prisoner called at PFZ's offices looking for the balance of his money, there were no funds to meet his claim. The situation had been reported to the board. Dr Mathani, the board chairman, had issued instructions that Francis was to attend the board meeting on Saturday when he would have the opportunity to give his side of the story.

On Saturday morning, armed with a flip chart and various papers, Carl and I arrived at the offices of Dr Mathani's company. The board consisted of Dr Mathani, four men and two women, one of whom was a member of parliament from a Kitwe constituency and the other a High Court judge from Lusaka. The management report was reasonably well received even to the extent that Dr Mathani acknowledged that we had let the board members off very lightly. The PFZ areas which had come in for most criticism in the report were the chaplaincy and the restaurant. The chaplaincy had few records and those it did have had not been kept up to date. Francis either did not know or would not tell us how many volunteers there were in care-groups around the country which undertook PFZ's core objective, the preaching of the Bible in prisons. From the information we had been able to glean from telephone calls to care-group chairmen, there were fewer care-groups than claimed and those still in being had a declining number of volunteers, nothing like the total of 700 claimed by Francis. The PFZ restaurant was not an income generator as had been planned, almost the opposite, and even the tuition it offered members of its focus group was very poor. Each different area of the organisation was looked at in detail and our recommendations were listened to although we did not know if any would be accepted. All of this took well over two hours during which time Francis was left to cool his heels sitting in the corridor outside the meeting room. We were thanked for our 'considerable' efforts and excused.

At the staff meeting after Monday morning's devotion, the members of staff were informed that Francis had been suspended from his duties as chaplain to PFZ until further enquiries were made. Later we were told that the balance of the money due to the ex-prisoner had been paid to him and that the board had asked for Francis's resignation. Maybe there were insufficient grounds for dismissal but resigning would allow him to say that he had left of his own volition and he certainly would not go quietly. Had he been dismissed it would have been harder for him to make derogatory statements about PFZ. I was sure that there was still a lot of unpleasantness to come and couldn't help remembering Lyndon Johnson's remark of J. Edgar Hoover, 'Better to have him inside the tent pissing out, than outside pissing in.' Lawrence, who had agreed to undertake the duties of director on a three-month temporary basis, had now been at PFZ for nearly six months.

Chapter 29

Shiwa Ng'andu

The rainfall levels in the Copperbelt were much lighter than in the previous year and reports from the south of the country were of almost no rain at all. As most of the maize is grown in the south this was affecting the crop yield resulting in a sharp rise in the price of mealie meal. A 25kg bag which had cost about K17,000 the previous year had risen to K45,000 and in some parts of the country to nearly K70,000. Nshima was not only the preferred choice of food of most Zambians it was also much cheaper than rice or other staple foods. As an average monthly wage was about K100,000, few families could afford a 400 per cent rise in their food bill so people were going hungry for longer periods. Many faced starvation. During a programme of economic reforms advised by the IMF and The World Bank, Zambia had sold off its stockpile of grain so there were no reserves. When the scarcity of meal became so severe that it was difficult to get, there were threats of riots. I changed my route between Zawi and the office to avoid passing the crowds waiting outside a milling company's yard in the hope of being able to buy meal. During this time Tony and Anna gave me a birthday present of a ticket to a champagne breakfast being held to raise money for the Society for Prevention of Cruelty to Animals (SPCA) which Anna was involved in. The breakfast was held in a guesthouse and while I appreciated that this fund-raising exercise had been organised long before the current food emergency it seemed incongruous to be fund-raising for animals while people starved.

A visitor at this time was Carole, Mike Bird's partner. At Mike's funeral in Liverpool, she had asked friends not to send flowers but instead to donate towards the street-children shelter in Kitwe where Mike had been planning to work, the building of which had been halted by his untimely death. Arriving in Zambia, she was considering how best that money should be spent. While getting acclimatised she spent some time in Ndola and like Carl and me was delighted when we got the opportunity to travel to Kapishya Hot Springs near Shiwa Ng'andu. Tony and Anna were accompanying a party of children from Simba International School on a camping trip to Kapishya during their Easter break and there was room in the school bus for another three. Under the guidance of Debbie Vrdoljak, another teacher at the school, these children were working towards getting their President's Award, similar to the Duke of Edinburgh Award project in the UK.

We left Simba School in convoy on the first leg of our journey, the 200 kilometre drive to Mkushi on the Great North Road. The school bus, driven by Debbie's husband Steve, a local businessman, led the way. Tony and Anna followed in a small truck loaded with camping gear and luggage and Debbie and her twelve-year-old son Jason brought up the rear in her 4WD. Arriving at Forrest Lodge for our overnight stay, the youngsters, aged between 14 and 18, had to set up camp as part of their President's Award challenge but the adults with the luxury of staying in thatch-on-brick chalets relaxed with a drink. Supper over, Debbie chased her charges off to their tents with instructions that she expected them all to be up and packed before breakfast the following morning.

The following morning the kids were up, their camp dismantled and the lorry packed but everything else was shambolic. The lodge staff were trying to cook breakfasts on a barbecue as the electric supply had failed but much worse was that Anna, who was six-months pregnant, had had a bleeding during the night. With only a lantern for light, Tony and she had spent a very anxious night and he had made many unsuccessful attempts to telephone her doctor for advice before eventually getting through. It was decided they should stay at Forrest Lodge until someone could drive from Ndola to take them home. The lodge was fully booked for the Easter weekend so we had to leave them there and travel on to Kapisha. Carl and Carole took it in turn to drive the truck.

With the late start and a journey of over 400 kilometres ahead of us, we wasted no time in hitting the road. To the north were the Lavushi Hills, undulating tree-covered countryside which gave every indication of being sparsely populated. At last, tired and with dust-choked throats we turned off the Great North Road to trundle down a rutted red dirt road. Being bumped about as the bus avoided the worst craters was punishing but there was pleasant relief from the heat of the afternoon sun when we passed through a grove of tall blue gum trees through which we sometimes caught a glimpse of the sunlit lake. Suddenly it felt as if I was back in Britain. The cottages and red brick clock-tower embellished gatehouse which welcomed people to Shiwa Ng'andu suggested an English country house, though one which had perhaps seen better days.

I had read Christina Lamb's *The Africa House* and if possible had wanted to visit Shiwa Ng'andu, the house which was the fulfilment of a dream of Stewart Gore-Browne, a well-connected but not too affluent army officer, who came to Africa in 1911 as part of the Anglo-Belgium Boundary Commission. In January 1914 after completing the mapping of the frontier between lands claimed by Belgium and those claimed by the British South Africa Company, he set off for Dar es Salaam to board a ship for the UK. When travelling through undeveloped countryside north of the Muchinga Escarpment he first saw Shiwa Ng'andu, the Lake of the Royal Crocodiles, an area he thought the most beautiful he had ever seen. Shortly after arriving at the lake he shot and killed a rhinoceros which had been charging through local villages bringing panic to the area. The local Bemba people called him *Chipembele* (Rhinoceros). He was told that his '*mupashi*,' his ancestral spirit, was watching over him and that he would have a long life. Three years working with the boundary commission had taught him much about African ways so he sought approval for his plans to build a dream house by the lake from Chitimukulu, the Bemba Paramount Chief, but in August that year Britain declared war on Germany and his plans had to be put on hold. He returned to Europe where during his service on the Western Front he often thought longingly about the peacefulness of Shiwa Ng'andu. David Livingstone's experiences of the lake were almost the exact opposite. He was seriously ill when he arrived there in 1867 and was distressed when Chitane, his pet poodle, a stray which had attached itself to him when he was in Zanzibar, was lost, possibly drowned but more probably eaten by one of the lake's crocodiles. Livingstone had become very attached to the little dog. When the trials and tribulations of illness and shortage of supplies depressed him the antics of the dog had always been able to raise his spirits. While he and some of his men were looking for the poodle his medicine case was stolen, adding to his problems. It is said that he cursed the lake, saying that it was evil.

Gore-Browne returned to Africa in 1920 when to took up a grant of 3000 acres of the free farm land which the British South Africa Company, which governed the region at that time, was making available to ex-soldiers. Later he purchased a further 10,000 acres at a cost of £500, a shilling (today's 5p) an acre. His plan was not only to build his dream house but also to finance his estate by extracting essentials oils from roses, geraniums and peppermint grown on the farm. Everything needed for the house and farm which could not be made locally had to be transported to Ndola, then the northern terminus for the railway from the Cape, before being carried by porters 650 kilometres over land and across crocodile-infested swamps and rivers, a journey which took at least three weeks. The house was completed by 1933 when it surpassed in grandeur every other building in Northern Rhodesia, even Government House. Many of the great and the good of that time wrote their names in his visitors' book. The Lake of the Royal Crocodiles became a regular stopping place for Imperial Airways flying boat service to Cape Town. Though the estate didn't generate the expected financial returns, Gore-Browne lived at Shiwa Ng'andu as a benevolent autocrat, enjoying the life of a nineteenth-century landowner. The estate had its own schools, hospital, post office and shops. There was even an airstrip. While he had great respect for the Bemba people and was uncomfortable with the prevalent colonial attitude of white superiority, he still expected those on his estate to conform to the lifestyle he demanded.

Elected to the Legislative Council of Northern Rhodesia in 1935, Gore-Brown worked tirelessly to improve the lot of the African people, something acknowledged by the authorities in the UK when in 1945 he was knighted. He felt strongly that far too much money was being withdrawn from Northern Rhodesia by the British government in tax and the British South African Company in 'royalties.' Before he retired from active participation in politics in 1951 he campaigned for concessions to be made to African demands and in the early days of the struggle for independence gave his support to the UNIP. At Gore-Browne's funeral in 1967 President Kaunda said of him that 'He was born an Englishman and died a Zambian. Perhaps if Africa had had more like him, the transition from colonial rule to independence would have been less traumatic.'

Once we had set up camp at Kapishya there was time to relax before supper. Debbie, Carole, Carl and I followed the narrow path through the bushes which led to the springs, a natural spa, a rocky pool separated from the river by a low wall and surrounded by raffia palms through which light filtered onto the blue-grey water. The warm springs bubbled up through the sandy floor of the pool. The sensation of hot sand giving way under my feet was unnerving at first and being unprepared for that I fell into the water with a splash. The others thought that hilarious until they found out for themselves that the sandy surface was anything but firm. If there wasn't a bit of rock to stand on, you floated.

The award participants set off on their two-day hike around the estate and as they had to do this unaccompanied Debbie and Steve moved around between the different groups ensuring that everyone was doing OK. Mark Harvey, Stewart Gore-Browne's grandson, who organised safaris and bird-watching trips to the Luangwa valley and the area around Lake Bangweulu from his home at Kapishya, arranged a white-water rafting trip for Carl and Carole on the river but insisted that this was too strenuous for me although he thought I would enjoy the last part of their adventure. A guide would walk with me to a suitable place where the rafters could pull in and pick me up. Feeling a bit like an Indian *maharanee*, I set off with my guide Clement and three dogs. While I carried a sunhat and a book, Clement carried a folding chair, a parasol, bottles of water and a small picnic. He ensured that the dogs did not stray too near the water's edge. Despite efforts to trace and kill a crocodile which had escaped from the lake into the river it was still around. After an hour we reached a grassy spot near the river where we sat chatting and dozing for the rubber dinghy was taking much longer than expected to get to this point. At last we watched as, caught in the current, it hurtled round a bend in the river and was thrown under the overhanging bushes on the opposite bank before at last pushing its way to where we stood at the water's edge. Carole, Carl and Elias, their guide, were tired, hot, dirty and scratched and when I heard tales of how they had had to get out and carry their rubber dinghy while also being pushed under spiky bushes I mentally thanked Mark Harvey for realising that the walk was a much better option for me. I think we all hoped the last bit of the river was, as promised, easier. While I climbed aboard, Clement once more tied the chair and parasol on his back and whistling to the dogs set off to walk back. When we thrust out into the current, I began to wish I had gone with him. Twice we had to lie almost flat on the bottom of the boat to get under trees. At one point we had to get out and walk while Elias pulled the dinghy along through shallow water. Later we passed the crocodile, at least four metres long, sunning itself on the bank. Our arrival at the farmhouse was spectacular. The current threw the boat under a tree at the side of a wooden chalet where visitors, Patrick and Catherine, were enjoying an afternoon beer on their veranda. Rising to the occasion they asked if we had dropped in for a drink.

The following day, Mark arranged for the three of us to go to Shiwa Ng'andu. Unfortunately his brother Charlie and sister-in-law Jo, who lived in the big house, were entertaining Mr and Mrs Young, the retiring British High Commissioner and his wife. The best Mark could organise was that we could walk round the outside of the house and the gardens after which Carl and Carole could climb Livingstone Hill behind the house. I could have a gentler walk up Bareback Hill to see the view of the lake from the special place where Stewart Gore-Brown had chosen to be buried yet I was fit, well-nourished and only seven years older than David Livingstone was when he arrived at Shiwa by way of the hill which now bears his name. In January 1867, Livingstone was near Shiwa but with the weather so bad that the cloud cover seldom lifted. That had particular importance to him for a few days earlier his precious chronometers had been damaged when the porter carrying them had fallen in the wet. Livingstone needed to make sightings to get accurate longitude readings. What was similar to that day in 1867 was that the weather was cloudy and damp and I didn't get the best view of the Lake of the Royal Crocodiles from the top of Bareback Hill.

My guide Isaac waited respectfully while I looked at the simple grave of Stewart Gore-Browne, asking only if I knew the meaning of the word 'Chipembele,' the engraving on the headstone. Nearby were the graves of John and Lorna Harvey, Gore-Browne's daughter. Many, including ex-President Kenneth Kaunda, believed that the Harveys had been assassinated. They were murdered in 1992 when gunmen broke into their house near Lusaka. John Harvey, a one-time hunter, realising that tourism could play a major part in Zambia's future had started to organise game-viewing safaris to the Luangwa Valley. He came up against powerful opposition when he became involved in an attempt to stop animal poaching and the ivory trade.

The dampness became a drizzle. Back at Shiwa House I sheltered under a tree but Charlie Harvey suggested I move out of the rain into the arched doorway of the house. It didn't take too much imagination to picture the grandeur there had once been. Ladies and gentlemen in evening dress would have taken the air on the paved patios in front of arched verandas, admiring the huge poinsettia trees covered in brilliant red blossoms in the formal gardens.

When we returned to the campsite at Kapisha it was no longer quiet and peaceful. The President's Awarders had returned from their two-day trek full of stories of their adventures. The following morning we broke camp at 08.30 and ten hours later we drove through the gates of Simba School in Ndola. Since Steve had had to attend a business meeting he left in the 4WD leaving Debbie to drive the bus. It was she who was first out the bus to greet Anna standing among the groups of parents waiting to collect their offspring. Apart from being told she must take more rest Anna was fine.

Chapter 30

High and Lows

Dragging myself awake and out of bed the following morning was quite something. I was still tired and very stiff after the long day's travelling but I did make it to the office on time only to be told the awful news that Robam's ten week-old baby had died of pneumonia. There was a real sense of shock but as usual when anything exceptional happened almost everyone was involved in making arrangements. In keeping with local traditions, Robam's employer, PFZ, was responsible for meeting the costs of the funeral. The bank balance was at zero so money had to be gleaned from all the different projects before there was sufficient funds to meet all expenses. Even the day's drawings at the restaurant were used leaving Idah with a problem the following day when she needed to buy fresh supplies. The staff had added personal donations and by the end of the day we had scraped together money for food, travelling expenses for Robam's family, flowers and fuel for the vehicles. There was no need for gravediggers' fees for the men would dig the grave themselves. All of this completely disrupted my newly installed accounting system where each project kept its own account books. No one appeared to have kept a note of how much money was drawn from each different project, but then a burial had to be paid for and that was far more important than account books.

At lunchtime I changed into a long-skirted dress which covered my legs completely for Regina and Mutinta had covered their skirts with chigenges as a mark of respect. I followed their lead when we visited the 'funeral house,' Robam and Mary's home. Only women went into the house. Chairs had been placed round a fire in the garden and the men stayed there with Robam. Mutinta and Regina kicked off their shoes outside the door. I did the same and followed their example when they crawled into the house on their hands and knees. The room was completely bare of furniture. Mary sat huddled on a makeshift bed of blankets in one corner, her legs covered with a bright coloured chigenge. Other women sat on the floor with their legs stretched out in front, their backs against the walls. No one spoke. The silence was broken only by a few smothered sobs and our whispered condolences as still on our knees we worked our way round the women, shaking hands with each one, including Mary, before joining those seated on the floor. The atmosphere was oppressive, almost unbearable. After some time four dark-suited men who had not removed their shoes came in. They sat down cross-legged, with their backs to Mary. The silence continued for about another ten minutes before one said, 'Shall we pray.' The prayers were long and in both English and Tonga, the language of the south of the country where Robam's family belonged. Shortly afterwards the pastors rose, shook hands with Mary and left.

After about a further half hour Mutinta indicated we could move. We shuffled round on our knees as we again shook hands with all the women. Another group of people had arrived and food needed to be prepared. Mutinta put large pans of water on charcoal burners to heat. Into those she stirred the mealie meal as I chopped onions and tomatoes for the relish. When some of the family came to take over, we left them to it. Mutinta whispered that they would say PFZ had been mean for we had not supplied any meat.

The men would keep a vigil outside all night. Some said that this was to ensure that no evil spirits came to claim the soul of the deceased; others said that it was a tradition followed from when wild animals roamed near the villages and the mourners had to protect the corpse. The funeral was held the following day. The cortege was led by the Hilux. The little white coffin was supported in the covered back compartment by four women dressed in blue jackets, blue and white chigenges with white scarves tied round their heads, the uniform of Robam and Mary's Seventh-Day Adventists

Church. At the cemetery, the coffin was gently lifted on to a plinth in the centre of an open area. A few of the women wailed hysterically but most sang hymns as the mourners grouped themselves, the men on one side of the plinth, the women on the other. After the short service the church attendants unscrewed the lid of the coffin and pulled back the covers from the baby's face. When all the other mourners had filed past the tiny white coffin, the baby's parents brought up the rear, but not together. Mary came first, supported by two women, then Robam. Usually immaculate he looked unkempt, the effects of his overnight vigil. The lid was screwed back on before the coffin was carried by four women to where a small grave had been dug. While the men stood round the open grave the women sat down on the mounds of other graves nearby. Many of these were new with the remains of withered flowers scattered over them and sometimes there was a cup or a plastic mug sitting on top of the mound just in case the spirit of the deceased needed a drink of water. Crosses made from two pieces of wood tied together had been placed near most with names and dates written in ink or burned on. Most showed ages of people in their twenties or thirties.

One lady spread her chigenge out so that I could sit down beside her without getting my dress dirty. The grandmother's wailing continued but the low murmur of the other women's hymn singing seemed more in keeping with the solemnity of the occasion. The coffin was lowered into the grave with little ceremony. Almost immediately the men lifted spades and after offering shovels of the earth to other mourners to touch, threw it on top of the coffin filling in the grave until a mound which was much larger than the little coffin we had buried rose above the ground. Then the women moved forward, tidying up the mound, patting the earth flat and smooth. A family friend acting as master of ceremonies took charge calling on Robam and Mary to lead the way in placing flowers on the grave. Their hands touched briefly, the only time they appeared to share their loss, as they placed a small circlet of flowers on the mound. One by one, other mourners were called to stick a flower into the fresh brick-red earth. Each of the PFZ staff had a red rose and we moved forward together, sticking the stem into the earth so that the flower stood up straight.

Returning to the funeral house, the previous evening's ritual of the shoes off and hand-shaking was renewed. However, with so many people waiting to be fed nshima, Maurice suggested there would be less to feed if those of the PFZ staff who wished to do so slipped quietly away.

At the end of April all VSO volunteers and staff in Zambia met for a three-day conference at the Andrews Motel on the southern outskirts of Lusaka. VSO now recruited in some of the more developed Third World countries and I shared a room with one of those volunteers, Priscilla King'oku from Kenya, who was working as a product development co-ordinator with a bee-keeping organisation in north-western Zambia.

I found the conference very exhausting. A bout of malaria a few weeks before had left me feeling tired and I was having problems with my hearing. The deterioration in it was so marked that I had made arrangements to travel home to Edinburgh immediately after the conference to consult an audiologist. A veil is best drawn over that flight home; my first port of call in Edinburgh was at the Tropical Diseases Unit of the Western General Hospital where dysentery was diagnosed.

Hindsight is a wonderful thing. It was only after arriving back in Zambia two weeks later that I realised I should have given myself a longer time in Edinburgh in which to recover fully. The flight back left me feeling drained and although I promised myself I would take it easy for a day or two, once back at work that was impossible. I had drawn up plans to help the restaurant where the staff had been told by the board that it would be axed if it was not profit-making by the end of September, but Idah, the manager, was in hospital. Although no one was ever going to say it I was sure that she was suffering from full-blown AIDS. She had shown many of the signs, weight loss, tiredness, skin problems, and I knew that both her husband and her child had died in the previous five years, often an indicator. Even in an organisation such as PFZ which tried to educate not only about how to avoid contacting HIV/AIDS but about not stigmatising someone who was HIV positive, everyone was still frightened of being pilloried if such an admission was made. When Mutinta and I went to the hospital to visit Idah we found her in a small side ward with two beds. Her bed was covered in a multi-coloured assortment of blankets and her head lay on a cushion, bedding provided by her family. The patient in the second bed was unconscious and looked very ill. When I remarked that she at least had a drip, Mutinta was doubtful that there was anything in it. Idah had been told that she needed a blood transfusion but that there was only one unit of blood available. The blood bank was almost empty for few would risk being a blood donor. There was a fear of contacting AIDS from a dirty needle or being told that the blood donated had been tested for AIDS and found positive. Idah was feeling too weak to eat so when we left the hospital Mutinta and I went looking for a food supplement. We managed to find a tin of it at a chemist's shop which cost K50,000 (at that time about £7). When we took it back to the hospital Mutinta stressed that it was for Idah alone and that we would check that she was getting it. 'You see,' she said 'they might well think it a waste to give it to someone who is dying.'

Dolores visited PFZ to discuss what would happen when Carl and I came to the end of our two year placements in four months' time. We had both indicated that we were prepared to stay for a further six months but that depended very much on the state of PFZ's finances and in my case on whether a new director had been appointed. At a meeting with Enias Chulu, the Vice-Chairman of the PFZ Board, Dolores spelt out VSO's terms.

The reception held at the High Commission in 2002 was a special one. It celebrated the 'Official Birthday of Her Majesty Queen Elizabeth II and the Golden Jubilee of Her Majesty's Accession to the Throne in 1952.' As guests were welcomed at the gates of the Residency in Independence Avenue, we were presented with button-holes of yellow roses in gold foil and little badges which marked the Golden Jubilee. Waiting at the end of the red carpet to receive their guests were the new High Commissioner and his wife, Mr and Mrs Timothy David. Mrs David, a tall elegant lady, was wearing a full length knitted silk dress in gold, in keeping with the jubilee theme of the lunch.

Photographs depicting the changes which had arisen during the 50 years of the Queen's reign including some photographs taken during State Visits to Zambia had been put on display. A further presentation showed drawings and paintings made by school-children of how they saw the same period. Ex-President Kenneth Kaunda was obviously delighted when he saw an excellent crayon drawing of himself. Schoolchildren, dressed as prominent figures during that time, wandered among the guests. A young look-alike of Margaret Thatcher, complete with blue suit, tied-bow blouse and black handbag, enjoyed the interest she was attracting.

The comfortable affluence of the High Commission stood in stark contrast to the reality of life back in Ndola. PFZ was still struggling financially. Two different donations were expected daily but hadn't yet arrived so with no money to pay the electric bill the office was working at subsistence level without either light or computers. I was processing office e-mails through my laptop at Zawi. When the money to cover the Tearfund's expenses arrived I had to keep reminding Robam that that money could not be dipped into for other uses. On the home front, things were much better. Anna was delivered of a healthy boy called Joshua, but known as Josh, and while I was in Lusaka meeting a group from Tearfund my landlord had had a new toilet bowl plumbed into my house. This was luxury, a toilet which did not leak and where the seat did not move each time you sat on it. Harriet also thought it great for it meant she had less cleaning up to do but she wasn't too pleased when Brian, now walking, took to stuffing the toilet roll down the bowl. Twice when I came home at lunchtime I found her trying to dry off a drenched toilet roll by hanging it on the clothes-line. But then nothing is ever safe from the attention of a fourteen-month-old boy.

One of the social highlights of Ndola took place shortly after the Tearfund's arrival. An Italian concert pianist who was visiting relatives in Ndola agreed to play at a concert in aid of one of the organisations helping street children. It was held in the hall at Simba International School, where the piano was an elderly upright. Considering the piano, the one on which the Simba children hammered out their music practice, was way below the standard of instrument he was used to our star pianist excelled himself. The evening was both a social and a financial success.

Having the previous year's experience in co-ordinating the Tearfund's visit, I had an idea of what to expect and what had to be organised. For the first weeks they followed a programme similar to the previous year, including the visit to Solwezi. Having explained to Mellbin what was involved, he acted as co-ordinator on that trip gaining experience which would be useful the following year when I had returned to the UK. I did accompany the team when they visited four prisons in Kabwe. At the first prison they had a great garden, growing cabbages, spinach, Chinese leaves, tomatoes and onions. Lunch of nshima and vegetables was being prepared probably the prisoners' only meal of the day. It took time to explain to the officer-in-charge why PFZ did not have the money to buy new mattresses and do something about the sanitation in the prison. He was genuinely concerned at the appalling conditions in his prison but really it was the prison service which should be upgrading these. His argument was that if PFZ had money to pay the salaries white people demanded it had money for what he wanted. He could not understand that Carl and I were not being paid 'white' salaries and what money we did get came from VSO and not from PFZ.

PFZ was trying to learn as much as possible about prisoners' sexual knowledge and behaviour. A list of 25 questions about health, particularly in relation to HIV and STDs, knowledge of health issues, sexual behavioural patterns and gender issues had been prepared and each time there was a prison visit someone tried to speak to as many prisoners as possible. Most were happy to answer the questions although how honest the replies were was a matter of judgement. Many said they were unfaithful to their wives/partners and that they had paid for sex. Too many thought it OK for a husband to rape his wife. Some said they did not enjoy sex but found it hard to abstain which begged the question of why they continued. We compared a sample of the answers I got to those given to other researchers for we wondered if because I was an elderly 'Mama' I would get a less truthful response. There didn't appear to be any variation although one prisoner who was acting as my interpreter did have trouble trying to explain 'masturbation' to another inmate who did not understand the word. I don't think I was supposed to see the physical demonstration which was given. At the end of the survey PFZ hoped to have a better understanding of the behaviour, knowledge and attitudes of the prisoners to sex, which would help the PFZ volunteers design more suitable teaching packages. Also underway was a move away from a medical focus to a more primary health one where the impact would be on trying to change the causes of ill health rather than treat them.

At one point, Marjorie Fwolishi, who had been taking a class on health education, looked quite distracted as she hurried past me, asking if I knew where Carl was for she was 'out of her depth.' Afterwards, I could see Carl and her talking to one prisoner. His story was that he was having visions of his wife. Apparently he had strangled her after being told to do so by a witch doctor. Carl told me afterwards that this prisoner was seeking psychological help. He definitely needed help but not the kind which could be given in a couple of hours.

Having stayed overnight at the Society of African Missions guest-house, the following morning it took us about half an hour to reach Mukabeko Maximum Prison, a very secure building with high walls painted white and topped with layers of razor wire. There were no smiles on the officers' faces as they checked and re-checked our documentation. Maurice, Dr Bosi and I were shown into the Commandant's office when we were told that the recently appointed Commissioner of Prisons wanted to be informed about our programme and also wanted to consult Dr Bosi. This involved returning to Kabwe where the Commissioner had his office. Once shown into his room, I remembered to bob a slight curtsey and support my right hand with my left when shaking hands for the Commissioner held an honorary place on the PFZ board. The chat about PFZ's programme took only a few minutes. His consultation with Dr Bosi took rather longer.

Back at Mukabeko, I was admitted to the Condemned Section, a prison within a prison, where the medical team were working. On one side of the small compound was a two-storey cell block, where heavy wire mesh covered the unglazed windows to prevent attempted escapes or suicides. The overcrowding was frightful for 268 prisoners were held in a few cells designed to hold no more than 50. Almost every prisoner was crowded into the compound area. All were dressed in prison garb, rough white cotton shirts and shorts. The variety of footwear for those lucky enough to have any varied between flip flops and Wellington boots. If the atmosphere in other prisons was depressing, here it was macabre. These prisoners were allowed increased rations because they were on death row. They were the best fed prisoners I had seen in Zambia. Many of the men wanted to talk to me. I supposed that because as an elderly musungo I was different or maybe they thought I might have some influence with the authorities which could help them achieve a reprieve. It was scary to think that I might have spoken to one or all of the men who were found guilty of the murder of the parents of Mark and Charles Harvey, whom I had met at Shiwa Ng'andu in April. It was possible for there had been no official executions since 1997, although no one knew when that situation might change.

The medical team had been given a spectacular traditional

welcome in dance, the tribal greeting for very honoured guests, before they set up tables on a dais in front of the officers' area which was shaded from the sun. Prisoners queued in front of different tables and if one climbed onto the dais without permission a blueband whipped him back into his place. Long-term prisoners were held in the outer part of the prison and it was with them that I became involved in the health education programme and the behavioural survey. During the afternoon, I had the services of a prisoner called Ennis as an interpreter. I never found out why he was a long-term prisoner, but then we were forbidden to ask questions. If a prisoner told us of his own volition, fine, otherwise, no comment. When at 16.00 hours a bell rang, everything stopped and the prisoners gathered in the central open area where a football match was in progress. There were 13 different teams in the prison playing each other in an in-house league and with over 1000 men in the prison there was great competition to get into a team.

In the next days we followed the same routine at the other prisons in Kabwe before moving on to the Remand Prison in Lusaka where our programme was held up because they were expecting a ministerial visit. Eventually we were allowed to take the bus inside the first gate and unload our equipment. The government minister did arrive but was called back to parliament almost immediately. The TV cameras went with him, which was a pity for PFZ would have welcomed some much needed publicity. At the end of a very tiring but successful week, the Tearfund members set off for a few days' relaxation in Livingstone before their flight home. I was just glad to be going home to a complete weekend off, the first in five weeks, with lots of hot water, my own bed and a flushing toilet.

Back in the office there was welcome news. The PFZ board had appointed a new Executive Director, Betlem Chonde, and although he was not expected to take up his appointment until the beginning of October, VSO would now extend my placement for a further six months until April 2003. When he made a two-day visit to meet the staff, Chonde asked if I would consider staying longer than six months. I said 'No.' Quite apart from whether VSO would extend my placement even further, I felt that two and a half years was long enough to be away from home and family. I tried to explain that my stay in Zambia created work and responsibilities for my family and friends at home and I did not think I should ask them to continue doing so beyond April. He appeared to think that a trivial excuse, saying he would ask VSO for someone to replace me. Since I was staying on to complete the aims of my placement, I could only think it unlikely that VSO would provide PFZ with another volunteer who had skills similar to mine. The board had also appointed a new chaplain. Starting in October, the Rev. Jim Mwewa would fill the vacancy which had been created when Francis Mpzeni was asked to resign in March.

Various grants and donations had either arrived or we had been given dates when they could be expected. When funds started flowing into PFZ's accounts once more, everyone worked hard to make up for the time we had lost through lack of funding. The exception was the staff at the restaurant. Although anything but well, Idah insisted on returning to work but her health continued to deteriorate and sadly we soon had another funeral to attend. The restaurant project needed a complete re-think or abolished completely. As most of the staff were ex-prisoners of family members of prisoners it was given a six-month reprieve. On a more positive note, while I was busy with the Tearfund team, Robam, Sambie, Melbin and Mutinta had continued working on plans for the craft-market we were trying to establish in the park on the last Saturday of each month. When in Lusaka I had visited the market held in the grounds of the Dutch Reform Church and had suggested to the management at PFZ that a market was perhaps a way for PFZ to use the park to generate income. Our first market was planned for Saturday, August 31. We had encouraged other NGOs and local organisations to pay for space where they could sell their craft goods. Getting people to know about the market took up a great deal of time and effort and we took it in turn to stand outside the Shoprite supermarket handing out flyers. Sambie and I went round the Ndola streets pinning notices to trees, and while I did a radio interview Maurice borrowed a loud-speaker system and he and Mutinta toured the streets advertising the great bargains which could be had. While it would be lovely to say our market was a great success, it wasn't. We had just over 30 stall-holders, selling everything from candles to hand-knitted toys, wooden carvings to paintings. We even had prison officers selling large cabbages grown in Kensenshi Prison gardens, but we did not get enough people through the gates. However, the stall-holders did see the potential and we all agreed that we would work even harder to spread the word before the market set for September 28. At Monday's debriefing on the craft-market, disappointment on our lack of success was expressed but there was acceptance that if we kept working at it a market in Ndola could prove financially beneficial to PFZ.

Chapter 31

Raise AIDS Awareness in Southern Africa

Each VSO in southern Africa had to complete an AIDS project working with a local partner. I asked Marjorie Fwolishi to be my partner and using some of the knowledge she had gained when visiting women prisoners she and I had started our RAISA campaign in the women's prisons in the Copperbelt earlier in the year. Our plans had to be put on hold during the Tearfund's visit but we had already completed research into what the women prisoners knew about AIDS and of contraception as a method of protection. We listened carefully to the difficulties women faced when men used physical, financial and cultural force to intimidate them. It wasn't all plain sailing. Maurice, with other errands to do in Kitwe, arranged a pick-up time with us when he dropped us outside the women's prison at Kamfinsa, a completely separate building but not far from that of the men. We were admitted to the reception area, a hall about eight metres by three, sited between two sets of gates. Once upon a time the walls had been painted a ghastly shade of dark brown, but little of that remained. Someone had stuck health posters on the walls but they looked as if they had been there as long as the paint. The officers were polite but very certain that they had been given no instructions to expect us. They could allow us to do our survey only if the officer-in-charge of the prison gave his permission and to get that we would have to walk to the men's prison. Arriving there, the gates were shut in our faces but some persistent hammering on the door eventually persuaded the gate-keepers to open it and let us into the reception area. It took even more persuasion to get through the next gate but eventually we were taken to the office only to discover that the officer-in-charge was in Ndola at the PFZ offices. His rather rude deputy, after insisting that PFZ were not giving his prisoners sufficient medical help, eventually provided the necessary permission but when we got to the gate leading back to the reception area, an officer stopped us from going through. Time was passing and we wanted to get on but the officer was adamant – we had to wait.

From the noise coming from the other side, we knew something was happening. Excited voices were shouting encouragement. It sounded as if someone was punching a balloon which had been filled with water. There were grunts and yelps, but no screams, just whacks and thumps and a choking noise. When the gates were opened we were hustled through but not before I caught sight of someone throwing a pail of water over a rather bloodied body. I learned later that an escapee had been returned by the police. His escape had deprived his cellmates of their privileges and they were being allowed to exact vengeance.

Back at the women's block, we were at last allowed through the gates into an open square from which at least six cell blocks led off. We were greeted by singing during which two older women performed a traditional dance of welcome. Answers to our questions were on the whole similar to those given at Kensenshi. One did tell me that she used a 'traditional method' of contraception. When I enquired later about this I was told that it involved tying a certain type of scarf round your waist while having sex.

Marjorie, with the help of Carl, had put together a programme about different types of contraception while emphasising that condoms were the only one which protected against AIDS. There was much interested giggling when Marjorie opened out a male condom and even more when she showed the women a female condom. She also offered some suggestions on how intimidation could be challenged. With further help from Carl, Marjorie and I put together the programme which we presented to the male prisoners. When we called it 'What women say about sex', the men's attention was assured. There was grumbling and mumbling when they watched role-plays which demonstrated some of the problems women faced but in the following discussions when they were reminded that the women in question could be their mothers, sisters or daughters as well as their wives, they became more sympathetic to the plight of women. We emphasised how women were more susceptible to contacting the AIDS virus because tearing of the vagina during sex, particularly dry sex, made it even easier for the virus to enter the bloodstream. Carl persuaded a local joiner to carve two wooden penises so that there could be demonstrations on the correct way to fit a condom. When explaining how a female condom should be inserted in the vagina, a cut-out from a plastic water bottle served as the model. After the talks, demonstrations and role-plays, the prisoners were encouraged to take part in a competition for the best drawing showing how women were exploited by men. The proud winner would be presented with a T-shirt bearing an AIDS message which when worn would remind his fellow prisoners of our visit and the information we had given about gender issues and safer sex. We learned quickly what caught the attention of the prisoners and adjusted parts of the programme to cover these. Quite by accident we found out that despite the protests that a woman should not be speaking about sexual matters, Marjorie could hold the men's attention better than Newton Zulu or Charles Kachali, two of the PFZ health volunteers, and conversely the women prisoners responded better when a male spoke to them.

When we set off one Wednesday morning, to take the programme to eight prisons in Central and Luapula Provinces, our party numbered six. Marjorie, Newton, Charles, Carl and I were accompanied by Sambie who came as driver/mechanic having got leave of absence from the micro-credit project for a week. He had completed a course on car mechanics and considering the age of the Hilux his recently learned skills could very well be needed. We were in almost a holiday mood as we drove out of Ndola at first light. While our journey was all about work, the only opportunities the Zambians health volunteers had to see other parts of their country were on occasions such as this trip. All four were intelligent and life had made them resourceful. While Sambie was on the paid staff of PFZ his monthly salary was not much more than the equivalent of £30 but as his connection with PFZ had started as a health volunteer I included him in that category. Newton had regular work with the street-children programme managed by Susanne Bradley but Marjorie and Charles scraped by on expenses of K10,000 (less than £1.50) they were given for a prison visit plus whatever temporary work they managed to get.

While most of the programme would be led by Marjorie, with help from Newton and Charles, Carl was there to supervise and adjust the programme as required and my role was administrator responsible for communicating with the prison authorities and local care-groups while ensuring we had accommodation and food. Marjorie, Carl and I travelled in the twin-cab with Sambie, and Newton and Charles lay on a mattress spread on the floor of the rear truck part of the Hilux, affectionately known to the PFZ staff as 'Penal Block' because those travelling in it were locked in from the outside. They used our luggage as pillows and passed the time playing gospel music on an old ghetto blaster.

We had just arrived in the small town of Mkushi, south of the DR Congo pedicle, our first port of call, when we got a puncture. Leaving Sambie with the Hilux, the rest of us set off on foot for the prison. Even at 09.30 it was swelteringly hot so none of us were too pleased when having walked over a kilometre on rough roads we were greeted with, 'You can't come in unless you have a letter of authority from the Commissioner of Prisons.' Assuring the officer at the gate that we did carry the necessary authority, which he was welcome to inspect, even photocopy if he wished, we were eventually taken to the office of the officer-in-charge, who told me that he had had a phone call that morning from his superior at Mansa, a prison on our itinerary and the senior one in the area, advising that we had no authority to speak to the prisoners. Although PFZ did not work in this part of the country as much as it did in the Copperbelt, letters advising of the proposed visit together with a photocopy of the approval which had been obtained form the Commissioner of Prison's office in Kabwe had been sent to each prison we intended to visit. Who, we wondered, was playing politics with us?

Even when we had proved our right to be at Mkushi it took time to make the necessary arrangements for nothing had been prepared for our arrival. Finally we were shown into a cell about 12 metres long by 6 wide, not much bigger than a large living room, where about 100 prisoners had been gathered. The men sat on the floor while two women prisoners sat on a bench at the side, with a female warder strategically placed between them and the men. There were many different answers to the question 'What is safer sex?' but the giggle rate rose when a wooden penis was produced and increased to laughter when the prisoner who volunteered to demonstrate how to put a condom on it got it wrong. There were even more giggles and the odd hand covering eyes when the female condom was shown. The water bottle cut to represent the vagina really brought out salacious comments from some, while the heads of other prisoners just about slipped back inside their tattered T-shirts. The women kept heads down but eyes up, ensuring that they didn't miss anything. When the questions started Marjorie fielded off the awkward ones yet kept the laughs going, helpful in reducing any tension felt by people unused to hearing sex discussed openly. That was just as well for the next part of the programme was looking at the flip chart drawings. To a background of guffaws and tittering, the bolder prisoners mentioned their pet names for various parts of the male/female anatomy but most studied our diagrams carefully. A few were too embarrassed to look and some among them complained that these matters should not be being discussed at all and certainly not by a female. Prison officers watching from the side-lines had great difficulty maintaining their dignity and distance. While they tried to show that they did not need this instruction, curiosity whetted their interest and most stayed close by watching what was happening rather than keeping a check on the prisoners. One said to me that he had not known that a woman could get pleasure from sex.

When it came to discussing gender issues, the women were separated from the men. Newton encouraged them to think how their sexuality was controlled by men. He produced coloured pencils and sheets on each of which he had drawn a circle, split into eight sections each representing a different way which they could use to protect themselves from contacting the HIV virus, such as fidelity to one partner or using a female condom. As they identified these areas, some of which required the use of negotiation or assertion, the women coloured in the appropriate section. That was followed by a short lesson on negotiation and some ideas on how to be assertive, such as making 'I' statements. Hopefully sometime in the future when they were back with their families they would remember.

Meanwhile the men were split into groups to discuss how they could help women protect themselves. Brought back into one large group, the prisoners read out the ideas identified in the smaller groups and argued about them. When we moved on to the role plays, which featured aggressive, assertive and passive behaviour, some of the prisoners who took part showed outstanding acting abilities. Whether the aggression shown was actually acting or just came naturally to them their thespian efforts brought roars of annoyance, disgust, approval and outrage at all the appropriate times which encouraged us to think that at least some of our message had been listened to and retained.

Before we said goodbye, we left paper, pencils and felt pens with the officer-in-charge promising to call in on our return journey to Ndola in a few days' time when we would select from the drawings, poems or stories produced by the prisoners the ones we felt best portrayed 'Helping women protect themselves from HIV/AIDS'. Just to add a little encouragement, Charles modelled the T-shirt with appropriate AIDS message which would be presented to the winner.

Sambie was waiting by the Hilux. While we were at the prison he had changed the wheel and taken the punctured tyre to be repaired, a patch welded on to the tyre and also with an inner tube inserted in it. Our next call was at Mkushi Farm Prison where prisoners at the end of their sentences in the main prison were housed until their release, about 20 kilometres along a very dusty rutted dirt track, a severe test for our spare tyre which seemed spectacularly lacking in tread. The officer-in-charge squeezed in among us, ostensibly to show us the way and ensure our welcome but really he was taking the opportunity to check on what was happening at the farm prison by hitching a lift. There were no funds in the prison budget for transport so if he wanted to visit the farm prison, he walked. The farm was completely without fences or bars and the 30 prisoners living there moved freely among the local villages which led to the possible rise in the HIV/AIDS rate in this area. Prisoners were gathered in from the fields and settled in the shade of a large jacaranda tree, a lovely location for our training. A few goats wandered past but the only serious disruption was when a cook, with the doubtful assistance of a dog, tried to catch a hen, which had escaped into the middle of our group. Its cry upon being captured left no doubt that it knew its fate.

We still had a journey of about 120 kilometres to Serenje, our overnight stop, and tried to make our departure as speedily as possible. It was dark by the time we arrived in that town and there was a bit of a panic when Carl discovered he had forgotten to pack the map and directions he had been sent by Ruth Brewer. Ruth and Molly Callaghan were VSO teacher-trainers at the Malcolm Moffat Teacher Training College in Serenje. They had made arrangements for Marjorie, Charles, Newton and Sambie to be put up at the college guesthouse while Carl and I stayed with them. Serenje, like many Zambian towns, was linear, one long street with buildings straggling both sides and some houses in rows behind. After many stops for directions we did eventually find the guesthouse and Carl and I left the others to get settled in as we set out with a guide to find Ruth's house. We made it safely having negotiated areas where new drains were being dug, prior to the start of the rainy season and got a great welcome from Ruth and Molly, not least because I had brought shoes and sandals for them from the PEP store in Ndola. In a recent burglary they had not only lost their bicycles, ghetto-blaster and tapes but also their shoes.

Although we were not due at Serenje Prison until 09.00 hours the following day, we had an early breakfast as Molly and Ruth's day started at 07.00 with a HIV programme before morning devotion at the college. Ruth was in charge of the HIV/AIDS instruction at Malcolm Moffat and during supper the previous evening had persuaded Carl, Marjorie and Newton to speak to the students about what PFZ was trying to achieve in its HIV education programme. The venue was the college hall complete with a stage, a microphone system and seating for about 500 students and lecturers. Carl spoke first and once the other two got into their stride they were great but I reckoned that it was lunchtime before Marjorie and Newton's heartbeats returned to normal.

Arriving at the prison, we repeated the previous day's programme, this time to about 150 prisoners. There was not a cell large enough to hold them all, so some stood outside and looked in through the bars of the unglazed windows. When Marjorie lifted her trouser covered leg and started to demonstrate how a female condom could be inserted, those outside fought for the most advantageous viewing places at the windows. Poor Newton became very embarrassed when, trying to insert the condom in the water-bottle, he announced, 'My fingers are stuck in the vagina.'

Our programme finished, we picked our way through the prisoners still sitting cross-legged on the floor before reaching the door where the air was still as hot but not quite so whiffy. Back in town we topped up the Hilux's tank with every drop of diesel we could squeeze into it before setting off on the 350-kilometre journey to Mansa.

The road north had been built by the Chinese in the 1960s. It travels over the low flood plain lands which border the Luapula River running for over 100 kilometres almost without bends. A ribbon of grey it stretched far into the shimmering distance narrowing to a pin-prick until it faded into the cloudless deep blue of the horizon. For a good part of our journey the only human inhabitants we saw were at a bridge over the river which was well guarded by the Zambian army because of its location near the border with the DR Congo. A collection of fishermen's huts stood at either end of the long low bridge. There was little to see, only flat bare boggy lands, where rows of termite mounds gave the impression of an immense cemetery. Listening to my Zambian colleagues speak about the technology which the Chinese had used to build this road and bridge and also to tunnel through rock when building the railway to Dar es Salaam suggested there was still a great respect for the help given to Zambia by China after the UN's embargo on Southern Rhodesia in 1965 effectively cut Zambia off from sea ports. But then China was looking for political dividends when assisting the economic development of countries in sub-Saharan Africa.

Mansa turned out to be a small pleasant town with tree-lined streets. We could see the prison but could not find a road into it. Eventually Sambie drove the Hilux over a ditch, a pavement and through a gap in the buildings and we were there. The chaplain greeted us enthusiastically which contrasted well with the grudging welcome of the officer-in-charge. Our evening visit was made only to establish our credentials and to make arrangements for the following day. Again there was a farm prison, 45 kilometres from the town, and even though it had not been included in our programme we were expected to visit it. We guessed that as the officer had made it clear he was not very interested in what we were doing this was his way of getting a free ride to the farm prison to see what was happening there. A quick discussion and we decided that if we split our resources and Sambie took Newton to the farm prison, Marjorie, Carl and Charles could take the programme in the main prison, and I could organise our food and cope with any organisational problems which arose. Doing so would mean we could keep to our timetable and not overstrain our budget too much.

Our accommodation was in a guesthouse recommended by members of the local care group. It was reasonably clean and relatively secure. We didn't lose anything. We might even have gained something for we were all rather itchy the following day. The lack of water was a problem but we were used to that. Once again it was 'Thank heaven for wipes,' but at K10,000 (less than £1.50) per person per night we could hardly complain. Food was not served so Marjorie, having visited a local market for supplies, cooked nshima and fish over a braii for supper.

Unlike the prisons in Mkushi and Serenje, we were not allowed to speak to all the prisoners, only those not involved in duties during our visit. In those circumstances we had to hope that our visit would be the subject of conversation after 'lights out'. Since the prisoners have so little to talk about we were fairly confident that we would get the coverage we wanted, although it might not be as accurate as we would have liked. Getting ready to leave for Samfra, the next stop on our itinerary, we had a disagreement with the chaplain who thought we should take him and a member of the local care group with us, perhaps the reason for his enthusiastic welcome. I wasn't sure where he thought we would put them – maybe tied to the roof – in Zambia anything is possible. No doubt he would have expected us to pay for their accommodation, meals and their bus fares back, which on our tight budget was impossible. When he waved us off it was with a definite sour look and we were in no doubt that because he was a member of a local PFZ care-group he would make a complaint to PFZ on our failure to co-operate with him. To him we were all part of PFZ so when we were in the area we should meet his needs and expenses. His request was both impractical and outwith our budget but that would never have occurred to him.

My guide book said that Samfra, a small town on the shore of Lake Bangweulu, was lacking in places to stay so finding accommodation was my priority when arriving there. The one small guesthouse we did find was perhaps not as clean as the one in Mansa but it did have a beautiful location right on the edge of the lake. It would have been lovely to have gone for a swim to wash off the layer of red dust which was caked on our sweat-soaked bodies but with the double risk of crocodiles and bilharzia in mind the ghastly windowless bathroom, lit by one solitary candle, was acceptable. There was hot water but no cold. A rather dilapidated pail was provided so that cold could be fetched from the oil drum of water sitting outside the toilet. At least that pail was better than the rusty one which served to provide water for the loo.

Once contact had been made with the prison, arrangements were made for the following day. The officer-in-charge was more flexible than his colleague in Mansa but again there was a farm prison, 34 kilometres from town. We agreed to complete our programme at both as long as we were allowed to start early. There was still time before nightfall to walk along the beach of fine white sand edging the waters of the lake, which looked more like a turquoise sea rather than a lake particularly as a mist lay on the water about three kilometres from the shore. It was the seaside without the salty smell of ozone. The lake is actually only 25 miles long but because of the swamps which surround it looks much longer. To my Zambian colleagues, none of whom had ever seen either the sea or a lake, it was awesome. Charles went crazy with excitement and dived in fully clothed as the rest of us paddled. We tried unsuccessfully to hire a boat to take us for a sunset cruise. All we found was a small dinghy whose owner agreed to rent it for an hour. Sambie, Marjorie and Charles couldn't get into it quickly enough but once they experienced the effort required to row a boat their enthusiasm dipped. The exhausting heat of the day had passed as had the sights and smells of the prisons. Now it was the smell of wood smoke which permeated the spicy mustiness of the sultry day. It was peaceful sitting in the shade, listening to the chirping of the tree frogs broken now and then by the raucous call of a fish eagle. There was a great deal of bird activity around the lake. It is one of the few relatively accessible places in Africa where the prehistoric-looking shoebills can be seen. A colony of around 500 live in the Bangweulu swamps nesting among the reeds in April/May. Other birds seen there include black and white egrets, different species of heron, ibis, plovers, marsh harriers, bee-eaters, flycatchers, rosy-breasted long-claws, open billed storks and pygmy geese, while during the rainy season when the floodwaters are high, visitors include wattled cranes, flamingos, pelicans and spoonbills. It is an ornithologist's paradise.

David Livingstone twice visited the lake. Late in 1867, having been delayed for various reasons, he headed south from Lake Mweru (Moero) to Lake Bangweulu during the rainy season in an attempt to establish that it was the most southerly source of the River Lualaba as suggested by his native guides. He then hoped to be able to follow what he thought as the Lualaba north from the lake until he could prove his (erroneous) theory that it was the Nile. (Stanley later proved it to be the Congo.) As was often the case during Livingstone's travels he was sick and his supplies were low. The weather was particularly inclement which made the taking of sightings difficult and also he was using the chronometers which became faulty after they had been dropped near Shiwa Ng'unda. They had been further damaged during an earth tremor which had occurred in July that same year. As a result of faulty readings Livingstone drew seventy miles of space on his map which was not actually there and in not realising that floods disguised the swamps south of the lake he calculated that Lake Bangweulu was much larger than it actually was.

Livingstone returned in December 1872, on what was his last journey. Because of the faulty readings from his chronometers, he was convinced that he was on the north-eastern side of the lake. He thought complete madness his guide's suggestion that to get to Katanga they travel in a south-westerly direction for he was sure that would take him right into the middle of the lake. Instead he made a disastrous decision and turned east which led him into swamps which stretched for almost 160 kilometres.

Rejoined by the others we watched the sun sink through the mist and over the horizon before heading back to the guesthouse to tackle the bathing problems. The general consensus was that since we were in a fishing village, it had to be fish for supper. Unfortunately fish was not a delicacy for the locals to whom it was probably a staple food and neither of the local restaurants had fish on their menus. I had to settle for nshima with a very tough beef. Walking back with my companions to the guesthouse through the dark village streets, lit only by small single lights in the windows of the thatched mud huts, I realised that there, in rural Africa, I was completely at ease. I felt at home.

Everyone was up bright and early the following morning. Sambie and Charles had risen before sunrise so that they could watch dawn break over the lake. It would have been fun to have a sail in the ancient rust-tub which trundled round the lakeside settlements but we still had prisoners to educate about HIV and gender issues. After a breakfast of eggs and sausages or in my case eggs only as with my blessing the boys divided my ration of sausages, we set off. Everyone was under instruction 'Don't waste time,' for we wanted to be back on the road by 12.00. The morning's programme went really well with everything going to plan. The farm contingent, Charles and Sambie, were no more than half an hour later than expected but they brought with them 20 bags of okra and a tiger fish, saying there was still some room in the Hilux. The tiger fish would at least help towards supper.

We found the one garage in the area that did have diesel but the staff were in no hurry to serve us and when I asked for a receipt I might just as well have asked for the keys to the pearly gates. We shook the poor Hilux back and forth so that the very last drop of fuel filled its tank. With the next filling station 320 kilometres away that last drop could well be very important. At last with nothing to do but pick up some food for our lunch and supper, we went to the market. But what had appeared a simple exercise became very difficult as most of the stalls were closed. Eventually with another hour lost and tempers becoming strained we were all glad to be leaving Samfra, agreeing to buy fish for supper when we stopped for a picnic lunch at the bridge over the Luapula River.

If Carl or I tried to buy the fish, or even if the others purchased it while Carl and I were there, the price would double, so just before the bridge Sambie stopped the vehicle. He, Charles, Newton and Marjorie got out and walked towards the fishermens' shacks, while with Carl at the wheel we drove across the bridge and stopped half a kilometre further on. When at last they did appear they brought several bags of dried fish having been on a shopping spree of their own.

We still had over 100 kilometres to go to the gates to the Kasanka National Park and we wanted to get there before nightfall. Even in the dry season the roads in the park were not good, especially for a vehicle like the Hilux which did not have a high clearance even when empty, and certainly not in its present over-loaded state. Roads in the park were little more than farm tracks where during the wet season wheels had gouged out ruts. These roads were difficult to drive over at any time but scary after dark even when using headlights. To give the Zambians their due, they did not understand just why it was so important that we arrive there before dark. They did not know where we were going, having only been promised that we would spend the weekend somewhere special, although even if they had known they still have taken their time when buying the fish. Bargaining was not something which could be hurried and buying the fish was an investment which would earn them money. We were challenging dusk as we hurtled south along the Great North Road and because of that were not as I had hoped able to visit the village of Chitambo where a simple stone monument topped with a bronze cross marks the place where Livingstone died. Seriously ill, it had taken him over two months to travel from Lake Bangweulu through the swamps to Chitambo, the same distance as we had covered in a few hours. Livingstone was desperately ill from malaria and dysentery but when it might have been expected that his African helpers would desert him, they didn't.

They carried him, even when as Livingstone noted in his diary 'the main stream came up to Susi's mouth,' eventually seeking shelter from Chief Chitambo. After his death his two closest followers, Susi and Chuma, having salted and dried his body with help from Chief Chitambo's people, carried it over 1,600 kilometres to Bagamoyo on the Tanzanian coast, a journey which took more than nine months. The plaque on a wall in Zanzibar stated that his body had been shipped home to Britain from there.

It was getting dark by the time we turned off into the park for the ten-kilometre journey to Wasa Camp. We were shown to our chalets, Sambie sharing with Charles, Newton with Carl, and Marjorie and me in the third. Having handed our supplies over to the camp cook, he prepared our supper, nshima, vegetables and fish, after which we settled down in chairs by the campfire. The Zambians did not enjoy that, saying it was too like a funeral. Gradually they slipped away to their beds.

It had been agreed that we would all have a lie-in on Sunday morning. Breakfast would be 09.00, very late for Zambians, after which we would hold a short service in line with PFZ's standing instructions. Then on to Luwombwa Camp where we could canoe on the river, fish, and hopefully see some game. In Livingstone's time animals roamed though out the land but after the devastation caused by big-game hunters in the nineteenth and early twentieth centuries and poachers in the twentieth, big game was now mainly restricted to the game reserves and national parks. Awake early I got up but found that Sambie and Charles had been up for hours. They were watching with binoculars from a hide outside the camp anything and everything that moved. Carl and I, mindful of PFZ's instructions, had prepared the morning devotion before we left Ndola. Sitting on the veranda in front of the dining-room chalet, we sang hymns from the PFZ songbook accompanied by noisy yawns from a hippo which was enjoying itself in a muddy pool nearby. When the rains came in a few weeks' time, that muddy pool would become a lake.

In a drive round parts of the park we passed antelope, baboons, monkeys and some fresh elephant dung but no elephants, disappointing for the Zambians who seldom get the opportunity to see the big game in their own country. Stopping at Luwombwa Camp, we went for walks, played football, saw crocodiles, canoed up and down the river and fished for bream, which we ate for lunch along with nshima. It felt like being on a Sunday School picnic. At about 16.00 we left on the return journey in the hope that we would see more game in the evening light when the temperature was lower. Rod, our guide, stopped at a hide, 18 metres up in a mululu tree and reached by a series of ladders made from tree branches. I had chickened out of climbing the ladders at Christmas. This time I had no let out. I went up mouthing silently (I hoped), 'Don't look down. One step at a time. Don't look down.' I was sure I was saying it out loud by the time I reached the first landing but I did climb all the way to the viewing point and the effort was well worth while. The view across the wide plain was superb for watching mostly types of antelope, impala, bushbuck, waterbuck, duiker and grysbok, though there were also a few zebra and some buffalo. There were still no elephants nor were there any of the very shy sitatunga which could sometimes be seen from that hide. We stayed until the sun had set, when I found getting down in the dark was if anything more threatening than the climb up.

On our second night, the Zambians were much happier sitting round the fire. They had persuaded the staff to lend them a braii rack and placed it over the fire to smoke some of the fish they had bought. It was one of the highlights of the week as we relaxed together. I left them still chattering away by the fire and from my chalet could hear their voices for a long time afterwards. Then it was a hippo which kept me awake as it grazed noisily outside the chalet.

Monday morning and we were on the road again. The engine was starting to splutter when we pulled into the filling station near Serenje. With the tank full once more we were off to the Farm Prison which was about 45 kilometres west from the town, almost on the border with the DR Congo. After our short break we had to get motivated again for our final prison visit of this trip. The programme went very well and the prisoners, so pleased we had come, made us a meal, the ubiquitous nshima and chicken. That gesture was really appreciated, the money saved helping to cover some of the expenses on the planned trip to Kabwe, when we would present the same programme to the prisoners there.

The Hilux was lying really low and groaning when we left the prison. The volunteers had bought even more vegetables at the farm. The fishy smell in 'penal block' had got so bad I was extremely glad I was not travelling in it but the Zambians would earn themselves some cash when they sold the vegetables and fish to friends and neighbours in Ndola. We made it safely home with only one stop, to buy even more vegetables, tomatoes this time. Perhaps it was as well we did stop for almost immediately after we pulled up the front nearside tyre gave a loud bang and deflated. The valve on the inner tube had sheared off. The wheel was changed in record time but as we crossed the River Itawa and drove into Ndola darkness was falling. During the past week we had travelled almost 2000 kilometres over a variety of road surfaces and had taken our programme to over 1000 male and 150 female prisoners as well as an uncounted number of prison officers. Once the Kabwe trip was completed the number of prisoners spoken to would double which was not at all bad on a grant of £670. The Kasanka visit had been an 'extra', a break which gave the four Zambians the chance to see something of their country.

Chapter 32

The Ending of a Strategic Plan

M r Chonde, the new director, having taken up his duties, wanted PFZ to have a strategic plan. At last we appeared to be making progress but unfortunately he focused only on that. It took priority over everything. Work in all departments suffered and that meant even less funding coming in which in turn made him critical of the managers. He was less than impressed when he visited PFZ's market in the park. We knew that Saturday, October 26, was not the best day for the craft market but all our advertising material had said that there would be a market on the last Saturday in each month until November so we went ahead with it as planned. And just as we anticipated, it was less successful than the previous two, partially because people were still waiting for their end of month salaries and also because of the Independence Day holiday on October 24. Many of those who had money to spare had taken the opportunity of the holiday to visit friends. When the first rains of the season arrived just before noon the stall-holders packed up early. Reports from Lusaka told of poor attendances at the very well established market there.

We did get funding from the PFZ Board for an Annual General Meeting although perhaps a better name might have been an Extraordinary Annual General Meeting, since there hadn't been an 'annual' one for about six years. It was disappointing when Chonde decided this was to be held on the last Saturday in November which coincided with the last craft market before the full force of the rainy season. As yet, there was no covered area in the park large enough to take the stalls so the market was being suspended until the return of the dry season in April. The PFZ staff hoped this market would make a good impression, something which would be remembered when it resumed. However, the organisation of both AGM and market was made difficult for three reasons. Mutinta, who had taken on the management of the park, was removed from her post. It appeared that her relationship to George Chanda had more to do with this than the reason given, that she had been employed as a secretary for the health department. The Venture had been stolen. Over the previous months it had been kept overnight at Robam's house. He said he had used it to attend a church meeting. When that finished and he went to drive home the Venture had gone. Keeping the vehicles from being stolen was a continual problem and because of that they were not supposed to be used at night unless the director had given permission, something Robam had not obtained. Chonde appeared more concerned by what he saw as the challenge to his authority than he was to the loss of the vehicle. After a series of angry confrontations between him and Robam, we were all called to a meeting when he upbraided all of us about not giving him the respect he was entitled to. With little insurance money available from the loss of the Venture there were no funds with which to replace it. Money was the root of yet another problem. With insufficient funds to pay the electricity bill, we were once more working without the use of computers and lights. My offer of putting e-mails through my laptop at Zawi as I had previously done was taken up but not as I intended. Chonde moved Regina's computer into my house and decided that he and Regina could work from there. Harriet was not amused for she had great difficulty working round them and wee Brian, toddling round dressed only in a small T-shirt and leaving the odd puddle on the floor, was getting in everyone's way. When I was having visitors I asked Chonde to move the equipment back to the office. He did, but with bad grace.

As the end of November approached electricity was restored in the office and preparations for the AGM and the market went ahead but always overshadowed by the preparation of the strategic plan which appeared to be getting nowhere. We spent hours talking about it but achieving little as Chonde insisted we move at a pace dictated by him. As the AGM approached Robam was glad of my help when it came to preparing income and expenditure statements and balance sheets. For the first time in two years I had access to all the accounts at the same time, although as in the case of all end-of-financial-year statements these were historical, a picture of what had happened rather than the current situation.

As representatives from care-groups around the country arrived in Ndola we had many visitors to the office all wanting to spend time speaking to the staff and asking to be driven to various places at a time when we were particularly busy. The venue for the AGM was the Anglican Cathedral hall which was conveniently near the park so preparations for it and the market could go ahead at the same time. The Hilux, laden with people and equipment, trundled back and forth across the town. By sunset on the eve of the AGM and the market we accepted that although there was much more we would like to have achieved, particularly in advertising the market, we had to be content and accept that the basics for both were in place. A supper for the care-group representatives and members of the PFZ board was held at the home of Peter Kanagamayagam, one of the PFZ board members, to which Carl and I were invited along with Chonde and Maurice. When we arrived most of the care-group representatives were seated on chairs set in a circle on the lawn. Chonde, who had shown few interpersonal skills in the office, chose to honour them by getting down on his knees and working his way round the group. While shaking hands with each representative he supported his right wrist in his left hand indicating his respect. It was an evening of hymns and prayers with everyone demonstrating goodwill to their fellow men and women.

Reports which came from the various members of staff who on the following day attended the AGM, suggested there had been few displays of peace and goodwill. All the usual recriminations were made against the staff at the office. Representatives appeared to believe that funds which should have been distributed to the care-groups were retained and used by the office staff. Very few of the groups appeared to feel that it was their responsibility to raise funds locally, something which would be difficult but not impossible. There was always a great expectation that funds would be donated by someone else with a complete refusal to believe that there were no such funds.

The market was still not as well attended as PFZ would have liked perhaps because the amount of advertising we had been able to do had been restricted by lack of time, no vehicle and little funds. While it went ahead in one part of the park, a buffet lunch was served to the AGM delegates in another part. When speaking to as many of them as possible, I tried to explain the fund-raising purpose behind the market. The response by some was 'When do we get our share of the proceeds?' At the end of the day, the market had generated sufficient cash to cover its expenses with little left for the PFZ coffers. At the AGM, delegates had voted to retain Dr Mathani as Chairman but Kalifungwa, the chairman of the Kitwe care-group, had taken over the responsibilities of Vice-Chairman from Chulu. Other than that only a few resolutions had been carried and not a lot appeared to have been achieved other than giving an opportunity for some to blow off steam.

It had been a busy weekend but a holiday was on the horizon. When the six-month extension to my placement was agreed, part of the new contract included travel home to the UK for Christmas. VSO notified me my flight home had been booked for December 12 with a return flight on January 4. Apart from bringing everything up to date before my holiday I had four events marked in my diary. The first was work, a three-day management course. The second was social, a weekend at Kasanka to watch some of the five million fruit bats which at the start of the wet season in late November are attracted by the unusual swamp vegetation near the Musola River. My companions were four of my VSO colleagues, Vicky Mulgatroyd, Sue, Ruth and Evelyn, a Dutch volunteer. We relaxed and lazed around in the hot humid December temperatures. The exceptions were our evening walks to watch the bats. During the day the straw coloured bats hang upside down on the mushitu trees where the combined weight of a number of them on the same branch often cause it to break from the tree. One bat weighs around 3lb and has a wingspan of about a metre. Five million of them hanging around break branches from a lot of trees. Taking care where we walked in the undergrowth we set off just before 18.15 hours to watch their evening flight. With so many branches breaking off trees more light filtered through onto the forest floor and that together with the fertilising effect of the bat droppings encouraged a growth in which many dangers, including crocodiles, lurked. One moment the pale evening sky was clear. The next it was black as the bats took off almost in unison. For around twenty minutes it was a fantastic sight, a dark vortex of swirling wings circled overhead before they split into groups to go in search of wild fruits.

Back at work on Monday morning, a visitor to the office, a wild-life ranger, told me that small colonies of the bats had been seen near Ndola. Harry, one of the ex-prisoners who worked at the park, had been discovered trying to poach a fruit bat. As they are a protected species, the punishment for poaching one was a three-year jail sentence. In mitigation Harry claimed that when he had taken his ailing child to a witch doctor, he had been told to catch a bat and draw a serum from its leg. His instructions were to cut his child's chest with a razor blade and rub the bat serum into the cut. The information that he worked for PFZ had saved him from being handed over immediately to the police. When asked to whom the ranger should speak to at PFZ, he had given my name. In these circumstances the ranger, feeling that a child's life might have been saved, was prepared to overlook the crime provided the seriousness of Harry's actions was made very clear to him. With Gift acting as interpreter I lectured Harry on the enormity of his crime, while fully aware that he had chosen me because he thought I would be the softest option at PFZ. A fifteen-minute harangue from me, no matter how forceful, was not a great hardship to him.

Afterwards I made sure he got money to take his child to a medical doctor.

The third was partly work and partly social. I was invited to speak to the Women's Institute (WI) in Ndola about my work at PFZ. The ladies from the white and Indian communities made me very welcome and the pattern of the meeting (I was asked to judge the entries for the home-baking competition!) reminded me of many such I had attended at home as a member of the Scottish Women's Rural Institute. It was there that I learned that Zawi, which sounded so African, was actually an acronym for Zambian Association of Women's Institutes and that, as I had thought, it had been built as sheltered housing but had been a casualty of the economic downturn in the 1970's when lack of funding had forced the WI to close the project and sell the property.

The fourth entry in my diary was a scribbled note, 'December 10, Chad and Joanna. 11.30.' While I assumed that Chad was Chad Kalobwe, the VSO Resource Manager in Lusaka, I didn't know the name 'Joanna.' When the usual timely confirmation of such a visit failed to come from the VSO office, and after having asked Carl if he had a similar entry, I dismissed the entry as something I had misheard. That was a mistake. For some reason, possibly lack of electricity or a telephone connection at PFZ, the e-mail advising a visit from Chad and Joanna had not been received. When they arrived unannounced (as far as PFZ were concerned) Chonde took exception to their visit by refusing to meet them as he had not been forewarned. Unfortunately, I mentioned that I had had a note in my diary. Before I had an opportunity to explain, I was given a severe lecture on not respecting his authority and dignity. In fact, Joanna was undertaking a study of how VSO worked in the field and if he felt such umbrage it would have been better if he had met her and complained about the lack of correspondence. Assuming that Chonde's indignation would blow over, I welcomed Chad's offer of a lift to Lusaka and left to enjoy Christmas and New Year in Edinburgh.

It was three years since I had celebrated Christmas with my

family and that made the 2002 festive season a memorable one but all too soon I was back in Zambia, enthusiastic to complete all the objectives of my placement. Chonde was not so enthusiastic about seeing me return. His umbrage at what he saw as a slight to his dignity had not blown over, rather it had intensified. Hoping to improve the situation I tried to apologise and explain what had happened but when I started to speak he turned away from me towards a filing cabinet at the back of his room. Other members of staff were equally unhappy, particularly about the security of their employment. Jim Mwewa, the chaplain, had taken up his duties and was working hard to try and improve the relationship between Chonde and the staff, an almost impossible task.

There was one very cheerful member of staff. Regina was radiant with happiness when I visited her at the weekend to congratulate her on the birth of her daughter, Mutale. When she handed the baby to me, her amusement at my nervousness was obvious. Mutale began to cry, perhaps sensing that I wasn't confident in the way I was holding her which became my excuse to hand her back to her mother.

On the following Wednesday we had what was known locally as 'London weather,' a grey sunless day. It had been wet earlier but in the evening when I walked home from work it was dry but swelteringly hot and humid, the build up to a tremendous thunder storm. I had almost half a kilometre to go when crossing Maina Soko Road into Independence Avenue I saw the first forked flashes of lightning and heard the ominous grumbling roar of thunder. The storm was still some way off but I wanted home before it broke overhead. Not quite running but walking as fast as I could I passed a group of street-children huddling under trees. Normally I got on well with the street-children. Most knew me as a friend of Susanne Bradley who ran their night-shelter. Many knew me by name and often if they were near the bakers when I bought bread I bought them buns, but recently a few were upsetting passers-by with nasty verbal comments. One or two of the older ones had taken to glue sniffing which made them belligerent. When abuse was shouted at me, I hurried on trying to appear unconcerned but not noticing a puddle of mud. As my feet slipped on it, I had to try and stop myself falling if at all possible for if I dropped my handbag and laptop they might be stolen before I could gather myself and them together. Later I described my actions as two cartwheels and three somersaults and it certainly felt like that, but at the end I was still upright and holding onto my possessions although my audience were roaring with laughter. I knew immediately that I had twisted my back. It hurt. As the rain came on I struggled home, soaked to the skin as well as sore, but I thought a hot bath and two paracetamols would put me to rights and they did ease the pain but the following morning I could hardly clamber out of bed. I asked Carl to make my apologies at the office before phoning Anna and asking her to take me to the clinic. The good news was that there was no new injury; I had aggravated an old one. I was also given a supply of pain-killers and antibiotics. It didn't seem to matter what the medical problem was in Zambia, provided the patient could pay antibiotics were prescribed. After being given a pain-killing injection I was told to go home and rest – come back after a week. Before going home, Anna took me to the office so that I could officially tell Chonde that I was on the sick list for a week. When he again turned his back on me, refusing to speak to me face to face, I questioned his sanity rather than his manners.

About ten days later, his behaviour became even stranger. Kennedy Phiri, who had replaced Dolores Long as my VSO Placement Officer, had made arrangements to meet with Chonde, Maurice, Carl and me to discuss what help VSO could give PFZ when Carl and my placements came to an end in April. Still officially 'ill' I arranged for a taxi to take me to the office for that meeting. Chonde informed Kennedy that he wanted someone with a proper management degree, someone who had qualified at the University of Bradford, for that to him was the only educational institution which produced properly qualified people though we never discovered why he thought so. There was also a peculiar reference to false claims about qualifications upon my part, something Kennedy took with more than a pinch of salt as he knew VSO had checked all my credentials before accepting me. Various other remarks made by Chonde at that meeting led Kennedy to say later that one or two things would have to be straightened out at PFZ before VSO would place other volunteers there. Life was becoming very frustrating. I couldn't work. There was little I could do at home and Brian, now twenty-one months, thought that I should play with him. In the past when I was at home at lunchtime, I had played little games with him or looked at a picture book. He couldn't understand why I could not even lift him onto my knee for lifting anything was one of the things I couldn't do. Without Anna, Susanne and Harriet my life at that time would have been awful. Anna brought food in for me, then, when I could move more easily took me shopping, refusing to let me lift even a tin of beans off a supermarket shelf. Both she and Susanne drove me back and forth to the clinic and invited me for meals as standing cooking was painful. Even my shared meals with Carl had stopped when his girlfriend, Vicky Shaw had arrived the previous year to stay with him. All in all I was fed up with life in general. With the pain in my back, sleep was almost impossible: I was relying on others for the basic requirements to get through the day; I couldn't even play with Brian (which made him tetchy); and most important of all my work at PFZ was suffering. Towards the end of the month I did manage to get back to the office but I realised that because of Chonde's attitude towards me I was never going to be able to complete my placement objectives. After discussing my health problems with Dr Banda at the clinic, I phoned Kennedy to ask his advice. I told him that I believed I was now wasting my time and VSO's money. We agreed that I resign from PFZ with effect from the end of February, two months earlier than planned.

After devotion on January 24 I handed my letter of resignation to Chonde. He appeared quite surprised. The staff were shocked and upset and I was touched by their concern. I agreed to Jim

Mwewa's suggestion that he set up a meeting between Chonde and me in the hope that Chonde would speak to me about the problems in our working relationship, but when he would not address me personally but started talking to me through Mwewa, saying 'Tell her —' I said the meeting was a waste of time unless he spoke directly to me. Another 'Tell her —' and I walked out of the room. Both men were stunned. As a woman I was supposed to sit there and listen. I felt sorry for Mwewa for he was trying to do what he saw as his Christian duty and I wasn't making it easy for him. Most of the others had gathered in the tailoring room and when I joined them there I tried to explain why I had taken this action. Little work was being done other than on the strategic plan, and that did not appear to be progressing. Fund raising had come to a stop and the organisation was about to hit another financial crisis. I felt that in putting in my resignation earlier than expected I might alert the PFZ board that the project work had almost ceased and that the staff, unhappy about the security of their employment, had begun to look for other positions. I think most appreciated what I was trying to do for both Mellbin and Maurice gave me a hug and Chama squeezed my hand when he passed by me. Dr Mathani, the chairman, did ask for a meeting with both Carl and me and we tried to tell him how we saw what was happening without bringing the personality conflict into our report. We were never sure if that meeting did alert the board to some of the problems PFZ was suffering but shortly thereafter Chonde called a meeting of the staff when Kalifungwa, the new vice-chairman and a friend of Chonde's, lectured us on not communicating with the director.

My flight home was booked for March 2 and I had to prepare to pack up my Zambian home and say goodbye to the many friends I had made in Ndola. At work I had begun to hand over projects in which I had been involved to other members of staff in preparation for my departure in April but that had to be accelerated. On Anna's advice I planned to have my farewell party early in February so that I had time afterwards to pack the items I was taking back to the UK and dispose of my household goods and unwanted clothes. My house was too small to hold everyone who wanted to wish me well and Anna moved the party to her house. She and I enjoyed preparing the food and between us provided a rather splendid buffet for a memorable evening of fun and laughter with good friends.

In one trip to Lusaka I combined an overnight stay with Sue Clay, a meeting with Kennedy Phiri, when I made my final report and we dealt with the formalities of my leaving, and attended a two-day seminar on AIDS in the company of Marjorie Fwolishi. Watching the confidence with which Marjorie took part in the discussions made me realise that if the PFZ organisation had not fully benefited from the work I had put in, at least some of the staff and volunteers had. When the seminar closed I joined Tony and Anna for a weekend visit to Lechwe Lodge, south of Lusaka, taking probably a last chance to view African wildlife.

One of the last things to be organised was the disconnection of my telephone and payment of the final bill. Having checked with Harriet that twenty-one-month-old Brian would walk the half kilometre to the telephone office, I suggested that I take him with me. He had been getting in his mother's way while she was ironing so was happy to let him go. Her instructions to him that he must behave were obeyed for he put his little hand firmly in mine as we walked out into Blantyre Road, where a white woman with a black baby, a reversal of normal roles, received many looks and smiles from passers-by. Remembering the problems I had had getting the telephone connected when I first arrived, I was prepared for it to take some time to arrange the disconnection of the service, but when Brian climbed up onto my knee while I sat at a desk I had the attention of three different clerks. There were other differences too. Like many other businesses in Ndola, small signs of improvement were beginning to show. The chairs for customers had been repaired while the office had had a coat of paint. Having paid my dues and thanked the staff, saying '*Natotela. Shalenipo mukwai*'

(Thank you, Goodbye) they came to shake my hand and wish me well. Brian skipped along by my side still keeping his hand in mine until we reached a small shack, Zawi's local shop. Among the eggs, buns and small bags of mealie meal on display were some caramel-type wrapped sweets and Brian stood in front of them, looked and waited. He obviously knew what they were but I was unsure about giving him a caramel. He wasn't moving and I couldn't lift him. He won. I bought five sweets telling him that he could have them only with his mother's permission. He was happy with that. Clutching one of the sweets in one hand, he took my hand in the other and we crossed the road back to Zawi. Harriet took charge of the sweets but saw no problems with him eating a caramel. Brian stood waiting and watching until she unwrapped one and gave it to him. I had become fond of both of them and would miss them.

Susanne helped me pack a box with mementos of Zambia and together we took it to the offices of Mercury in Ndola for transportation back to the UK. At my final visit to the medical clinic in Ndola, Dr Banda advised that lifting anything heavy might aggravate the injury to my back and suggested that I ask the airport for assistance with my luggage when travelling home. My last day was a very busy one. I had already packed most of the items which I would need on the journey home or wanted to take back with me. My professional books were left at the office. Marjorie and Harriet got the clothes and shoes I was not taking home and they together with the other health volunteers divided up the remainder of my household goods sharing curtains, sheets, blankets, plates, mugs, pots and pans.

I wanted to say thank you to everyone at the office. Over the twenty-eight months I had been there, they had all been so kind to me. Having got Chonde to agree that the staff could stop work for half an hour for cake and a soft drink, I arranged with Paterson's bakery to make me a large sponge cake. Chama went with me to the garage to collect two crates of cold soft drinks and at 15.30 work stopped as many staff and volunteers crammed into the health department to watch me cut the cake into slices. Eyes followed the knife as I cut into the sponge. To some of those watching, a piece of cake was a treat, a luxury which seldom came their way. Regina joined us, bringing baby Mutale with her, a ghetto-blaster was produced and we partied in the office garden to tapes of African music for much longer than the official half-hour but then Chonde was not in his office.

At 17.00 the staff took me to the PFZ restaurant where we enjoyed a meal together. Again Chonde was absent but Peter Kangamayagam came to represent the PFZ board. Sambie and Mwewa were both in Lusaka but I had arranged to meet with them there before leaving for the airport. When I said goodbye, I said how much I had enjoyed being with them and how much I would miss them. I added that while I had tried to abide by their customs I was going to take my leave of them in true British fashion. I gave each a hug and a kiss on the cheek which left the men looking sheepish, a bit like embarrassed schoolboys, but they accepted that I was paying them a compliment. Chama asked if I would like to say 'Goodbye' to him again, making everyone laugh. When Carl and I walked back to Zawi in the warm evening air, Mutinta joined us for part of the way. We spoke about the change in temperature I was going to experience when I arrived back in the UK. News reports had spoken of snow.

At Zawi it was a last hug for Harriet and a cuddle for Brian before Susanne arrived to collect me and my luggage. The children had already been given little gifts, some sweets, a pencil and rubber, but they gathered round as Susanne lifted my backpack and holdall into her vehicle. With a Pied Piper tail of kids, I crossed the garden to say goodbye to Carl and Vicky before leaving with Susanne to spend my final night in Ndola at her home. It was an early start next morning. Although it was PFZ's responsibility to take me and my luggage back to Lusaka, the problems at the office had made me accept Susanne's offer to drive me there.

At 07.15 on Sunday, March 2, I checked in at Lusaka Airport

for my BA flight to Heathrow. Jim Mwewa was there, along with Susanne, to load my luggage onto the security scanner. Jim said a short prayer. With a hug from him and a kiss from Susanne I was on my way home. I glanced round while walking out to the plane. Towards the horizon the pale lilac of distant hills shimmered hazily in the morning heat.

Chapter 33

Sharing Skills, Changing Lives

Once at home reverse culture shock kicked in. The streets of Edinburgh felt strange. The shops were full of goods, people rushed in and out, spend, spend, spend, but with frowns rather than the smiles I had grown used to. After my experiences in Zambia, I found the amount of food available difficult to deal with. I remember staring for some minutes in a branch of Tesco at so many different types of coffee before walking off confused, unable to make a choice. Then again, when I got treatment at St John's Hospital for the injury to my back, my fellow patients seemed to do nothing but moan about the National Health Service, unaware how fortunate they were to have such a facility. I was perplexed by the change in lifestyle I had to deal with, so different from that which I had experienced in Ndola. It took time to readjust but with the support of family and friends gradually I did.

For two and a half years I had lived and worked with Zambians and had seen how difficult it was for them when they lacked what we take so much for granted, education, food on the table, employment, support services in times of trouble. They have a far greater prevalence of life-threatening diseases, e.g. AIDS, malaria, cholera, meningitis, than we in the developed world. Being a volunteer with VSO broadened my understanding of some of the problems confronting people in Third World countries. I got great personal satisfaction in having coped with the challenges of life in Zambia. I had stepped outside of my loss of John and shown myself capable of meeting the future head on.

In sharing my knowledge of management and accountancy with my Zambian colleagues I helped them towards building careers. Marjorie Fwolishi, who had performed so well at my last VSO

AIDS seminar, wrote me saying how much my presence at PFZ had motivated her to encourage the male members of the health volunteer team to accept that she could be every bit as effective as them. In a country where jobs were hard to come by Mutinta and Marjorie found employment with mining companies, Mutinta in administration and Marjorie in health education; Sambie moved to an NGO which helped vulnerable women and children; Mellbin became a teacher at a local technical college. Maurice moved on to become a placement officer with VSO in its Lusaka office.

Prison Fellowship Zambia has survived. Once more under the direction of Ennocent Silwamba who had replaced Chonde and with whom I had expected to be working when I first arrived in Zambia, PFZ is again undertaking its mission in the prisons with the help of new people in charge of the chaplaincy, finance and administration of the health programme. The monthly market has been retained, hopefully now an established fund-raiser. Regina, who was widowed shortly after I left, has taken charge of a project aimed at helping prisoners' children. In 2006 she spent a few weeks with PF England learning about their programmes on children's welfare during which she found time to visit me in Ratho. With a little financial help from my friends in the UK, Regina, Marjorie, Zele (a health volunteer) and Sambie, have undertaken further study through the University of Zambia's distance learning programme.

I made a return visit to Ndola in 2007 when I was warmly welcomed by these four as well as Mutinta, Mellbin, George and Chama. The sad news was the deaths of Robam, Gift, Knox and Francis Mpzeni. I enjoyed meeting Harriet, who keeps in touch by letter, and six-year-old Brian. Debbie and Steve Vrdoljaks were wonderful hosts in Ndola and at their new venture in the lower Zambezi, Wild Tracks.

After a break of four years I saw many improvements in the economy: new shopping centres, mining activity in the Copperbelt, more land given over to agriculture and a huge increase in tourism, particularly around Livingstone and the Zambezi. Where there were few facilities for tourists on the Zambian side of the Victoria Falls in 2000, now there are many hotels and game lodges together with all the ancillary services. It is still a country in the grip of poverty but that grip is slowly but surely being loosened.

Voluntary Service Overseas' objective of having its volunteers share their skills with people less fortunate than themselves does change lives. My own experience proved it. Zambia itself needs an educated workforce and VSO volunteers are helping towards that goal. The practical help they give ripples outwards as people pass on their training. And it can be a life-enhancing experience for those who volunteer.

Bibliography

Personal Diaries

Letters sent to family and friends

Chris McIntyre, *Zambia, The Bradt Travel Guide*, Bradt Travel Guides Ltd

Lizzie Williams, *Footprint Tanzania*, Footprint Books

G.H.N. Haantobolo, *Senior Secondary History of Central and Southern Africa,* Times Printpak (z) Ltd

Dick Hobson, *Tales of Zambia*, The Zambia Society Trust

Tim Jeal, *Livingstone,* Wm. Heinemann Ltd

Barbara Kingsolver, *The Poisonwood Bible*, Harper Collins

Christina Lamb, *The Africa House*, Penguin

John M. MacKenzie (Advisory Editor), *David Livingstone and the Victorian Encounter with Africa,* National Portrait Gallery

Stephen Taylor, *Livingstone's Tribe, A Journey from Zanzibar to the Cape*, Flamingo

Hannilie Zulu, *Nomeon*, Zulu Publications